Items should be returned on or before the last date shown below. Items not already requested by other borrowers may be renewed in person, in writing or by telephone. To renew, please quote the number on the barcode label. To renew on line a PIN is required. This can be requested at your local library.
Renew online @ **www.dublincitypubliclibraries.ie**
Fines charged for overdue items will include postage incurred in recovery. Damage to or loss of items will be charged to the borrower.

Leabharlanna Poiblí Chathair Bhaile Átha Cliath
Dublin City Public Libraries

Dublin City
Baile Átha Cliath

Leabharlann Shráid Chaoimhín
Kevin Street Library
Tel: 01 222 8488

Date Due	Date Due	Date Due

MAKING UP THE NUMBERS

SMALLER PARTIES AND INDEPENDENTS IN IRISH POLITICS

DAN BOYLE

The History Press

First published 2017

The History Press Ireland
50 City Quay
Dublin 2
Ireland
www.thehistorypress.ie

The History Press Ireland is a member of Publishing Ireland,
the Irish book publisher's association.

British Library Cataloguing in Publication Data.
A catalogue record for this book is available from the British Library.

ISBN 978 1 8458 8954 8

Typesetting and origination by The History Press
Printed and bound by CPI Group (UK) Ltd, Croydon, CR0 4YY

Contents

Introduction

In the thirty general elections that have been held in the Republic of Ireland (and its earlier incarnation as the Irish Free State) since 1922, close on 44 million votes have been cast. Nearly three-quarters of these votes have been won by the two parties created from the constitutional cleavage that brought the State itself into existence: Fianna Fáil and Fine Gael.

Only one political party has contested all of these elections – the Labour party. Winning some 11 per cent of the vote, the existence of the Labour party has led many political scientists to label Irish electoral politics as a two-and-a-half-party system.

An important factor in recent Irish elections has been the strength of the 'others' vote. In this category the votes of candidates of minor parties and independent candidates have on occasion, and in recent years with increasing regularity, fractured the traditional template. The 'others' category has been more likely to bring a change in govern-ment formation when a minor party (or parties) breaks from the pack. At over 15 per cent this has been a vote that has been very influential in the final determination of parliamentary seats, and often in the ultimate composition of governments.

This 'others' vote is in need of further analysis. While Ireland has had a tradition of 'independent' candidates contesting election without party affiliation, three-fifths of the 'others' votes were for candidates of 'minor' parties, political parties that sought to break the hold of the three traditional parties. Even when the votes of independent candidates are removed from the 'others' vote, the remaining proportion of votes for minor parties is comparable to the Labour party.

The Irish voting system – Proportional Representation Single Transferable Vote (PRSTV) – allows for the significant representation of minor parties and independents, but it also gives a greater benefit to larger parties. Notwithstanding this, seats in Dáil Éireann won by 'others' still outnumber those won by the Labour party.

Of the 551 seats won by 'others', 304 of these seats were won by candidates of other parties; 140 of these seats were won by the six parties that have participated in government. This, and consequent analysis of vote and seat share, indicates a significant and influential political presence of 'others' resulting from Irish elections, and within this sector a predominance of minor parties as a grouping capable of involvement in the formation of government.

The dominance of the Fianna Fáil party in Irish elections, particularly in the period 1932–2011, might suggest that Ireland has been close to being a one-party predominant party system. However, Fianna Fáil's total dominance has always been somewhat undermined, in that despite lengthy unbroken periods of government (1932–48, 1957–73 and 1997–2011), several of these single-party governments were minority administrations; since 1989 the party has been unable to enter government without a coalition partner.

Neither can the Irish party system be said to be bipolar. The traditional second party, Fine Gael, has only twice come close to winning a majority of seats in the Irish parliament (November 1982 and 2011). In its earlier version, as Cumann na nGaedheal, the party managed single party governments without ever holding a majority of seats, helped in no small part by the abstentionism of anti-treaty republicans.

Defining the Irish party system as a two-and-a-half-party system is convenient and is certainly closest to reality. But it is more correct to state that it is a party system in transition, and that that transition has been evolutionary. Part of that evolutionary road of transition is a journey from being a two-and-a-half-party system to a two-and two-halves-party system, and ultimately to a multiparty system.

However, up until 2016, no clear competitor to the Labour party as the second 'half' in a two-and two-halves system has been apparent.

There has been a litany of minor parties that have not persisted, and neither have they consistently had the levels of electoral support enjoyed by the Labour party. In individual elections the Labour party has been relegated to fourth position (by the Farmers party in 1923, the Centre party in 1933, in terms of votes but not seats by Clann na Poblachta in 1948, by the Progressive Democrats in 1987, and most recently by the modern manifestation of Sinn Féin in 2016), but no minor party has yet outpolled Labour in consecutive elections.

Within the 'others' category there is competition occurring between competing candidates of minor parties, and between minor parties and independent candidates, this competition not unlike the election competition between the largest parties or two half parties, selecting the best potential challenger to the two-and-a-half party system.

While Irish party politics, according to Peter Mair, represents 'a rather incongruous strain within the relatively clear cut patterns which exist within the rest of Western Europe', it may be that Ireland has taken longer to settle on a pattern that has been more prevalent elsewhere.

More likely, within the 'others' vote in Irish elections is a character that often refuses to conform to type. This unpredictably, this eccentricity, this eclectiveness, is found in the individual and collective stories of those who have sought votes and presented clear alternatives to the existence of a political mould, while offering alternatives as to why that mould should be broken.

Pre-Independence

The last all-island Irish parliamentary election – the Westminster election of 1918 – put in place templates that were rarely diverged from, in either jurisdiction, over the next seventy years.

Twentieth-century Irish politics had begun to slip into a comfortable predictability. John Redmond had come out best from the Irish Parliamentary Party's internecine fallout over the deposing of its leader, the much-vaunted 'Uncrowned King of Ireland', Charles Stewart Parnell. Redmond had solidified support for the Irish Parliamentary

Party and sidelined factions led by Tim Healy, and breakaways like the All for Ireland group led by William O'Brien.

The coming together, influenced by Arthur Griffith, of Sinn Féin in 1907 seemed unlikely to upset the comfortable complacency that surrounded Irish politics. As editor of the *United Irishman* newspaper, Griffith had floated ideas such as parliamentary abstentionism as a policy, believing it to be effective in helping Hungary gain additional status within the Austro-Hungarian Empire.

Griffith formed a number of political vehicles to promote his ideas. The first of these was Cumann na nGaedheal, a vehicle that was later to assert itself more prominently. A second grouping was the National Council. It was at a gathering of this organsiation in 1905 that began the formalising of a Sinn Féin policy. In 1907 Cumann na nGaedheal combined with a similarly inclined northern Ireland based organisation, the Dungannon Clubs, to form the Sinn Féin League. Later that year the National Council came on board to form the Sinn Féin party.

While this was occurring a discontented Irish Parliamentary Party MP became supportive of the new party. C.J. Dolan, MP for North Leitrim, resigned from the Irish Parliamentary Party. In 1908 he became the Sinn Féin candidate in the subsequent by-election. Despite a respectable 27 per cent of the vote for Sinn Féin, the new Irish Parliamentary Party candidate, in this two horse race, succeeded in winning more than twice as many votes.

There was to be no big bang for this incarnation of Sinn Féin. By 1910 its Ard Fheis was poorly attended. It was not possible to elect all the party officers from among those present. Small footholds were gained in electing some councillors at the local elections of 2011, but of itself these were not enough to register on the Irish public's conscientiousness. Sinn Féin 'Mark I' would soon be seen to have served its purpose.

It may have attracted wider public interest had the party's executive acted on a proposal made by William O'Brien. O'Brien, a nationalist MP for Cork, had expended much of his political capital trying to reunite the Irish Party. Having been largely successful in doing so, he became dissatisfied with what resulted and this led to his own breakaway in forming the All for Ireland League. He approached Sinn Féin proposing co-operation but, despite Griffith being well disposed, the idea did not find wider favour within Sinn Féin.

Sinn Féin had not even the capacity to contest the Westminister elections of 1910 – a year of two general elections. Those elections slashed what had been a comfortable Liberal majority and placed them level with the Conservatives, whose numbers also included Irish unionists. For the first time since Parnell, the Irish Parliamentary Party had leverage within the House of Commons.

By 1914 a Home Rule Act was on the British statute books. A largely self-governing Ireland, albeit partitioned, was soon expected to come into being. Then came the Great War. This was to cause an interregnum in general elections for the Westminster parliament. Because of the war no general election would be held from the second election of 1910 until 1918.

Parliamentary by-elections continued. Several dozen such by-elections were held in Ireland during this period. Most were uncontested. The few that were indicated some changing winds that were subsequently to make greater sense in 1918.

In 1915 a by-election was held for the Dublin College Green constituency. The Irish Party was challenged there by an independent Labour candidate, Thomas Farren. He performed very creditably, winning almost 43 per cent. The effect of the Dublin Lock Out of 1913 had been felt.

The Irish Labour Party had been established in 1912 after a meeting in Clonmel, County Tipperary. It was established as the political wing of the Irish Trade Union Congress. It even created a military wing in the form of the Irish Citizens Army, this had been created as a response to the 1913 Lock Out. It maintained a presence in the febrile atmosphere of the time.

The party participated in local elections, succeeding in having a number of councillors elected. It did not officially contest any of by-elections that took place between 1910 and 1918. Regarding the 1918 general election, it took a position that it would not contest, seeing the election as a referendum on national sovereignty. According to the political scientist, Brian Farrell, the failure of the Irish Labour Party to contest the British general election in Ireland in 1918 helped copper-fasten the role of the party as the third wheel of Irish politics.

The 1912 meeting was not the first attempt by founder, James Connolly, to establish an Irish left-wing party. At the turn of the previous century, in 1896, he helped to create the Irish Socialist Republican Party. While it was really only Dublin based, with less than 100 members, it did contest local elections. It also published its own newsheet, *The Workers' Republic*, which called for an independent republic long before Sinn Féin found itself able to.

Connolly, even as a full-time organiser, found it difficult to make headway. He even managed to anger a small number of the activists who had been attracted into the party. They in turn sought to create the Irish Socialist Labour Party. Neither vehicle survived past 1904 when Connolly left Ireland for economic reasons, returning in 1910.

What did upset the apple cart was the little local difficulty of the Easter Rising. This may have had limited political effect, if it had not been for how the British Government reacted to the event. The summary executions of the leaders of The Rising evoked huge public sympathy. The political reaction became even more pronounced as British spokespersons and politicians attributed the nous behind the rebellion to a shadowy Sinn Féin involvement.

It was a huge back-handed compliment. What existed of Sinn Féin had had no involvement in The Rising. The suggestion that it had been was a huge credibility boost. It revitalised what had been a moribund organisation and introduced new membership, while pointing to a political route to pursue.

The British establishment mistook being outside the system for radicalism. Even at that stage Sinn Féin had not committed itself to defining what kind of Ireland it aspired to in the event of independence being achieved. The surviving leaders of The Rising joined the party, giving it some revolutionary cachet. Then, at its 1917 Ard Fheis, newly admitted member Éamon de Valera became the party's new President. A compromise motion was adopted, through which the Irish people would become free to choose their own government by referendum; and with that, Sinn Féin Mark II was born.

A series of by-elections provided an opportunity to test the extent to which the Irish political landscape was changing. The first such by-election was in November 1916. Sinn Féin did not participate in the West Cork by-election. It was a more traditional Irish parliamentary by-election between John Redmond's Irish Party and William O'Brien's All for Ireland League. This had been an O'Brienite seat. The party ended up having both an official and an unofficial candidate. William O'Brien endorsed Frank Healy, who had been imprisoned at the Frongogh internment camp in Wales for the crime of having 'associated' with Sinn Féin. He had not been endorsed by Sinn Féin because he did not intend to abstain his seat should he be successful. O'Brien's endorsement of Healy had caused difficulty for his local members, one of whom ran as an independent.

The by-election was won by the Irish Party's Daniel O'Leary with a margin of fifty-six votes, due to his opponent's vote splitting. The non-involvement of Sinn Féin was complacently seen by the Irish political establishment as thinking the effects of the Easter Rising would not be so pronounced.

In February 1917 a by-election was held in North Roscommon. Sinn Féin had a greater presence, but it remained an unofficial one. George Plunkett, father of Joseph Mary Plunkett (an executed leader of the Easter Rising), announced his intention to contest. He was a papal knight, giving him a right to style himself a count. Despite having impeccable revolutionary credentials, Plunkett ran as an independent. His election literature made no reference to Sinn Féin. One potential reason for being reluctant in seeking or taking an endorsement, was a supposed animus that existed between him and Arthur Griffith.

The implied support was deemed to be sufficient. Plunkett won comfortably, shocking the Irish Party in the process. Once elected he announced his intention to become an abstentionist MP, something he had not referred to at all during the campaign. Later that year he joined Sinn Féin.

The first of these by-elections to have a fully fledged, official Sinn Féin presence was the South Longford by-election of May 1917. It was a campaign that was not without controversy. The result was marred by accusations of intimidation. The returning officer at first announced the election of the Irish Party candidate. He was then called upon to examine a bundle of votes that may or may not have been counted.

The method of persuasion was unusual. The writer and journalist Tim Pat Coogan, in his biography on Michael Collins, quotes then Sinn Féin activist Alasdair MacCába as saying: 'I jumped up on the platform, put a .45 to the head of the returning officer, clicked back the hammer and told him to think again.' This produced the result of Joseph McGuinness becoming the first directly elected Sinn Féin MP, by a margin of thirty-seven votes.

Later 1917 by-elections in Clare East and Kilkenny City were won comprehensively and without controversy by Éamon de Valera and W. T. Cosgrave respectively. In 1918 the Irish Party seemed to stem the tide by winning three by-elections in a row. In March party leader John Redmond died and was replaced by John Dillon.

Sinn Féin began to campaign successfully on the issue of being against conscription. This helped the party win the remaining two by-elections before the general election, the last of which in East Cavan saw Arthur Griffith being elected as the successful candidate.

The general election in December 1918 gave Sinn Féin a number of advantages. The eight-year gap between elections had seen the infra-structure of the Irish Party wither away in many parts of the country. As a result twenty-five Sinn Féin candidates were elected without being opposed. Ultimately seventy-three Sinn Féin MPs would be elected. Winning seventy-three seats out of a total of 105 MPs has been described as a Sinn Féin landslide. Drilling into the results the election is less emphatic than it has subsequently been portrayed.

Unionist candidates won one in every four of the votes cast. Irish Party candidates one in every five. In an election that had been cast as a referendum on national sovereignty, Sinn Féin candidates won less than half the contested vote (47 per cent). If the vote had been contested in the other twenty-five constituencies a probability existed of the Sinn Féin vote exceeding 50 per cent. Nevertheless, it was because of the 'first past the post' electoral system that this election gave the appearance of being a landslide.

What the results also showed was the extent to which partition had taken root in Ireland. Most of the Unionist vote and a substantial part of the Irish party was gained in Ulster. Five of the Irish Party's six seats were won there. The only other Irish Party seat came in the Redmondite stronghold of Waterford, where Captain William Redmond won the seat with a margin of less than 500 votes.

Only 6 per cent of the vote in this election was attributed to 'other' – those other than Sinn Féin, the Irish Party or Unionists. The Labour Party had decided/been encouraged not to contest this election. A number of Belfast activists did not support this policy. They decided to contest several constituencies, being successful in electing three MPs. Each described themselves as Labour Unionists.

The breakaway first Dáil met in Dublin's Mansion House in January 1919. No Unionist or Irish Party MP attended. Twenty-seven of the seventy-three Sinn Féin MPs, now named TDs, were in attendance. Twenty-seven 'others' were listed as either being imprisoned or expelled by foreign powers. These TDs went on to propose, debate, then approve a democratic programme.

This programme was drafted with the help of the Labour Party leader, Thomas Johnston, none of whose members would be present to approve its contents due to not contesting the 1918 election. The numbers present and the prior attention given to it attached some element of controversy to the programme. No subsequent Irish government has shown any commitment to its contents.

On the same day as the first Dáil met, the Soloheadbeg ambush took place in County Tipperary. It resulted in the deaths of two RIC policemen. This event was seen as the opening salvo in the Irish War of Independence.

The final pre-independence engagement of Sinn Féin with election to the Westminster parliament took place in March 1919. The party contested the North Londonderry by-election. Its candidate was Patrick McGilligan, later to be a government minister. He was not successful.

The political response of the British government was to produce a number of pieces of legislation designed to undermine the legitimacy of Sinn Féin hegemony in Irish politics. The first of these was the Local Government (Ireland) Act of 1919. This allowed for elections to take place in January 1920 for urban areas, followed by elections in June for rural councils. The elections took place under a new voting system, that of the Single Transferable Vote/Multi-Member Constituency system.

These elections offered the first opportunity for political diversity to be practised under the new and impending dispensation. The triad that had contested the 1918 Westminster election – Sinn Féin, the Irish Party and the Unionists – were now joined in contest by the Labour Party and independent candidates.

The Labour Party performed well, particularly in urban areas. The remnants of the Irish Party performed best in the six Northern Ireland counties. The election saw many independent candidates being elected. Of around 1,800 council seats that were available, Sinn Féin won around one-third of these seats. Labour held about one-fifth, marginally more than the Unionists (whose vote was very concentrated in the six Northern counties). Irish Party/Nationalists won about 15 per cent of seats, again mainly in Northern Ireland. A similar amount of independent/non-aligned councillors were elected.

An interesting feature of these elections was the existence of a number of councils that would soon fade from being. In the Greater Dublin area alone, separate councils existed in Blackrock, Dalkey, Killiney Ballybrack, Pembroke and Rathmines and Rathgar. The last two of these, Pembroke and Rathmines and Rathgar, returned Unionist majorities in 1920.

The second piece of British government legislation was the Government of Ireland Act in 1920. This entrenched partition, confirming two separate home rule parliaments for Northern Ireland and Southern Ireland. Elections for these parliaments were also to be held under the STV system.

Sinn Féin decided to participate in these elections but not to recognise any home rule parliament. The party chose to see this process as elections to the Second Dáil of an independent Ireland. The elections were held in May 1921. In the twenty-six counties, other than the Dublin University constituency where four Unionist candidates were nominated, all other nominations were of Sinn Féin candidates, leading to no votes being cast.

In Northern Ireland an election did take place. This was dominated by the Unionists. Irish Party/Nationalists won six seats as did Sinn Féin. Five of the successful Sinn Féin candidates had also been nominated/elected in other constituencies in the Southern twenty six-counties.

The Second Dáil would then consist of 125 members, all representing Sinn Féin. In June of 1920 a truce was proposed to bring about an end of hostilities in the Irish War of Independence. This truce came into effect in July. This allowed the Second Dáil to sit in August. The main business conducted was the progressing of the selection of a delegation to negotiate with the British government. As part of this process the Dáil voted to enhance the office held by Éamon de Valera, promoting him from Head of Government to that of Head of State, to allow the ensuing negotiations to be portrayed as occurring between two distinct nations.

The negotiating team returned with an agreed but controversial treaty for the next session of the Dáil held in December. A month of bitter debate followed until a close majority approved the treaty in January. A later formal sitting of the House of Commons for Southern Ireland was convened to formally ratify the Treaty. This one and only sitting was boycotted by anti-Treaty TDs. As a result the Treaty was passed unanimously.

De Valera resigned as President, being replaced by Arthur Griffith. The Second Dáil had done its work. Its impact would be felt for generations. Elections for the Third Dáil would take place in June 1922 to be followed by more turbulence in the form of a bloody eleven-month Civil War.

1

Towards Government in Ireland

The 1922 General Election to the Third Dáil can be considered to be the first example of a pluralistic election of the new Irish State. The vehicle of Sinn Féin was now subdivided into two parts, not on ideological grounds, but instead on a vexed area of political strategy. Other than the Labour Party, there were interest groups organising themselves politically and presenting candidates to the electorate.

The largest of these was the Farmers Party, the political arm of the Farmers Union. On a smaller scale a Businessmen's Party (otherwise known as the Business and Professional Group) stood five candidates in Dublin and in Cork. Twenty independent candidates, hardly an influx, presented themselves for election.

Seven constituencies which between them carried thirty-four seats were uncontested in this election. These were the constituencies of Clare, Donegal, Kerry/Limerick West, Leitrim/Roscommon North, Limerick City/Limerick East, Mayo North and West and Mayo South/ Roscommon South. The seats were equally divided between the pro- and anti-treaty factions as per an agreement between Éamon de Valera and Michael Collins. The Dublin University constituency was also uncontested, as was tradition.

Ninety-four of the 128 seats were won by the competing factions of Sinn Féin. Fifty-eight of these were won by pro-treatyites, thirty-six by the anti-treaty faction. Labour, in its first Irish parliamentary election, had a very successful campaign. The party stood eighteen candidates in half of the twenty-eight constituencies, winning seventeen seats. The party won two seats in four constituencies – the eight-seat constituency of Cork Mid, North, South, South-East and West; Kildare-Wicklow; Waterford-Tipperary East and Wexford. Its Dublin North West candidate, John James O'Farrell, was the only Labour candidate who failed to be elected. The 21 per cent of the total national vote won by the party would long remain its high-water mark in Irish parliamentary elections.

The Farmers Party succeeded in having seven TDs elected in what was its first parliamentary election. Like Labour it took a targeted approach. It stood thirteen candidates in eight constituencies, securing its seven seats. It could have but did not secure an eighth seat in the Cavan constituency. Its candidate, Patrick Baxter, was the second of four candidates in this three-seat constituency. He was 400 votes short of the quota after the first count. The other candidates were pro-treatyites led by the poll topper Arthur Griffith, who won more than two quotas and easily helped elect a second candidate. The third pro-treaty candidate was also brought over the line, having been 5,000 votes behind the Farmers' candidate on the first count. This was the first successful use of effective vote management under the new voting system.

The first Farmers Party parliamentary party consisted of party leader Denis Gorey, elected in Carlow/Kilkenny; John Dineen in Cork East and North East; Daniel Vaughan in the omnibus constituency of Cork Mid, North, South, South East and West; John Rooney in Dublin County; Richard Wilson in Kildare/Wicklow; Daniel Byrne in Waterford/Tipperary East and Michael Doyle in Wexford.

The Business and Professional Group, trading as the Businessmen's Party, succeeded in having one TD elected. He was Michael Hennessy, elected for the Cork East and North East constituency. He was not that effective a flag bearer, as by the time of the following election he had become a candidate for another political party.

Nine independent TDs were elected. Five of these were from the two University constituencies. Four others were from three Dublin constituencies, two from the one constituency of Mid Dublin.

Each of these four independent TDs carried interesting stories. Saddest of these was Darrell Figgis, who topped the poll in the Dublin County constituency with a personal vote that was twice the quota. Up to a month before the 1922 election Figgis had been a prominent and active member of the pro-treaty faction of Sinn Féin. During the War of

Independence a serious rift developed between Michael Collins (then Minister for Finance in the Provisional Government) and Figgis, centred around remuneration for Oireachtas members, particularly for members of the government. Despite this, Figgis continued to have a high profile within Sinn Féin. He was vice chair to Michael Collins's chair of the Constitution Committee established in January 1922 to agree a draft constitution, but ended up being its effective chairman as Collins only attended its first meeting.

After the approval of the Treaty, Figgis (who was strongly opposed to the Collins–de Valera Pact) launched a personal initiative to encourage the Farmers Party and the Businessmen's Party not to contest certain constituencies so anti-treaty candidates might be prevented from being elected. The leadership of Sinn Féin, still hopeful of maintaining a unified party after the election, moved to expel Figgis. He was successful, but not as successful, in being elected to the Fourth Dáil, after which his personal life took several tragic turns.

Myles Keogh was elected an independent TD for the Dublin South constituency. A physician and a surgeon, he was an enthusiastic supporter of John and Willie Redmond. Over the next fifteen years he would have a varied career in Irish politics.

The two independent TDs elected for the Mid Dublin constituency shared the distinction of holding the office of Lord Mayor of Dublin over a period of sixteen years between them. The poll topper, and incumbent Lord Mayor since 1917 was Laurence O'Neill. His time in Dáil Éireann would be brief, but he would go on to to hold other public office in the Free State Senate and later Seanad Éireann.

The second independent TD elected in that constituency would begin an even longer political lineage. Alfie Byrne carried a direct link to the Irish Party. He was elected to the House of Commons, after a 1915 by-election, as an Irish Party MP. He continued in that office until the 1918 general election. He would go on to be active in Irish political life for over forty years, being most associated with being the Lord Mayor of Dublin, an office he held for nine years in succession. Through reputation and strength of personality, rather than the holding of any policy positions, he created something of a micro political party. Three of Alfie Byrne's sons would also become members of Dáil Éireann.

None of those elected in June 1922, no more than anyone else in the country, would have a very enjoyable year. Little more than a week after the election, the Provisional government (encouraged by the British government) had decided to act against an anti-treaty force that had been occupying the Four Courts building since the previous April.

There followed many skirmishes throughout the country, with the most intense fighting occurring in the first few months. The imposition of martial law, with military tribunals given the right to approve the execution of seventy-seven anti-treaty fighters, raised anger levels among the opposition. Greater firepower helped the Free State government achieve eventual military success. Victory is a term that could not be applied in these circumstances.

In parallel, the political process continued. The anti-treaty TDs elected in June would not recognise the Dáil as being legitimate. They would be abstentionist TDs. Their absence would give the pro-treaty elements a majority in the new assembly.

A nuanced exception to republican abstention was the presence of Laurence Ginnell, who sought to sign the members register, but refused to take his seat in a parliament that had been defined by the government of a foreign country. He found himself formally removed from the chamber.

Ginnell had already had an interesting political history. First elected as an Irish Party MP in 1906, he was expelled for having enquired too intensely into the party's finances. He subsequently stood as an independent nationalist, being elected on that ticket in 1910. He acquired a reputation as a campaigning MP. He strongly opposed the British government on its war policy. The reaction to the 1916 Rising he argued was counter-productive. These stances moved him closer towards Sinn Féin. He joined the party as part of the 1917 intake.

In the 1918 Westminster general election he contested and was elected for the Westmeath constituency. In 1921 he was part of the Sinn Féin slate that comprised the Second Dáil. He was opposed to the treaty and was given responsibility by de Valera to represent the anti-treaty cause in the US and South America. He returned to participate in the 1922 election, succeeding in being elected. After that he headed to the US again and died in Washington DC in April 1923.

The new Dáil met for the first time on 9 September 1922. The sitting took place after a month in August, where events occurred that would dramatically alter the course of Irish politics. It was ten days that shook the country. On 12 August, Arthur Griffith died. Ten days later Michael Collins was assassinated. Promoted to fill their absence was W.T. Cosgrave.

The first business of the Third Dáil was the election of the President of Dáil Éireann, into which Cosgrave was assumed in an acting position. The debate which accompanied the motion showed a parliament unsure of its purpose or how it was supposed to proceed. Born from a desire to create a modern, independent nation, its workload was being determined by processing legislation created and approved by a 'mother' parliament in London.

A feature of the debate was how non-Sinn Féin TDs were contributing to the discourse. Active in this debate were Thomas Johnson of the Labour Party, Denis Gorey of the Farmers Party and the independent Darrell Figgis. The record of the sitting states that the motion electing W.T Cosgrave was approved, but did not say which deputies were in support. Within the debate Thomas Johnson declared his intention, and that of the Labour Party, to call a division, and with that his willingness not to support the motion.

On 25 October in the Dáil the Constitution for the Irish Free State/ Saorstát Éireann was adopted. The debate on the Constitution had been wide ranging. There were questions on whether there should be a constitution at all and whether then was the time to adopt a constitution, given the turmoil in which the country was finding itself. Many of those who had been elected did not participate in its consideration.

The Third Dáil's adoption of the Constitution was itself dependent on the British parliament doing the same. This was done in December 1922, after which the provisions of the Constitution took effect. These saw the Irish Free State being given dominion status (as existed with Canada and Australia) within the British Empire. The British King would be Head of State, to be represented in Ireland by the office of Governor General. This would be former Irish Party MP and Parnell *bête noir*, Tim Healy.

The uncertain political environment, into which the evolving Irish State was being created, was underscored by the assassination of pro-treaty TD Sean Hales as he left the Dáil on 7 December. This was stated to be an act of reprisal for the execution of anti-treaty prisoners by the government.

The most commented upon feature of the new constitutional set-up was the requirement for members of the Dáil to undertake an Oath of Allegiance to the British Crown. This was to continue to be a reason for republican abstention from the parliament. It was also to be the reason behind the first defection from the Labour Party's Dáil representation.

Patrick Gaffney had topped the poll for the Carlow/Kilkenny constituency by a considerable margin. In his wake came the soon to be head of government W. T. Cosgrave, as well as the leader of the Farmers Party, Denis Gorey. Gaffney had participated early in the life of the Third Dáil, but refused to accept the taking of the oath, becoming an abstentionist TD. In doing so he removed his affiliation from the Labour Party, which had remained in the Dáil, then delared himself to represent the interests of the Communist Party of Ireland.

A Communist Party was set up in Ireland in 1921. It was a successor to the Socialist Party of Ireland, which itself had been an offshoot of attempts by James Connolly around the turn of the century. These socialists/communists saw themselves as trying to pursue a deeper form of socialism than that being promoted by the Labour Party.

Roddy Connolly, son of James, preferred the deeper socialism. He had developed close contacts with the new communist regime in Russia. Through this he became convinced of the need for a communist party in Ireland. The defection of Patrick Gaffney should have been seen as something of a coup, as an epoch-making moment. It does not seem to have been so. It should be noted that the current incarnation of the Communist Party of Ireland makes no reference to Patrick Gaffney in its party history.

In the meantime the Civil War was winding towards its conclusion. A truce was called on 30 April 1923. The Third Dáil had been the protagonist in a civil war, elected a government and introduced a Constitution, but would soon have its own life shortened. On 9 August the proceedings of the Third Dáil were brought to an end and the election for the Fourth Dáil took place at the end of that month.

The Treaty vote brought an end to Sinn Féin 'Mark 2'. De Valera seemed to recognise this and chose the name Cumann na Poblachta-The Republican Party to contest elections to the Third Dáil. The Collins/DeValera Pact made this name change moot. Part of the national conversation at that time was about whether or not political parties themselves were necessary. The existence of other political parties, and the interest groups they sought to represent, made the need to organise more necessary.

In April 1923 W.T.Cosgrave launched Cumann na nGaedheal – a name used twenty years earlier by Arthur Griffith. This would be the party title used by pro-treatyites in future elections. Supporters of Éamon de Valera would be referred to as republicans but called themselves Sinn Féin, much to the annoyance of the pro-treatyites. The decision to hold on to the Sinn Féin name was in effect the establishing of a new political party. This would be Sinn Féin 'Mark III'.

While Civil War hostilities had ceased, the atmosphere for these elections remained highly charged. The government continued to treat anti-treatyites as combatants. De Valera came out of hiding to campaign and found himself arrested and then interned. As a political tactic it proved unproductive. While the pro-treaty vote remained static, the republican vote increased by almost 6 per cent.

The Fourth Dáil increased in numbers by twenty-five members. Cumann na nGaedheal received five extra seats. The Republicans won another eight seats. The biggest winner was the Farmers Party which more than doubled its Dáil membership to fifteen seats. The Businessmen's Party won two seats, which was the number also won by a sister party, the Cork Progressive Association. An additional four seats were won by independents.

The big losers were the Labour Party which saw its vote halve in percentage terms. The party failed to win any of the additional seats and its numbers reduced by three. This also meant that the party became smaller than the Farmers Party, and was no longer capable of calling itself the main opposition party.

The improvement in the Farmers Party performance could be put down to adopting a different electoral strategy. Other than the two university and two other Dublin constituencies, each constituency was contested by the party. Sixty-five candidates were run, several in many constituencies, with the transferred votes helping to win additional seats. Its unsuccessful candidate in 1922 from the Cavan constituency (in the absence of Arthur Griffith) topped the poll.

The second Farmers Party parliamentary party consisted of party leader Denis Gorey, elected in Carlow/Kilkenny; Patrick Baxter in Cavan; Conor Hogan in Clare; John Dineen in Cork East; Daniel Vaughan in Cork North; Timothy O'Donovan in Cork West; John White in Donegal; John Conlon in Kildare; Patrick Hogan in Limerick; Patrick McKenna in Longford/Westmeath; Patrick Mulvany in Meath; Michael Heffernan in Tipperary; Nicholas Wall in Waterford; Michael Doyle in Wexford and Richard Wilson in Wicklow.

John Rooney failed to hold the seat won previously in Dublin County. Daniel Byrne who had been elected a TD in 1922 for the Waterford/East Tipperary constituency, chose not to stand in 1923. This election was the high-water mark for the Farmers Party.

Michael Hennessy was elected for the Businessmen's Party in 1922 but then defected to Cumann na nGaedhael, standing successfully on its behalf. In 1923 the Businessmen's Party restricted itself to standing four candidates in three Dublin constituencies, with one further candidate standing in Tipperary. It succeeded in having two candidates elected – William Hewat in Dublin North and John P. Good in Dublin County. While the party did manage to double its representation, it did not manage to strengthen its support. Both Hewat and Good benefitted from Cumann na nGaedheal not being able to manage its vote in either constituencies. General Richard Mulcahy was the Cumann na nGaedheal poll topper in Dublin North. His vote equalled almost four quotas. In Dublin County, Kevin O'Higgins performed similarly well. In neither constituency did Cumann na nGaedheal win the number of seats its vote would have entitled it to. Hewat and Good were the beneficiaries. Good had previously been an unsuccessful Unionist candidate in the 1918 Westminster general election.

In Cork, a sister party of the Businessmen's Party – the Cork Progressive Association – also won two seats in similar circumstances. Contesting the Cork Borough constituency the votes of Richard Beamish (from the noted brewing family) and Andrew O'Shaughnessy were between them slightly shy of a quota for a seat. O'Shaughnessy was particularly adrift, having amassed a first count total which was only 10 per cent of the vote he required. Both again were beneficiaries of a lopsided Cumann na nGaedheal ticket. Here poll topper J.J. Walsh had about two-and-a-half times the vote he needed, which was not effectively redistributed to his party colleagues.

Thirteen independent TDs were elected, three of these for the Dublin University constituency. Of the independents elected in 1922, Laurence O'Toole did not re-contest. With O'Toole's absence Alfie Byrne's vote increased, seeing him easily being re-elected. Myles Keogh saw some slippage in his support but was also re-elected. Darrell Figgis almost suffered a fall from grace. Having been a poll topper in 1922 he now won the eighth of the eight seats in his constituency, his support having fallen by over 12,000 votes.

The seven new independent TDs were John Cole in Cavan; John Daly in Cork East (who ran as Independent Labour); Major James Sproule Myles, a poll topper in Donegal; Major Bryan Ricco Cooper in Dublin County; James Cosgrave in Galway; John Lyons in Longford/Westmeath (again as Independent Labour) and Captain William Redmond in Waterford.

John Cole's election in Cavan would be his first in thirty-four years of contesting elections there, where he experienced as much failure as he did success. A member of the Orange Order, he served as Grand Master of its County Cavan branch. His success had been at the expense of his namesake, outgoing Cumann na nGaedheal TD, Walter Cole, who had been elected on Arthur Griffith's coat tails in 1922. In Cork East John Daly was to begin a journey of riding several horses, a journey shared by several independents elected in the early years of the Dáil.

In Donegal Major James Sproule Myles's poll topping would be a regular feature in successive elections. His military service had been during the Great War, during which he was awarded a Military Cross. He also had the distinction of having been an Irish international rugby player.

Of similar lineage was Major Bryan Ricco Cooper. He was born in India and was from a military family. Educated in Eton, he followed his father into a career in the British Army. In January 1910 he was elected as an Irish Unionist MP for South Dublin, losing that seat in the second election in December that year. During the Great War he served in Gallipoli. Among his supporters was the poet W.B. Yeats, who encouraged him to contest the 1923 election.

Like Cooper, James Cosgrave was also a part of the elite club of people who had been members of the British House of Commons and of Dáil Éireann. He had been elected on behalf of the Irish Party in a 1914 by-election, but had not defended the seat in the 1918 general election.

John Lyons was elected a Labour Party TD for the Longford/Westmeath constituency in 1922. He became the second person to distance himself from the Labour parliamentary party, when successfully contesting the 1923 election as an independent labour candidate.

Captain William Redmond was to become the fourth TD in the Fourth Dáil to have also served in the British House of Commons. Of the four candidates he was the one with the most impressive dynastic lineage. He was the son of John Redmond, leader of the Irish Party until his death in 1918. His parliamentary career began in 1910 when he was elected as an Irish Party MP for the East Tyrone constituency. In keeping with his father's policy of encouraging army recruitment as a mean of ensuring Irish home rule, William served on the Western Front during the Great War. On the death of his father he resigned his East Tyrone seat to contest the Waterford by-election, in which he was successful. Nine months later he was again successful in the 1918 general election. He did not participate in the first Dáil, continuing to sit in the House of Commons. There he strongly criticised British military actions during the War of Independence. He continued to operate as an MP until the new constitutional arrangement had been agreed.

Holding 9 per cent of the national vote, independents were becoming a significant presence in Irish political life. Several trends were emerging from this presence. Electing independents was being seen as a preferred route for the Unionist minority to be represented. For isolated Irish Party politicians, it represented a route back. For those elected but unhappy with the parties they were representing it was an alternative, or at least a transitory, political space.

Relative proportionality, helpful for the election of independents and candidates of smaller parties, was being achieved through the existence of several large multi-seat constituencies. For this election there was a nine-seat Galway constituency, three eight-seat constituencies in Donegal, Dublin North and Dublin County and five seven-seat constituencies in Dublin North, Kerry, Sligo/Leitrim, Limerick and Tipperary.

One who had followed this third option was Patrick Gaffney, elected as a Labour Party TD for Carlow/Kilkenny in 1922. Despite a brief flirtation with the Communist Party of Ireland, Gaffney contested the 1923 election as a Republican Labour independent and polled 10,000 fewer votes.

The 1923 election also saw the appearance of a new political party. In 1922 a group called the Land League of Unpurchased Tenants had been established. This became the National Democratic Party. It stood four candidates in three constituencies, making it more local than national. Their collective performance, winning around 6,000 votes, did not convince it of the value of democracy much either. Formed to respond to what the party felt were unmet needs within farming communities, the success of the Farmers Party revealed that there was no particular space available. The party disbanded not long after the election.

One of its candidates was Patrick Belton. In 1922 he had stood unsuccessfully as an independent candidate for Longford/Westmeath. In 1923 his constituency was Laois/Offaly. He went on to have an eclectic electoral career, as well as siring a dynasty of several members, across a number of generations, each of whom would achieve some level of political success.

The fourth Dáil met for the first time on 19 September 1923. With the continued absence of anti-treaty TDs, W.T. Cosgrave was the only nominated candidate to be President of the Executive Council.

2

Towards a Normal Politics

Over a five-year period there had been four parliamentary elections and a set of local elections. From here there would be a pause in national parliamentary elections. However, there would be a larger number than usual of by-elections that would keep the evolving democracy on its toes. In the early days of the Fourth Dáil, by-elections caused by a number of deaths and resignations occurred. These were usually of Cumann na nGaedheal members, and were relatively easily held by the government.

In the year that followed the general election, ten by-elections were held. All were caused by changes within the Cumann na nGaedheal parliamentary party. The party won eight of these contests, with abstentionist republicans (one of whom was future Taoiseach, Sean Lemass) winning the other two. A Businessmen's Party candidate, Matthew Good, scored an impressive 9,000 votes in a by-election for the Dublin County constituency.

The biggest political crisis of 1924 was the Army Mutiny, brought about by the government's handling of the standing down of a large part of the national army, then deemed surplus to requirements. The crisis created something of a power play within the Cosgrave government, with Cosgrave seeking to stay aloof while others in his cabinet, like Mulcahy and O'Higgins, adopted a more gung-ho approach.

Cosgrave's caution failed to keep either his cabinet or his parliamentary party together. In October 1924 the government's refusal to reinstate army officers brought about the resignation of nine Cumann na nGaedheal TDs. Included in their number was the then Minister for Industry and Commerce, Joseph McGrath.

This group became known as the National Group. Other than McGrath they included Sean Gibbons, Sean Milroy, Frank Cahill, Sean McGarry, Daniel McCarthy, Thomas Carter, Alex McCabe and Henry Finlay.

Along with the Army Mutiny, the National Group was also unhappy with the lack of perceived progress with the Boundary Commission (established to agree the border between Northern Ireland and the Irish Free State), which some had hoped might provide a route map towards a United Ireland.

Armed with this two-item manifesto the National Group resigned en masse from Dáil Éireann. The intent was to create a mini general election in seven constituencies represented by the TDs (four of the TDs represented two constituencies). Those constituencies were Carlow/Kilkenny, Cavan, Dublin North, Dublin South, Sligo/Leitrim, Mayo North and Roscommon. The by-elections were held on 11March 1924.

The National Group was also referred to as the National Party, although it was difficult to sense any long-term political strategy in the bringing about of these by-elections. Only one of the nine, Sean Milroy, contested. Curiously, his candidacy was not for the Cavan constituency for which he had been elected, but instead he was put forward for the Dublin North constituency. Here he finished fifth of the five contesting candidates, with less than 5 per cent of the vote.

Cumann na nGaedheal won seven of the nine seats being contested. Republicans won the other two seats, both of which were in two constituencies (Dublin North and Sligo/Leitrim) where two seats were available. The biggest political casualty of these events, Joseph McGrath, went on to to found the Irish Hospital Sweepstakes, an act that ended up making him an extremely wealthy man.

Local elections occurred in 1925. These would be the first local elections held in the Irish Free State. The attitude of the Cumann na nGaedheal government to these units of local democracy was somewhat distrustful. Rural District Councils had been abolished, reducing the number of units of local government that existed.

Cumann na nGaedheal did not formally contest these elections. Party members contested as independents. Sinn Féin took a more proactive approach to these elections. While refusing to recognise Dáil Éireann, it strongly participated in local councils.

These contrasting approaches to local government by Cumann na nGaedheal and Sinn Féin fed the Cosgrave government's distrust. This distrust was an obvious factor in the circumstances that led to the subsequent short-term removal of Dublin Corporation and Cork Corporation.

The first election for the Senate of the Irish Free State also took place in 1925. The original Senate had been put together in 1922 by a combination of nomination and election by an electorate that consisted of members of the Dáil and the newly nominated Senators. Among the nominated members was the poet and playwright, W.B. Yeats.

Of the sixty members of the 1922 Senate, forty-two Senators identified themselves as independent. Thirteen of these had been elected – Richard Butler, John Counihan, Edward MacLysaght, Éamonn Mansfield, George Nesbitt, William Barrington, Eileen Douglas, James Douglas, Alice Stopford Green, (Sir) John Griffith, John MacLoughlin, William Molloy and Maurice Moore.

Eamon Mansfield, an independent who had been supported by the Labour Party, was a Senator for five days. Elected on 7 December, he wrote a letter of resignation on 12 December. (He may have been persuaded by a threat issued by the republican side in the Civil War to assassinate any member of the new Senate.)

There were four female members of the 1922 Senate, two elected (Eileen Costello and Alice Stopford Green) and two nominated (Ellen Cuffe, the Countess of Desart, and Jennifer Wyse Power). Three of these were independent Senators; the fourth (Wyse Power) was an executive member of Cumann na nGaedheal, until when frustrated at the performance of the party in government, she sat as an independent in 1925.

Costello and Cuffe had been members of the Gaelic League, Cuffe having served as its President. Wyse Power had been active in Cumann na mBan. Cuffe had the distinction of being the only member of the Jewish community to sit in the Senate. Stopford Green was a noted historian who had been associated with the Howth Gun Running in 1914.

The Farmers Party succeeded in having one Senator elected in 1922, Thomas Linehan.

The 1925 election was for nineteen of the sixty Senate seats. Candidates could only be nominated through Dáil Éireann or by existing nominated members of the Senate. This led to seventy-six candidates being nominated. The entire country was treated as a single nineteen-seat constituency. In an added complication the electorate was restricted to voters over 30 years of age. These complications led to a turnout of less than one-quarter of the electorate.

As with the local elections Cumann na nGaedheal did not formally contest, encouraging 'supporters' to do so. In not attending Dáil Éireann, Sinn Féin chose not to nominate candidates, thus boycotting the election. Of the seventy-six candidates who were nominated, seven were nominees of the Farmers Party, three of whom were elected. These included Michael O'Hanlon (the General Secretary of the party), Thomas Linehan and James Dillon (not the future government minister).

The Labour Party nominated eight candidates, of whom three were elected. Cumann na nGaedheal supporting candidates won ten Senate seats. Twenty-five of the seventy-six candidates were non-aligned. Three of these succeeded in being elected – Henry Barniville, Sir Edward Bellingham and Sir Edward Bigger.

The final two by-elections of the Fourth Dáil occurred in February 1926. These were for the constituencies of Dublin County and Laois/Offaly. The Dublin County vacancy had arisen as a result of independent Darrell Figgis TD taking his own life in October 1925 – the final in a series of tragedies that dominated the closing years of his life.

A month previously he had sought, unsuccessfully, to change his mandate to become a member of the Irish Senate. He had been subject to political controversy through his membership of a committee examining radio broadcasting. The minister responsible for this area, J.J. Walsh (known himself to favour private rather than State ownership of any broadcasting company), accused Figgis of peddling influence, forcing Figgis's resignation.

In November 1924 his wife Millie had taken her own life by shooting herself in the back of a taxi cab. A number of months later a new partner in his life, Rita North, died in the UK after a medical procedure. One of Figgis's last actions was to attend and to give evidence at her inquest in London. A week later he was to take his own life there.

The Dublin County by-election was won by the Labour Party's William Norton, who would later become leader of that party. Norton's election was helped by transfers gained from an independent candidate, Patrick Belton, who had polled 8,975 votes. This vote was far in excess of the combined total of National Democratic Party votes won by four candidates (of whom Belton was one) in the 1923 general election.

Dublin County was the third constituency Belton had by now contested in a four-year period. Another interesting feature of the Dublin County by-election was the absence of a republican candidate, as Sinn Féin was experiencing financial difficulties. In Laois/Offaly Cumann na nGaedheal comfortably held the seat.

As elections to the Fifth Dáil neared, political activity became more fevered. Several new political parties were produced in 1926. January of that year saw the founding of Clann Éireann (Family/Party of the Irish). The main motivation in setting up that party was because of those who were unhappy with the findings of the Boundary Commission which maintained the existing border with Northern Ireland. This resulted in parts of Derry, Tyrone, Fermanagh, Armagh and Down – that had hoped to be brought into the Irish Free State – being left within the jurisdiction of Northern Ireland.

Those feeling unhappy included Cumann na nGaedheal TDs Professor William Magennis who represented the National University of Ireland, Pádraig O'Máille from Galway and Christopher Byrne from Wicklow. O'Máille had survived the December 1922 attack that had resulted in the killing of Sean Hayles TD.

While all three were participants in the Fourth Dáil, the new party dedicated itself to getting rid of the unpopular Oath of Allegiance. Some who had associated with the new party had been involved with the National Group formed in the Army Mutiny aftermath. The independent Republican TD, Dan Breen, seemed to have a similar relationship.

As a party leader, Maginness does not seem to have been ideally suited. Possessing a pompous personality, his obsessions with censorship and with protectionism rarely developed into a wider policy agenda. In late 1926 Clann Éireann absorbed the National Protectionist League, making the issue more central in its priorities.

The Boundary Commission report and the Oath of Allegiance were also the issues that were exercising Éamon de Valera as President of Sinn Féin. The copper-fastening of partition, with republicans deliberately choosing to remain aloof from the process, was proving deeply frustrating to de Valera. He resolved then sought to convince the Sinn Féin organisation of the necessity of a policy change on abstentionism.

Throughout 1925 Sinn Féin struggled with the issue. Some within the party even considered entering the Dáil on a one-off basis to vote down the Boundary Commission report. De Valera did not believe this to be a credible course. As the party prepared for its 1926 Ard Fheis, de Valera was determined he would seek a change of policy. Weighed against him were the traditionalists of the party who viewed abstentionism as a religious article of faith.

As if to emphasise the religiosity of the issue, an amendment to the motion de Valera and the Sinn Féin leadership were putting to the party's conference was tabled by the party's Vice President, Fr Michael O'Flanagan. The party gathered for its Ard Fheis on 9 March 1926 at the Rotunda Building in Dublin.

Debate on the motion carried into a second day:

> That once the admission oaths of the twenty-six and six- county assemblies
> are removed, it becomes a question not of principle but of policy whether or
> not Republican representatives should attend these assemblies. And the amend-
> ment: That it is incompatible with the fundamental principles of Sinn Fein as it
> is injurious to the honour of Ireland, to send representatives into any usurping
> legislature set up by English law in Ireland.

The vote on the O'Flanagan amendment saw 223 delegates in favour with 215 delegates being against. However later, when the amendment was included along with other agreed changes, the meeting voted 179 to 177 against.

De Valera had not secured the support of his party for the new policy. At best the position of the party seemed confused. For de Valera this Ard Fheis was an each-way bet. Had he been successful, Sinn Féin 'Mark III' would have been his vehicle for progression. In losing he was able to walk away and distance himself from a movement whose refusal to be flexible was proving to be permanently self-defeating.

The inaugural meeting of de Valera's new party, Fianna Fáil (Soldiers of Destiny), was held at La Scala Theatre, Dublin, on 16 May 1926. After the confused vote at the Sinn Féin Ard Fheis it was clear that the bulk of its membership and its organisation, and as would soon be discovered its public support, had followed de Valera into Fianna Fáil. Sinn Féin 'Mark III' was over.

With the Irish Free State entering into its fifth year of life, the old guard of the Irish Parliamentary Party was considering how it should and could play a greater role in the political life of the new State. William Redmond TD, as the inheritor of this mantle, issued a manifesto for a new party, the National League. His co-author, and co-sponsor, was Thomas O'Donnell, former Irish Party MP. In September 1926 the new party was launched at the Redmondite stronghold of Ballybricken Hill in Waterford.

At this event were several former Irish Party MPs. Two other TDs, Alfie Byrne of Dublin North and James Cosgrave of Galway, were former Irish Party MPs. Byrne did not seem attracted to the new party but Cosgrave was recruited. Redmond attempted to widen the appeal of the new party by introducing a private members' bill aimed at improving the legal position on town tenants.

Meanwhile, things were not going well for the main opposition party. The main problem for the Farmers Party was that it was difficult for it to find issues on which to oppose the government. Some discussions were entered into with the newly formed National League, but the talks came to nothing. More effort was put into talks on a potential merger with Cumann na nGaedheal. Agreement to this merger was reached between the party negotiators, but was vetoed by the sponsors of the Farmers Party – the Farmers Union. The failure to ratify this merger led Farmers Party leader Denis Gorey to cross the floor to join Cumann na nGaedheal. He was subsequently replaced as Farmers Party leader by Michael Heffernan.

The potential for the Businessmen's Party/Cork Progressive Association also receded in the Fourth Dáil. The Cork TDs O'Shaughnessy and Beamish, having initially sat as independents, took the Cumann na nGaedheal whip in 1924. Neither would seek election to the Fifth Dáil. The same was true of Businessmen's Party TD William Hewat. John Good was the only one of this group to contest the following election, and that was as an independent.

In January 1927 an interesting development occurred with the first abstentionist TD, Dan Breen from Tipperary, taking the Oath of Allegiance to sit and participate in the Fourth Dáil. Elections for the Fifth Dáil were called for 9 June 1927. The Fourth Dáil had sat for four years.

3

Change is Possible

The results of the election for the Fifth Dáil saw little difference in the support given to Cumann na nGaedheal or Fianna Fáil. Cumann na nGaedheal managed to stay marginally in front, winning forty-seven seats to Fianna Fáil's forty-four. There was a difference of little more than 15,000 votes, or 1.2 per cent of the national poll, between the two parties. The collective vote of the two parties was 53.6 per cent of the electorate, giving other parties and independents quite a significant share of the vote.

The Labour Party gained significantly in terms of seats but only marginally in terms of vote. The party returned to twenty-two seats but was still 10 per cent behind its 1922 high-water mark. The Farmers Party, coming into this election with a newly appointed leader and with its confidence badly dented, lost three seats. The eleven seats won could still be seen as something of an achievement.

Former leader Denis Gorey was barely elected as a Cumann na nGaedheal TD in the Carlow/Kilkenny constituency he shared with the President of the Executive Council, W.T. Cosgrave. Gorey won less than 1,000 votes, 12,000 votes behind Cosgrave whose surplus helped to elect Gorey.

Joining Michael Heffernan in the Fifth Dáil were Richard Holohan (elected ahead of Denis Gorey in Carlow/Kilkenny); Patrick Baxter (re-elected in Cavan); Thomas Falvey (who replaced Conor Hogan in Clare); previous TD John Dineen was replaced by David O'Gorman in Cork East; Daniel Vaughan was re-elected in Cork North as was Timothy O'Donovan in Cork West; John White in Donegal was another re-electee. The Kildare seat of John Conlon was lost, but Michael Carter won a new seat in Sligo/Leitrim, while new candidates failed to hold the party's seat in Limerick, and in Longford/Westmeath Patrick McKenna lost out to his party colleague Hugh Garahan. In Meath the party's seat was lost to Labour; Michael Doyle retained the Wexford seat, but the Waterford and Wicklow seats were lost.

The National League performed respectably on its first outing, winning eight seats with a little over 7 per cent of the national vote. The party had thirty candidates contesting the election. Party leader William Redmond topped the poll in Waterford. His former Irish Party colleague, James Cosgrave, elected as an independent in Galway in 1923, was unsuccessful but the party did win a seat there through William Duffy. John Horgan won a seat for the party in Cork Borough. Daniel McMenamin was elected in Donegal. Vincent Rice was successful in Dublin South. James Coburn was another poll topper in Louth and John Keating won a seat in Wexford. Finally in Sligo/Leitrim, John Jinks (who was later to achieve some degree on infamy) became a TD.

Sinn Féin 'Mark IV' stood fifteen candidates in just over half the constituencies. The leadership of what now, in effect, was a new party was somewhat convoluted. John J. Kelly, a former President of the Gaelic League, was selected to become President of this version of Sinn Féin. He was an abstentionist TD until 1923, but he was not a candidate in this election.

The highest profile of the candidates was the party's Vice-President, Mary McSwiney, sister of republican martyr and former Lord Mayor of Cork, Terence McSwiney. A case can be made for Mary McSwiney being considered as the first female leader of an Irish political party. McSwiney was also one of several Sinn Féin candidates who were family members of republicans who had lost their lives in the conflicts of the previous decade. Also in this category were David Kent in Cork and Cáitlín Brugha in Waterford. The concept of blood sacrifice not being in vain seemed to inform the 'not an inch' intensity of these republicans.

Kent and Brugha were elected. Mary McSwiney in Cork Borough was not. Austin Stack in Kerry, Oscar Traynor in Dublin North and John Madden in Mayo North made up the five TDs elected for this version of Sinn Féin. The party won short of 4 per cent of the national poll.

Clann Éireann had formed during the Fourth Dáil. It would be contesting this election with three outgoing TDs, each of whom had been elected as Cumann na nGaedheal TDs in 1923. In total the party would stand eight candidates in seven constituencies. Five of these candidates would finish bottom of the poll in their constituencies. The party nominated two candidates to contest the Longford/Westmeath constituency. Between them they secured less than 1,000 votes, securing the bottom places after the first count there. Nationally the party won 5,527 votes, less than half of 1 per cent of the total poll. This would be the party's only election.

This election saw the first instance of a specific interest group take the form of a political party to progress their interest. The Irish Association of the Blind created a Blind Men's Party presenting two candidates for election. The party won 0.1 per cent of the national vote. Why the needs of blind women were not being campaigned for does not seem to have been addressed.

Sixteen independents were elected to the Fifth Dáil, three TDs more than in 1923. Dublin University continued to select its three independents. In Cavan John O'Hanlon topped the poll with 4,300 votes over the quota. It was his first general election, although he had been a Farmers Party candidate in the National Group by-election of 1925, when he secured a significant vote.

John Daly was again elected on an independent Labour ticket in Cork East. In Cork North Dan Corkery (not to be confused with the author Daniel Corkery) was elected as an independent republican. Jasper Wolfe completed a trio of Cork independent TDs, winning a seat in Cork West. Corkery had been an IRA commandant, while Wolfe was a previous President of the Incorporated Law Society. He was also the owner of the *Cork County Eagle and Munster Advertiser*, successor of the *Skibbereen Eagle*, the newspaper which had kept its eye on the Tzar of Russia.

There were poll-topping performances by James Sproule Myles in Donegal and Alfie Byrne in Dublin North. Byrne's performance was particularly impressive, exceeding the quota there by over 10,000 votes. Myles Keogh was re-elected, less spectacularly, in Dublin South. The last of the Businessmen's Party TDs, John Good, was elected to the Fifth Dáil as an independent for the Dublin County constituency. This was the constituency he shared with Bryan Ricco Cooper, who was comfortably re-elected, exceeding the quota by finishing second to Cumann na nGaedheal's Kevin O'Higgins.

The Limerick constituency returned an independent TD in the person of Gilbert Hewson. He was a future relation of Paul Hewson, who would become prominent in the entertainment industry as Bono of U2. Alexander Haslett was elected in Monaghan with the designation of an independent farmer. His voting base should more rightly be seen as representing the Protestant minority in the border county. He also acted as Grand Master of the Orange Order there.

Arthur Clery was elected to represent the National University of Ireland. He was more than something of an outlier. He believed in, and had even promoted, partition in Ireland as a political solution. He was also opposed to the Anglo Irish Treaty, seeing it as a means for the island of Ireland to be reabsorbed into Britain. Roscommon returned Michael Brennan as an independent TD. It was the start of a twenty-four year association he had with the constituency.

John Cole was unsuccessful in holding the independent seat he had won in Cavan in 1923. John Lyons did not defend the seat he had won in Longford/Westmeath. Dan Breen's taking of the Oath of Allegiance and his seat in Dáil Éireann did not win the support of enough of the voters in Tipperary.

With the personnel of the Fifth Dáil now established, there would follow twelve of the most highly charged weeks in Irish politics. On 23 June the Fifth Dáil convened to elect a new government. The outgoing Cumann na nGaedheal government, while still the largest party, had only secured forty-seven of the 153 seats. Fianna Fáil with its forty-four seats, the five Sinn Féin TDs, and independent republicans, Arthur Clery and Daniel Corkery, continued to practise abstentionism. Even in a Dáil of 102 active members, Cumann na nGaedheal would be in a minority government. With the re-election of Michael Hayes as Ceann Comhairle/Speaker, the party still was five seats short of a working majority.

The debate on the election of President of the Executive Council saw W.T. Cosgrave make an early contribution, acknowledging the difficulty of the situation. Thomas Johnson on behalf of the Labour Party made his opposition to Cosgrave quite clear. Other speakers for the Farmers Party and several independent TDs stressed the need for continuity.

The vote was sixty-eight to twenty-two in Cosgrave's favour. Labour voted against. The National League abstained. The eleven Farmers Party TDs supported Cosgrave, as did eleven independent TDs. These included Michael Brennan, Alfie Byrne, John Daly, Bryan Ricco Cooper, Alexander Haslett, Gilbert Hewson, Myles Keogh, James Sproule Myles, John O'Hanlon, William Thrift (Dublin University TD), and Jasper Wolfe.

A second division was called on the composition of the government. The numbers opposed to the government increased to thirty-one. Labour was joined by three independents – Alfie Byrne, Gilbert Hewson and Jasper Wolfe. The National League split on the vote and five of their TDs voted against the government. One, Vincent Rice, voted with the government. Two, John Horgan and John Jinks, did not vote. It did not auger well for party discipline.

The third assassination of a member of Dáil Éireann in less than five years occurred on 10 July. Kevin O'Higgins was Vice President of the Executive Council and had been seen as the hard man of the Cosgrave government. In 1924 he was the de facto head of government during the Army Mutiny, when Cosgrave had taken sick leave. As Minister for Justice he had, during the Civil War, signed the execution warrants of seventy-seven republican prisoners, an act that had made him a target from that point on. He was 35 years of age.

On 17 July Constance Markievicz, republican icon, died. Her death, at 59 years of age, was due to complications following appendicitis. There was no political reason behind her death but there would be political consequences. A month previously she had been a candidate in the general election, being elected for the Dublin South constituency. She was elected as a Fianna Fáil TD, having chaired the inaugural meeting of the party a year previously.

The insider/outsider approach of Irish politics was mostly being felt at this period. As a government minister, O'Higgins was given a state funeral. Markievicz was not, causing considerable unhappiness in republican circles. This was despite her involvement in many of the key historical moments in the life of the nation over the previous fifteen years. From the Dublin lock out in 1913, through membership of the Irish Citizens Army, involvement in the 1916 Rising, election as the first woman to be elected to the British House of Commons and from there membership of the First Dáil, the second woman ever to hold ministerial rank as Minister for Labour in the provisional government (1919-22), to membership of the second and fourth Dáil, hers was a life worth noting.

On 26 July, in a move that had somewhat heightened the prevailing mood caused by these events, a second abstentionist TD, Patrick Belton, took the oath and his seat in Dáil Éireann. In June, having previously contested two other constituencies under Independent and National Democratic Party designations, he succeeded in being elected a Fianna Fáil TD for the Dublin County constituency. On that day he broke party ranks to find himself then expelled from his new political home.

Little more than two weeks later de Valera himself was to recognise the oath as an 'empty political formula' and lead Fianna Fáil into Dáil Éireann on 12 August. The Fianna Fáil number had been diminished by the death of Markievicz and the explusion of Belton, but had been augmented by the recruitment of independent TD Daniel Corkery also entering Dáil Éireann, for the first time on that day.

De Valera had been encouraged to come to this decision after legislation had been passed by the Cosgrave government, which now required candidates to announce their intention to take up their seats upon being nominated for election.

The arithmetic of the Dáil had changed dramatically because of this. Discussions took place between Labour, the National League and Fianna Fáil on the possibility of replacing the Cumann na nGaedheal administration with a Labour/National League government that would be supported externally by Fianna Fáil.

The first phase of this campaign was to bring down the government via a vote of no confidence. This was moved by Labour Party leader Thomas Johnson. The continuing abstentionist TDs, vacancies caused by the deaths of O'Higgins and Markievicz, and the inability of the Ceann Comhairle as speaker to vote, meant that 143 TDs were available to vote. The movers of the motion were confident that they could win the support of the seventy-two needed to vote against the government.

Cumann na nGaedheal gained the support of the Farmers Party TDs. All available independent TDs also supported the government. In something of a coup, the government had also managed to convince The National League TD Vincent Rice to support it. This would give seventy-one votes, but the opposition was confident it still had the numbers.

When the vote was taken it was seventy-one votes each. The National League, having already suffered one defection, had literally lost another of its TDs, John Jinks. The National League's TD from Sligo/Leitrim, did not participate in the confidence vote. This created all manner of stories that sought to explain his action. He acquired some level of infamy because of it, and quite a deal of international media attention.

The more lurid stories recounted that he had been kidnapped by government supporters and brought to a nearby hostelry, where he was fed with copious amounts of alcohol. The truth, the banal truth, was that Jinks never felt inclined to support the no confidence motion. In his resignation letter to National League leader William Redmond, he explained his reasons for not voting:

> I could not, in view of recent events, remain any longer a member of a party from which my political outlook so distinctly differs. On the recent issue of the proposed alliance between Fianna Fáil, Labour, and National League, I was not, to my great surprise consulted before action (improper action) was taken by you in favour of the proposed pact. All these things taken into consideration, I see no alternative open to me but to take the course I have now decided upon.

With a tied vote the Ceann Comhairle was obliged to vote with the government. On surviving the vote of no confidence W.T. Cosgrave proposed a lengthy adjournment with the house due to return in October 1927. Part of the reason for this was to allow two outstanding by-elections to take place. These were for the Dublin County and Dublin South constituencies and took place on 24 August.

Both were won convincingly by Cumann na nGaedheal. A subplot saw Fianna Fáil overwhelmingly defeat both Sinn Féin candidates, but with the combined vote still less than that being achieved by Cumann na nGaedheal.

W.T. Cosgrave, emboldened by these by-elections victories, by overcoming the vote of no confidence in the Dáil and by strengthening his parliamentary party through the defections of independent TDs John Daly, Bryan Ricco Cooper, Myles Keogh and rebel National League TD, Vincent Rice, now decided to call a snap election to try and strengthen Cumann na nGaedheal's position. The Fifth Dáil had lasted 98 days. Elections for the Sixth Dáil would take place on 15 September 1927.

4

Change is Coming

The second general election of 1927 saw a restoration of the dominance of the political parties born from the Civil War. Cumann na nGaedheal won an additional fifteen seats. Fianna Fáil added thirteen seats to its total. All the other political parties shipped losses. Labour lost nine seats to return thirteen TDs. The second general election within a three-month period had put enormous pressure on smaller parties, particularly on their finances and organisational capacity.

The failure of its party leader Thomas Johnson to hold its Dublin County seat was of greater disappointment for Labour. A few weeks earlier Johnson had been presenting himself as an alternative President of the Executive Council. The mantle of Labour leadership passed on to T.J. O'Connell.

The decline in the Farmers Party continued with the party nearly halving its parliamentary size, now standing at six TDs, down from eleven. The Farmers Party in Dáil Éireann now consisted of Richard Holohan in Carlow/Kilkenny; Daniel Vaughan in Cork North; Timothy O'Donovan in Cork West; John White in Donegal; Michael Jordan in Wexford (he had defeated sitting TD, Michael Doyle); and party leader Michael Heffernan in Tipperary. Those who lost out included Patrick Baxter in Cavan (lead spokesperson in the Fifth Dáil for the party until Michael Heffernan became appointed leader); Thomas Falvey in Clare; Hugh Garahan in Longford/Westmeath and Michael Carter in Sligo/Leitrim. David O'Gorman was unsuccessful in Cork East in winning back the seat of his party colleague John Dineen.

Farmers Party TDs may have had some solace in seeing their former leader, Denis Gorey fail to hold his seat in Carlow/Kilkenny. W.T. Cosgrave may have anticipated this situation when he chose to stand for election in Cork Borough as well as Carlow/Kilkenny. He was successful in both, opting to represent Cork, necessitating a by-election in Carlow/Kilkenny.

National League support collapsed. The party stood only eight candidates in this election, when three months previously it had presented thirty people for election. Six seats were lost. Some, such as that of the Sligo/Leitrim seat of John Jinks, and that of Cumann na nGaedheal defector Vincent Rice in Dublin South, were uncontested by the party (Jinks stood as an independent, finishing bottom of the poll, while Rice was defeated under his new party designation). This saw only two National League TDs being elected – party leader William Redmond in Waterford and James Coburn in Louth.

John Horgan in Cork Borough along with John Keating in Wexford failed to hold seats won in June. Neither Daniel McMenamin in Donegal nor William Duffy in Galway stood again. Although in Galway, James Cosgrave did try again in less favourable circumstances to be elected, he finished second bottom of the poll. Behind him was another former TD, Pádraic O'Máille, once a flag bearer for Clann Éireann.

The two by-elections in August 1927 saw the last appearance of Sinn Féin in an Irish election for a considerable time. Legislation that then required declaring the acceptance of any seats upon nomination for election had undermined abstentionism as a tactic for them. One candidate, Kate McCarry, standing in the Donegal constituency, did style herself as an independent Sinn Féin representative, but she finished bottom of the poll.

Twelve independents were elected, down from sixteen elected the previous June. Cavan elected two independent TDs, restoring John Cole (who had lost a previously held seat in June) and re-elected John O'Hanlon. Jasper Wolfe was comfortably re-elected in Cork West, being just sixteen votes shy of the quota. In Donegal James Sproule Myles once again topped the poll. Alfie Byrne in Dublin North was also comfortable, exceeding the quota on the first count. Dublin County elected two independents, John Good being re-elected, with Joseph Murphy being elected for the first time. In Monaghan Alexander Haslett was re-elected, as was Michael Brennan in Roscommon. The three Dublin University professors of Alton, Craig and Thrift were again returned.

Gilbert Hewson had the dubious distinction of being the only independent first elected in the June election seeking re-election, but he failed to be elected. Abstentionist TD Albert Clery did not re-contest the National University of Ireland constituency. Others elected as independents in June had chosen to join political parties. Dan Corkery in Cork North had chosen Fianna Fáil and was successful. Bryan Ricco Cooper and Myles Keogh were both elected as Cumann na nGaedheal TDs in Dublin County and Dublin South, respectively, Cooper topping the poll. Patrick Belton, elected as a Fianna Fáil TD but expelled when he took his Dáil seat without the party's approval, did not retain the Dublin County seat as an independent.

September 1927 saw another attempt for a communist party to infiltrate, at least electorally, the Irish political system. This time it was in the form of Jim Larkin, of Dublin Lockout fame. As an earlier version of the Communist Party of Ireland had petered out, Larkin set up the Irish Workers League, which became the Irish affiliate of Communist International. The party stood three candidates, each in Dublin constituencies. The candidates included Jim Larkin standing in Dublin North, and his namesake son standing in Dublin County. John Lawlor was the party's Dublin South candidate.

The party won a respectable 12,699 votes, most of which were gained in Dublin North and helped elect Jim Larkin on the first count by exceeding the quota. The performance of Larkin Jr. in Dublin County was a probable factor in the Labour Party leader, Thomas Johnson, losing his seat there.

The Larkin triumph was extremely short-lived, however. A long-running feud between him and Labour and trade union activist, William X. O'Brien (not the All For Ireland MP), had seen O'Brien win a libel action against Larkin. By demanding payment of this award, Larkin was made bankrupt, unable to take up the seat he had won. An irony of this situation was that O'Brien was an intermittent member of Dáil Éireann. He had not secured re-election in the bid for the Tipperary seat he had won in June 1927. Earlier, between 1922-23, he had been a Labour Party

TD for Dublin South. The Larkin/O'Brien feud would continue to torment the Labour Party for several decades to come.

Even with Larkin's non-admission and Cosgrave's dual seat-winning, Cumann na nGaedheal would still be some dozen votes short of achieving a working majority. The Sixth Dáil convened for its first meeting on 11 October and Michael Hayes was again elected as Ceann Comhairle. W.T. Cosgrave was the only nomination for the position of President of the Executive Council. A division on this saw seventy-six TDs supporting the nomination, with seventy TDs being opposed. Cosgrave had secured the support of his own party, the Farmers Party, and all of the independent TDs. Opposed to his nomination were Fianna Fáil and Labour. The two National League TDs did not participate in the vote. The nomination of the members of the Executive Council would not take place until the following day, when a similar division occurred.

In addition to naming the eight other members of his cabinet, W.T. Cosgrave announced his intention to appoint five Parliamentary Secretaries, TDs who would not be sitting in cabinet but would have certain ministerial functions devolved to them. One of these appointments was given to Michael Heffernan, leader of the Farmers Party, who was appointed as a Parliamentary Secretary to Minister for Post and Telegraphs, Ernest Blythe, who was also the Minister for Finance. This would be the first instance of a shared approach to government in Irish politics. It could not be considered a formal coalition, as Heffernan was not a member of cabinet.

The first by-election of the Sixth Dáil was held in November for the Carlow/Kilkenny constituency Cosgrave had decided not to represent. It provided an early opportunity for former Farmers Party leader, Denis Gorey to get back into the Dáil. It was not an easy opportunity. In a two-horse race his winning margin over his Fianna Fáil opponent was only 273 votes, about half of 1 per cent of the total poll.

Among the bills that Cosgrave wanted to pursue early in the life of this Dáil were two bills that sought to modify the democratic mechanisms of the State. The first of these was a Local Government (Amendment) Bill. This sought to hold all local elections on the same day in June, with councils then serving a three-year term. These elections would then take place in 1928. They would be for every local council in the country, with the exception of the two largest councils, Dublin Corporation and Cork Corporation, which continued to be suspended.

The second piece of legislation was a Seanad (Amendment) Bill. This sought to remove the public voting component for subsequent elections to the Senate. This diminution of democracy was opposed by the Labour Party. Fianna Fáil opposition was based on its belief that the Senate itself should be abolished.

In April 1928 the Dublin North by-election, brought about by Jim Larkin's disqualification, took place again. This time his son Jim Larkin Jr was the candidate and while he secured a higher vote than his father had in the September general election, with only one seat available, he finished here a distant third. The by-election was won by the former National League TD (now Cumann na nGaedheal candidate) Vincent Rice. He had been unsuccessful in September but here won over 50 per cent of the vote.

In June 1928 local elections were held. For the period until the 1967 general election it has been very difficult to fully assess the political impact of local elections in Ireland. Election results were never centrally collated. Analysis has depended on results given in local newspapers, archives of local councils (some of which were subsequently abolished) or those of political parties.

In 1928 the trends indicated that Fianna Fáil was the most success-ful party. Cumann na nGaedheal continued with its half in/half out approach, electing some officials and endorsing other government sup-porting candidates. The Labour Party was not as successful as it had been in 1925. The Farmers Party did do better than had been expected and many independents continued to be elected.

The Local Government election cycle did not fit with attempts at forming new political parties since the signing of the Treaty. None of those that had been formed – The National Democratic Party, Clann Éireann or the National League – were in existence long enough to contest local elections. By 1928 the National League, while still repre-sented in the Dáil, was now effectively bankrupt.

The Seanad election in December, under the new restricted voting system, would further entrench these trends. Despite the party's opposi-tion to the Senate, Fianna Fáil had six Senators elected. Four Senators were elected under a Cumann na nGaedheal banner. The Labour Party also managed to have its former party leader, Thomas Johnson, elected.

Six independent Senators were elected. Chief among these was Alfie Byrne, who resigned his Dáil seat. Others included Ross McGillycuddy, also known as The McGillycuddy of the Reeks, Walter Nugent (Sir) who had previously been an Irish Party MP for South Westmeath, John Bagwell, who had been first elected in 1922, and Andrew Jameson (perhaps better known for his association with the whiskey distillers, John Jameson and Co.). The final elected independent Senator was (Sir) Bryan Mahon who had originally been appointed in 1922.

Two other independent Senators had been elected in by-elections prior to 1928 – Pat Hooper and Samuel Brown. Brown had previous experience, having been elected in a 1923 by-election, but was unsuccessful in 1925.

By 1928 the Farmers Party group of Senators had dispersed. Michael O'Hanlon and James Dillon now represented Cumann na nGaedheal. Thomas Linehan was by now sitting as an independent Senator.

The ascension of Alfie Byrne to the Senate required a by-election to be held once again in Dublin North. Jim Larkin would not contest this by-election. It would be another two-horse race between Cumann na nGaedheal and Fianna Fáil. The government was represented by the brother of Kevin O'Higgins, T.F. O'Higgins. Fianna Fáil ran a recent convert, Oscar Traynor, who had been one of five abstentionist TDs elected for Sinn Féin in June 1927. It was to be a close-run thing. With a valid poll of almost 57,000 votes, O'Higgins came clear with a margin of 151 votes.

Seven years into the life of the new state there were signs of political duopoly taking root. While this was beginning to occur at Leinster House, some diversity could be found at local level. Elections for a newly restored Cork Corporation in 1929 saw Fianna Fáil, Cumann na nGaedheal and Labour all came within 100 votes of each other, yet between them the three parties won only eight of the available twenty-one seats. Of the other thirteen seats, seven were won by independents. Six successful councillors described themselves as Business candidates, this being the city that had elected two TDs for the Cork Progressive Association only six years previously.

The Cosgrave government had passed a specific piece of legislation for the newly convened council. The Cork City Management Act took away many of the executive decision-making rights of elected councillors, giving them instead to an appointed chief executive to be called the City Manager. Superficially based on an American system, it would develop into a uniquely Irish approach to local government, which more appropriately would be local administration.

The death of the Fianna Fáil deputy Samuel Holt brought about a by-election in Sligo/Leitrim in June 1929. Sean Mac Eoin won the seat on behalf of Cumann na nGaedheal, helping somewhat to strengthen the position of the Cosgrave government.

There were four Senate by-elections in 1929. Nugent Everard (Sir) had been nominated to the Senate in 1922 but had failed to be elected in 1928. He was re-elected in the first by-election caused by the death of Cumann na nGaedheal Senator (and TD until 1927) William Sears. Cumann na nGaedheal reversed this setback by filling an independent vacancy caused by the death of Alice Stopford Green, with Kathleen Browne being the successful candidate.

The other two by-elections saw independents fill independent vacancies. The first was the return of Laurence O'Neill, who served for seven years. He had been Lord Mayor of Dublin and had briefly (1922-23) also been a TD. He filled a vacancy caused by the resignation of Henry William Edmund Petty-Fitzmaurice, otherwise known as the Marquess of Landowne. He had succeeded to his father's seat in the British House of Lords in 1927. Between then and 1929 he had the distinction of serving simultaneously in the parliamentary chambers of two different jurisdictions.

The final Senate by-election of 1929 saw Richard Butler fill the vacancy caused by the death of the first by-election victor, Nugent Everard, who had died three months after being elected.

There were two Dáil by-elections in 1930. Neither involved candidates of minor parties or independents. Fianna Fáil held the seat in the Longford/Westmeath constituency. The vacancy had been caused by the death of its TD, James Killane. This would be the first by-election won by Fianna Fáil.

The by-election in Dublin County was held after the death of Bryan Ricco Cooper, initially an independent but finally elected as a Cumann na nGaedheal TD in 1927. The party comfortably held onto the seat.

The only other by-election of the Sixth Dáil was for the Kildare constituency. Here Fianna Fáil won the seat that had been held by the late Labour TD, Hugh Colohan.

The triennial local elections were due to be held in 1931. The Minister for Local Government, Richard Mulcahy, produced the Local Elections and Meetings (Postponement) Bill, 1931. This bill sought to postpone most of the elections due in 1931 until 1934 on the contentious reason that the intention was to restructure local government. The bill also included a provision to postpone the 1932 annual meetings to elect new mayors and chairs to various councils, so that such changes would not coincide or interfere with events linked with the anticipated Eucharistic Congress. Elections did go ahead for the Waterford and Limerick Borough Councils as well as elections for one-third of the membership of Cork Corporation.

Three other changes took place in the Senate during this period. Two independent Senators, Bryan Mahon and Patrick Hooper passed away. Their vacant seats were filled by new Cumann na nGaedheal Senators. The balance was somewhat restored with the election of a new independent Senator, Arthur Vincent, who filled a vacancy caused by the death of a Cumann na nGaedheal Senator, Patrick Kenny. Arthur Vincent had been responsible for donating Muckross House and Estate to the State.

Elections for twenty-two Senate seats took place in 1931. The newly elected Senators took up their mandate from December. Six independent Senators were elected – Eileen Costello, James Douglas, John Griffith, Ross McGillycuddy, Laurence O'Neill and Arthur Vincent. All had been re-elected. Newly elected as a Cumann na nGaedhael Senator was Hugh Garahan, who had previously been elected as a Farmers Party TD.

The alternative to the emerging duopoly in Irish electoral politics was being created on the fringes of political life. Behind several of these initiatives was the totemic figure of Peadar O'Donnell. O'Donnell from Dungloe in County Donegal had become radicalised, not only becoming consumed with the notion of Irish independence, but also being convinced of the need for widespread social change.

As a teacher on Arranmore Island he helped unionise many migrant workers, who departed from the island for large parts of each year. Unable to form a viable Irish Citizens Army unit in that part of the country, he became active instead in the IRA during the War of Independence.

In 1923 he was elected as an anti-treaty abstentionist TD. While not active in Dáil Éireann he became involved in many social change initiatives. He became a member of the Army Council of the anti-treaty IRA, editing its publication *An Phoblacht*, was responsible for setting up the Irish Working Farmers Committee, as well as the Anti-Tribute League. The latter advocated the non-repayment of land annuities, an issue that would later absorb Irish politics.

O'Donnell's main initiative during this period was to facilitate the establishment of a republican left wing front, known as Saor Éire. At a well-attended meeting in Dublin, a programme for the putative grouping was agreed. O'Donnell was appointed as leader with the meeting, chaired by the former TD, Sean Hayes, a former pro-treaty member of Dáil Éireann.

The Army Council of the anti-treaty IRA lent its support to the emerging organisation, considering it a better alternative to the existing moribund version of Sinn Féin. Many of those who attended were not only prominent in Irish republican circles, but also included those who would subsequently advance republican politics in other ways.

The Cosgrave government considered the formation of the movement more of a threat than its potential suggested. The government moved swiftly to introduce legislation, Constitution (Amendment No. 17) Bill, 1931, to proscribe Saor Éire. This Act was passed in October 1931. Not many other pieces of legislation were passed by the Sixth Dáil. A general election was called for February 1932. The Sixth Dáil was the longest such Dáil in existence.

Changes Occur

The 1932 general election results finally replaced Cumann na nGaedheal as the largest party in Irish politics. The party lost four seats, with Fianna Fáil winning an additional fifteen, easily passing its rival.

The Labour Party was reduced to seven seats. It again lost its leader, Thomas O'Connell, who failed to be elected from the Galway constituency. The Farmers Party had also lost its leader, but through a more tested route. Michael Heffernan was appointed a Parliamentary Secretary. This proved to be an absorption mechanism that saw him resign his Farmers Party leadership, standing unsuccessfully in the 1932 election as a Cumann na nGaedheal candidate.

What was left of the Farmers Party stood only six official candidates and only three were successful. Daniel Vaughan and Timothy O'Donovan were elected in the Cork North and Cork West constituencies. The third elected Farmer TD was John O'Shaughnessy in Limerick. Vaughan and O'Donovan had been re-elected. John O'Shaughnessy was a first-time TD. The unsuccessful candidates included former TD David O'Gorman in Cork East, and first-time candidates in Kerry and Laois/Offaly, Patrick Trant and Daniel Kennedy.

Four candidates stood as independent farmers. All were former Farmers Party TDs. John O'Hanlon was successful in Cavan. Richard Holohan in Carlow/Kilkenny, Michael Carter in Sligo/Leitrim and Michael Doyle in Wexford failed to be returned to Dáil Éireann. In Cork East a previously unsuccessful Farmers Party candidate, Brook Braiser, was elected as an independent TD.

The National League ceased to exist in 1931 when its party leader took the decision to join Cumann na nGaedheal. He was successfully re-elected in 1932 under that ticket. The other National League TD, James Coburn, chose to contest the election as an independent and was successful.

The Irish Workers League sought again to secure a foothold in Dáil Éireann. Its candidate team were the Larkins, senior and junior, in the Dublin North and Dublin South constituencies. Between them they secured less than 5,000 votes, most of these being won by Larkin senior.

Fourteen independents TDs were elected in 1932, up two from September 1927. Three of these were the consistent Dublin University complement. Two were independent labour – former Labour TDs Richard Anthony in Cork and Daniel Morrisey in Tipperary, both in dispute with the party. Two had been associated with the Farmers Party, another was originally elected for the National League.

Jasper Wolfe was elected in Cork West. James Sproule Myles delivered his usual poll-topping performance in Donegal. On this occasion he was joined by James Dillon, son of the last Irish Party leader John Dillon, grandson of John Blake Dillon of *The Nation* newspaper and the Young Ireland movement of 1848.

Tiring of the Senate, Alfie Byrne resigned his seat in 1931 and re-contested the Dublin North constituency where he was re-elected with an excess of more than two quotas. John Good was once again elected in Dublin County. The last of the independents to be elected in 1932 was the colourful Frank McDermot in Roscommon. He would play a telling role in the immediate political history of the country.

Fianna Fáil had succeeded in winning the highest number of seats of any political party in any Dáil election (after a 10 per cent increase in its vote), yet in the Seventh Dáil it still could not be guaranteed to form a stable working government. The new Dáil convened on 9 March 1932. The newly elected Ceann Comhairle was Fianna Fáil's Frank Fahy. Following his election, Fianna Fáil still required another five votes to secure de Valera's election as the new President of the Executive Council.

The social programme of Fianna Fáil appealed more to Labour. It had voted against Cosgrave in the previous and other Dáils. The party would now support the election of de Valera. The Farmers Party split, two voting against de Valera, John O'Shaughnessy voting for. De Valera also secured the support of independent farmer TD, John O'Hanlon. Most surprisingly (on the basis that he was the leader of the largest group in the Dáil) he was supported by newly elected independent TD James Dillon. Another newly elected TD, Frank McDermot, chose to abstain. De Valera was also elected President of the Executive Council by eighty-one votes to sixty-eight. The new government was approved without a division.

The peaceful transition of power was a mark of maturity in the life of the new State. Some Fianna Fáil TDs had entered the Dáil chamber that day carrying revolvers, in fear that that transition would not be achieved.

Cumann na nGaedheal, in government for the opening decade of the State's existence, had cultivated its image as the party of the establishment. This allowed it in turn to portray Fianna Fáil as the anti-establishment party, with which Fianna Fáil felt quite comfortable. When campaigning against Fianna Fáil, the outgoing government characterised its opponents as being essentially communist in nature.

Fianna Fáil was acquiring a voting base that was proving more successful than Labour in securing the support of working-class voters in town and cities, and that of agricultural workers and small farmers in rural communities. The flag bearer of the radical republican left, Peadar O'Donnell, encouraged supporters of his agenda to vote for Fianna Fáil.

Having secured Labour support to achieve election as President of the Executive Council, de Valera set about implementing his agenda. The Oath of Allegiance was abolished. Land annuity payments to Britain were stopped, initiating an economic war between the two countries. De Valera also took the post of Minister for External Affairs, actively promoting an independent foreign policy through the League of Nations.

In the meantime, the threads that remained from what had been the National League and the disintegration of the Farmers Party, were still to be resolved. Outside of the three remaining Farmers Party TDs, six of the elected independent TDs had been elected through support received from local farmers organisations. Attempts were made to weave this into a more cohesive national organisation.

On the initiative of Frank McDermot a meeting was held in September 1932 with representatives of farmer organisations from all over the country. This was followed by a subsequent meeting where it was agreed to establish a National Farmers and Ratepayers League which held its first convention in October, with representatives of twenty of the twenty-six counties.

This convention stated the aims of the League to be the promotion of agricultural interests; the elimination of the bitter memories of the Civil War; and to abolish partition by abolishing the animosities which were the causes of partition. It was agreed to decide at a future meeting whether the League should call itself The National Party or The Centre Party.

Some, like independent TD Alfie Byrne and independent Senator Arthur Vincent, felt that a strengthened Cumann na nGaedheal might allow a route for those promoting this new party to pursue. W.T. Cosgrave was open to having such discussions. Frank McDermot was not, believing the purpose of the new party was to keep a distance from either Civil War party.

This was all happening during the development of a quickly changing political environment. De Valera had achieved one of his immediate political goals in having his preferred candidate, Dónal O' Búachalla, appointed as Governor General. No sooner had he been appointed to office, when de Valera requested the holding of a general election to give Fianna Fáil the opportunity of obtaining a stronger mandate. This election was planned for January.

The National Centre Party was having to establish and organise itself in the middle of an election campaign. After a meeting with James Dillon, McDermot and Dillon agreed to set up a National Centre Parliamentary Party. Dillon's participation surprised some. His association with the old Irish Party, and his earlier support for the National League, were countered by his voting for de Valera to be President of the Executive Council.

McDermot and Dillon gave the new party something of a cosmopolitan gloss. Both were barristers. Both had lived and worked outside the country and were acquiring reputations as being among the better orators in Dáil Éireann.

The first advertisements which appeared under the name of National Centre Party outlined a ten-point list of principles. They stressed the need for individual liberty and individual ownership. They sought more influence for the agriculture community over government policy. They also called for a new spirit and atmosphere in Irish politics.

Establishing a new party was not made any easier by alternating in promotional material the names of National Centre Party with that of the National Farmers and Ratepayers League. To many voters the new party seemed more like the latest manifestation of the Farmers Party.

Nevertheless, the party managed to secure twenty-six candidates to contest twenty-one of the thirty constituencies. The party performed well, electing eleven TDs, and becoming the third largest party in the Eighth Dáil.

Regarding the bigger picture, de Valera's election gamble had paid off. Fianna Fáil returned with five additional seats, winning a shade under 50 per cent of the vote. The decline of Cumann na nGaedheal continued apace. The party lost nine seats and close on 5 per cent of its popular vote. It was not a successful election for the Labour Party either, having to contest a general election under its third leader in three elections.

At least on this occasion William Norton managed to be re-elected. The party won an additional seat to bring its Dáil contingent to eight TDs. However, it also slipped to its lowest ever share of the national vote (below 6 per cent) and for the second time had become the fourth largest party in the Dáil.

Outside of Fianna Fáil strengthening its chokehold on power, it was the National Centre Party that was the story of that election. Other than its totemic figures Frank MacDermot in Roscommon and James Dillon in Donegal, the party succeeded in having Richard Holohan (former Farmers Party TD) elected in Carlow/Kilkenny. The party ran two candidates in the Cavan constituency, but it was not the outgoing independent TD (and former Farmers Party candidate) John O'Hanlon who was elected, but his running mate Patrick McGovern.

In Cork East the National Centre Party recorded a success that pointed a way towards an interesting political future. Its successful candidate, William Kent, had been elected a Fianna Fáil TD in the September 1927 election but failed to be re-elected in 1932. He had been reselected as a Fianna Fáil by-election candidate when the formation of the National Centre Party piqued his interest.

His family history was particularly interesting. His brother David was elected as a Sinn Féin abstentionist TD in June 1927 election. Another brother, Thomas had been executed in 1916 for his part in a shootout all three had taken part in, resulting in the death of a Royal Irish Constabulary officer outside the Kent family house.

One of the last Farmers Party TDs, Timothy O'Donovan was successful for the National Centre Party in Cork West. Patrick Rogers won a seat for the party in Sligo/Leitrim. John Finlay was another new TD in Laois/Offaly. Charles Fagan successfully carried the flag in Longford/Westmeath. Richard Curran became the party's TD in Tipperary. In Waterford former Farmers Party TD, Nicholas Wall was elected for the new party.

The National Centre Party experiment was not universally successful. Two of the last three Farmers Party TDs, Daniel Vaughan in Cork North and John O'Shaughnessy in Limerick, were not elected as National Centre Party candidates. Another former Farmers Party TD, Patrick Baxter, stood in Clare (he had previously stood in Cavan) but failed to win a seat.

It may have been different if the first attempt to establish a Centre Party had been successful. In 1931 the politically promiscuous Patrick Belton tried to establish such a party. The main planks of this party were to de-rate agricultural land and to break the currency link with sterling. The party never took root. Belton would contest the 1932 elections as an independent in the fourth constituency he had contested, Dublin North. He was again unsuccessful.

In 1933 he succeeded in that constituency as a Cumann na nGaedheal candidate, making him the only person to be elected for both Fianna Fáil (June 1927) and Cumann na nGaedheal. Not only was this the fourth Dáil constituency he had contested, it was his third different political party (he ran with the National Democratic Party in 1923). He also had contested several elections unsuccessfully as an independent.

Successful independent TDs saw a downturn in the 1933 election. Five fewer were elected, with the share of the national vote being more than halved. Part of the reason for this was the number of previous independents who had chosen the vehicle of the National Centre Party in this election.

Of the nine independents elected in 1933, three were the usual suspects from the Dublin University constituency. Richard Anthony once again saw off the official Labour challenge in Cork Borough. His independent labour colleague in Tipperary from the 1932 election, Daniel Morrissey, chose not to contest in 1933.

Becoming as regularly monotonous as the Dublin University TDs was James Sproule Myles, once again elected and topping the poll in Donegal. In Dublin North, a constituency shared with Fianna Fáil's Seán T. O'Kelly and Cumann na nGaedhael's Richard Mulcahy, Alfie Byrne was once again elected. The same was true of John Good in Dublin County. Alexander Hassett was re-elected again in Monaghan.

The former National League TD James Coburn was re-elected as an independent TD in Louth. His erstwhile party leader, William Redmond, had been elected as a Cumann na nGaedheal TD in 1932. He had passed away before the 1933 election, and his Waterford seat was won by his widow Bridget.

Jim Larkin Senior once again contested a general election, this time as a strict independent and not as an Irish Workers League candidate. He was again unsuccessful.

The furniture of the Eighth Dáil having been established, it then had to select its new government. This was done on 8 February 1933. Fianna Fáil became a technical minority government with the re-election of Frank Fahy as Ceann Comhairle. In again securing the support of the Labour Party, the rest of the Dáil divided against the Fianna Fáil nominee, Éamon de Valera. With the support of Labour, de Valera won eighty votes in the Dáil, the highest level of support ever won for that office.

6

Blue is the Colour

Throughout 1932 the first Fianna Fáil government relaxed a number of legislative restrictions that had affected anti-treaty members of the IRA. This had the effect of raising the temperature at public political events. Cumann na nGaedheal complained that its public meetings were being attacked as part of an anti-treaty IRA campaign they titled 'No Free Speech for Traitors'.

As a reaction a security force was created to protect Cumann na nGaedheal meetings. Named the Army Comrades Association (ACA) the group was soon to develop a political dimension. T.F. O'Higgins was called on to become its leader. Within months the organisation would claim 30,000 members.

On being re-elected President of the Executive Council, de Valera sought to replace the Garda Commissioner, Eoin O'Duffy. O'Duffy had been a pro-treaty TD in the early life of the State, but for the last decade had led the country's police force. With the ascension of Fianna Fáil into government, he was not seen as being appropriately cooperative and found himself being removed from office.

He was given an immediate political opportunity to respond to these events, when he was asked to lead the Army Comrades Association in 1933. He immediately styled the organisation into his own image. An admirer of Benito Mussolini and the Italian Fascists, O'Duffy introduced stylised uniforms, based on blue shirts. He encouraged the straight arm salute favoured by European fascists. His rebranding was complete when he renamed the organisation, the National Guard. The organisation would undergo two further name changes, firstly to become the Young Ireland Association, finally to end its life as the League of Youth.

In August 1933 O'Duffy sought to organise a show of strength by holding a major demonstration in Dublin. The government declared this demonstration illegal. While the event did not go ahead, parallel events did take place elsewhere in the country. This gave the de Valera government a pretext to ban the National Guard.

O'Duffy's heightened public profile coincided with attempts to create a more cohesive opposition to Fianna Fáil. The National Centre Party (which had been less than a year in existence) had entered into talks with Cumann na nGaedheal on the possibility of establishing a new political party. Into these talks was introduced Eoin O'Duffy (representing the Young Ireland Association, the renamed National Guard) making a tripartite arrangement. In September 1933 that new party, Fine Gael (United Ireland), was formed. It chose an unconventional leadership structure. O'Duffy, not a TD, was chosen as leader. W.T. Cosgrave was to be its parliamentary leader.

Frank MacDermot became a Vice-President of the new party. At the concluding meeting of the National Centre Party MacDermot told his members that they would be entering as equals into the new alliance. He cannot have been aware of the vampiric qualities of Cumann na nGaedheal. The recent election had given clear evidence of that through the candidacies of two former Farmers Party leaders, Denis Gorey and Michael Heffernan. Both had stood as Cumann na nGaedheal candidates, without success.

The O'Duffy experiment lasted less than a year. He was forced from office in June 1934, having been seen to embarrass the party on more than one occasion. He mitigated the political absence by forming his own National Corporate Party. The party never took off and the Spanish Civil War would later consume more of his attention.

The first significant electoral test in this period was the local elections of 1934. In these elections Fianna Fáil won about 40 per cent of the available seats, Fine Gael about 32 per cent, with Labour gaining about 10 per cent of the councillors elected. Of the others, most were independents, although Sinn Féin did have some councillors elected.

The anti-treaty IRA were again engaged on whether a political wing could be established and whether it could prove effective. A convention of its members decided, by a single vote, against setting up a new party. Those who disagreed left to form their own organisation. In April 1934 in Athlone an inaugural meeting of the Republican Congress was held. Once again Peadar O'Donnell was its prime initiator.

The group established a national office and that prerequisite of any republican socialist group – its own newspaper. In the local elections of that year, two councillors were elected under a Republican Congress banner.

These initial encouraging signs were not followed up with any sustainable organisational development. Within two years, after recriminations on what strategic approach should be followed, another attempt at republican socialist party-building withered on the vine.

Later in 1934 elections were held for twenty-two Senate seats. Five independent Senators were elected. Each had been previously elected. The only significant change was that Jennie Wyse Power was now elected as a Fianna Fáil Senator. She had been sitting as an independent Senator, having originally beenchosen for Cumann na nGaedheal. Among the new Fine Gael Senators elected were former Farmers Party TDs Patrick Baxter and Richard Wilson.

In June 1935 the first significant by-elections for the Eighth Dáil were held in the Dublin County and Galway constituencies. Both by-elections were caused by the deaths of two Fine Gael TDs. Each by-election was a two-horse race between Fianna Fáil and Fine Gael. Dublin County was successfully held by Fine Gael but Galway was lost to Fianna Fáil. The success in Galway allowed Fianna Fáil to become the first single-party majority government in the history of the State.

A significant political resignation occurred in 1935 when Frank MacDermot resigned from Fine Gael. Amongst other things he thought the party too consumed with the British Commonwealth. He sat as an independent for the remainder of this Dáil.

Meanwhile de Valera's patience with the Senate of the Irish Free State was beginning to run thin. The composition of the Senate did not allow for a Fianna Fáil majority to exist there. Some of this concerned the length of the term of offices for Senators, which at nine years had already been reduced from twelve. The limited electorate made the Senate practically self-perpetuating. The method of election, with approximately one-third of members being elected every three years, meant a chamber that rarely coincided with its sister house in Dáil Éireann. All this meant that the Senate was not adaptable for de Valera's purposes.

Having stymied too many of his proposed constitutional changes (although The Senate only had the power to delay legislation by twenty months) de Valera decided that a new Constitution was needed and that the Senate had to go. To this end he produced The Constitution (Amendment No. 24) Act (1936), the death warrant for the Senate of the Irish Free State.

In its short life it had provided a valuable platform for alternative debate. However, in truth, its powers had been eroded from the date of its first meeting. Only once, in 1925, and for only nineteen of its sixty seats, was the Senate subject to a public vote. A power it had never utilised, but which was now being taken away from it, was the ability to directly put questions to public referendum.

In August 1936 two further Dáil by-elections were held in Galway, again, and in Wexford. Once again the by-elections were caused by the death of two Fine Gael TDs. Fianna Fáil won both by-elections, thus strengthening its Dáil majority. Sinn Féin offered a slight third-party challenge in these by-elections. Its two candidates won less than 4,000 votes between them so it seemed to have been a toe-dipping exercise for the party.

De Valera's priorities now lay in having a new Constitution adopted. This would be done by holding the first referendum in the history of the State, in conjunction with a general election for the Ninth Dáil. These ballots would be voted on on the first day of July.

Prior to this general election de Valera had tilted the playing pitch in his favour. The size of the Dáil was decreased by fifteen members. A total of 138 seats would now be available. The number of constituencies was increased, particularly adding to those of a smaller size, but with fewer seats available. These changes were designed to be more helpful to the largest party.

Fianna Fáil's vote dropped by almost 5 per cent, as did that of Fine Gael (although officially this was its first general election). Labour and the independents seemed to benefit equally from this shift. So, little changed in the Dáil arithmetic. Fianna Fáil won precisely half the available seats. Fine Gael lost eleven seats to stand at forty-eight. Labour had a fillip, moving from eight to thirteen, while eight independents were elected.

There was one less independent TD in the Ninth Dáil. In Cavan John Cole returned, having last been elected in September 1927. In Clare Thomas Burke was elected as an independent farmer. In Cork Borough, Richard Anthony held off the official Labour candidate for a third election in a row. James Sproule Myles won a seat in the new Donegal east constituency, again topping the poll.

The large Dublin North constituency was replaced with two new constituencies of Dublin North East and Dublin North West. Alfie Byrne contested Dublin North East where he was the poll topper. A second independent was elected in the constituency – James Larkin Senior. Fine Gael's big beast, Richard Mulcahy, lost out there. In Dublin North West a second member of the Byrne family stood as a candidate – Alfie'e son Alfred Patrick, who exceeded the quota. A dynasty was born. In Dublin South, Joseph Hannigan, a medical doctor and first-time candidate, secured a seat.

Of the outgoing independent TDs John Good did not contest in 1937. He had had five successful election campaigns, after having been first elected as a Businessmen's Party TD in 1923. Alexander Haslett failed to secure another term as a TD for Monaghan.

Patrick Belton stood again as an independent, having been elected a Cumann na nGaedheal TD in 1933, and reverted to a previous constituency in Dublin County. In 1936 he founded the Irish Christian Front, ostensibly to support the nationalist side in the Spanish Civil War, but this additional profile did not help his electoral chances.

How had the National Centre Party candidates elected in 1933 fared in 1937 as Fine Gael candidates? Neither Frank MacDermot in Roscommon nor William Kent TD from Cork East chose to test the proposition, as both retired from Dáil Éireann.

James Dillon was elected in Monaghan, while Patrick McGovern was successful in Cavan. Also elected were Timothy O'Donovan in Cork West; Patrick Rogers in the new Sligo constituency; John Finaly in Laois/Offaly; Charles Fagan in the new constituency of Meath/Westmeath and Nicholas Wall in Waterford.

This represented a relatively high success rate for the party. Two former National Centre Party TDs were unelected in this election – Richard Curran in Tipperary and Richard Holahan in the new

Kilkenny constituency. The Fine Gael candidate elected in Kilkenny was the former Farmers Party leader, Denis Gorey.

Elsewhere, the last remnant of the National League party was also being assimilated into Fine Gael. Having been twice elected as a National League TD, and subsequently as an independent on two further occasions, James Coburn, a TD for Louth, was elected on behalf of Fine Gael.

The referendum on adopting a new Constitution revealed an interesting result. A turnout of 76 per cent was significant. The 56-44 per cent vote in favour seemed significant. However, spoilt votes, at 10 per cent of the total poll, indicated a significant protest against The Constitution. When spoilt votes were added in, the in favour margin was wafer thin.

Armed with his new constitution, de Valera set about putting his new systems into place. The new Dáil met on 21 July. Frank Fahy was again selected as Ceann Comhairle which once again put Fianna Fáil into a minority position. The new Constitution would not come into effect until 29 December. This meant that the Dáil had to once again elect a President of the Executive Council. For the third successive time, de Valera secured the support of the Labour Party. He also gained the support of Jim Larkin, making his election quite comfortable.

The new Constitution allowed for elections for the new Seanad, successor to the previous Senate, and was put in place in early 1938. This was to be the Second Seanad, the first to be elected under the new electoral system of candidates being selected from vocational panels. Independents did surprisingly well under this system, as political parties had yet to develop the art of solid block voting.

Nine independent Senators were elected to the Second Seanad – Thomas Condon, John Newcome, Ross McGillycuddy (a member of the First Senate), Michael Twomey, Seamus O hEocha, and James Douglas (another member of the first Senate). The other three elected independent Senators represented the Dublin University constituency (subsequently elected to the Seanad rather than the Dáil). These were Ernest Alton, Joseph Johnston and Robert Rowlette.

A feature of the new Seanad was the facility for a sitting Taoiseach to directly nominate eleven members. Three independents were within the first group of Taoiseach's nominees – (Sir) John Keane, William Magennis and Douglas Hyde. Keane had served throughout the term of the First

Senate. Magennis was a former Cumann na nGaedheal TD who then led the short-lived Clann Éireann party (his colleague in that exercise, Pádraic O'Máille, was elected to the Second Seanad as a Fianna Fáil Senator).

Douglas Hyde was only to serve as a Senator for a matter of weeks. In May 1938, as the sole nominee, he was elected to become the first President of Ireland, an office that made the position of Governor General redundant.

Another curious Taoiseach's nominee was Frank MacDermot. MacDermot had founded the National Centre Party, taken it into an alliance with Cumann na nGaedheal to form Fine Gael, but subsequently resigned to sit as an independent for the remainder of that Dáil. He later took the Fianna Fáil whip when offered that appointment.[*]

The political agenda concentrated on resolving the continuing Economic War with Britain. This was causing considerable hardship within Ireland and was the main factor in bringing about a decrease in Fianna Fáil support at the general election.

The mood was to resolve the issue as quickly as possible. By April 1938 an Anglo-Irish Trade Treaty had been agreed and was approved by Dáil Éireann. This involved a cash settlement from the Irish Government to Britain, but also saw the return of four 'Treaty' ports to Irish control.

The ending of the impasse, despite the hardship it had caused, brought about an improvement in the government's fortunes. Just as he had done in 1932/33, with less than a year into the life of the Ninth Dáil, de Valera sought to call another general election to try to improve Fianna Fáil's majority. The election was held on 17 June.

The gamble paid off spectacularly. Fianna Fáil secured more than 50 per cent of the vote. The party would be the first ever elected with a working majority over the combined opposition – a majority of fifteen seats. Fine Gael continued its decline, losing a further three seats. Labour

---

[*] The *Oireachtas Members Database* does not give the affiliation of several members of that Seanad. They would include John Greene, Martin O'Dwyer, Michael Conway, John Gaffney, Frederick Hawkins, Gilbert Hughes, James Johnston, Thomas McShea, David Walsh, Patrick Keohane, and Peadar Toner Mac Fhionnlaoich.

yo-yoed once again, losing almost one-third of its parliamentary party. One fewer independent TD was elected to this Dáil.

Six of the eight independent TDs elected in 1937 were re-elected in 1938. The two people who lost out were left-wing independents. In Cork Borough, the Labour Party finally won its battle with Richard Anthony, taking the seat he had held. In Dublin North East, Jim Larkin Senior lost out to Fine Gael's Richard Mulcahy (who had to endure a brief sojourn in the new Seanad). One new independent, Patrick Cogan in Wicklow, was elected.

Bunreacht na hÉireann (The Constitution of Ireland) specified that elections to Seanad Éireann had to occur within three months of an election for Dáil Éireann. This meant that the Second Seanad was ended after only ten sittings. Despite the proximity of the two elections there was some change in the membership between the Second and Third Seanad.

Of the independents elected, the three Dublin University Senators, along with Ross MacGillycuddy and James Douglas were returned to office. Four others were unsuccessful. One new independent Senator, John Counihan, was elected. The new Senators listed as being unaffiliated were James McGee, Dominick MacCabe, Martin O'Dwyer, Thomas Delany, Joseph Brennan, Peter Trainor Kelly, Frederick Hawkins, James Johnston, Peter Lynch, Patrick Keohane and Peadar Toner Mac Fhionnlaoich.

The Senators nominated by the Taoiseach were largely those who had been nominated to the Second Seanad.

7

'Others' Return

The 1930s was a bleak period for 'others' in Irish politics. Between Fianna Fáil's consolidation, Fine Gael's decline and the Labour Party's oscillation, there was developing an all-too-narrow framework for Irish politics. Attempts at new party development were limited to the fringes, never escaping from those confines. The one serious attempt at a new party, the National Centre Party, ended up being a transitory vehicle for the creation of Fine Gael. The number of elected independents was also being whittled down, with bailiwicks becoming entrenched around the fortunes of a number of individuals.

The international political environment was heading, inexorably, towards global conflagration. Perhaps this uncertainty fed another attempt for a fourth party to emerge in Irish electoral politics. That party would be the third attempt to establish a farming-centred party, in a state that had yet to achieve twenty years of existence. These were the circumstances into which Clann na Talmhan (Family/Party of the Land) was created. Being the third in a number of failed attempts did not seem to auger well. However, there were factors that indicated that a different approach might achieve other levels of success.

In June 1939 a meeting was held in Athenry, County Galway, to try to achieve such an effect. The western locale was significant. Previous agrarian parties had pivoted around a more eastern axis. The type of farmers represented at this meeting were also different, being mainly smallholders as opposed to the 'ranchers' who had been the more adept at political representation. The platform spoken about here also seemed wider, more infused with a social democratic bent.

The first electoral test for the new party came in May 1940 when a by-election in Galway West was held. The Clann na Talmhan candidate was Michael Donnellan, leader of the party. Fine Gael, organisationally weak, had decided not to contest the election, the first that was uncontested by the party in either of its incarnations.

This meant that Donnellan was the only challenger to Fianna Fáil. Donnellan had already served as Fianna Fáil councillor on Galway County Council, before becoming disenchanted with the party. The by-election was won easily by the government candidate, although Donnellan had secured a significant vote, which if repeated would put him in the frame in a future Dáil election.

Also in 1940 yet another attempt was made to establish a republican party to compete with Fianna Fáil. Coras na Poblachta (The Republican Plan) was another collection of former IRA activists. They did at least seek to develop a policy that went beyond the reunification of the national territory. These included some ideas that were getting a first airing, ideas that eventually would be seen to be implemented.

Among these ideas were proposals to break the link with the British pound, and the nationalisation of banks and the making of bank officials into civil servants. In education, the party proposed free education for all children over primary age as a right, and for university education when feasible. Also called for was the introduction of children's allowances.

Meanwhile the Second World War was raging, a period known in neutral Ireland as 'The Emergency'. De Valera's policy of neutrality had won widespread acceptance within the country's political system. However, it was not without some questioning voices. Chief among those was James Dillon. While being a passionate advocate against neutrality, Dillon also found himself at odds with his own party. In 1941 he resigned the Fine Gael whip to sit once again as an independent.

Local elections, which had already been delayed by several years, were held in 1942. These results were not collated at a national level, making analysis difficult. A new political party was formed in 1942, but did not contest these elections. This was Ailtirí na hAiséirghe (Architects of the Resurrection), the furthest right wing exponents of any Irish political party. Its founder, Gearóid Ó Cuinneagáin, was born in Belfast, where he was brought up to form a strong attachment to the Irish language.

This obsession was to inform many of the policies he, and subsequently his party, espoused.

These aims included the banning of English being spoken in public, combined with the total revival of the Irish language across Ireland. A virulent anti-Semitic strain ran through the party which saw it call for the removal of Jews from Irish society. The parallel logic of this position also saw the party call for the installation of a Catholic-based dictatorship. Support for the Axis powers in the Second World War also set the party apart.

Ailtirí did attract some significant supporters. Cumann na nGaedheal stalwarts, former government ministers and TDs, Ernest Blythe and James Walsh approved of what the new party was saying. Among those who sought membership were Seán Treacy, the future Labour Party/ Independent TD and Ceann Comhairle of Dáil Éireann, as did the novelist Brian Cleeve and the journalist/broadcaster and author Breandán Ó hEithir. Perhaps it was a youthful romanticism with the emphasis on language that attracted some of these people as members. In most cases their political positions were to develop otherwise.

A fellow traveller of Ailtirí was the infamous Oliver J. Flanagan. While supportive of many of Ailtirí aims, Flanagan chose a different political vehicle for himself. It is difficult to portray Monetary Reform as a political party, certainly as a national one. It did not seem to operate much outside of the Laois/Offaly constituency, or highlight members other than Flanagan.

He was acquiring a somewhat eclectic reputation, but with it a high public profile. Stories were told of him cycling to meet potential voters, his bike adorned with a sign at the front (saying 'Here comes Oliver') and another at the back (saying 'There goes Flanagan').

His opinions, however, were very much in accord with those of Ailtirí. He publicly made a number of anti-Semitic statements. Some of these he believed were masked by his support of the international Social Credit movement, which while it sought to describe political problems and their solutions in how currency was dealt with, attribute some of these difficulties to the 'international Jewish banking conspiracy'.

An alternative Ireland did exist, an Ireland where a second chamber in Seanad Éireann allowed for some independent thinking to occur. In

November/December 1942 the Taoiseach's nominee (Sir) John Keane secured a four-day debate:

> That, in the opinion of Seanad Éireann, the Censorship of Publications Board appointed by the Minister for Justice under the Censorship of Publications Act, 1929, has ceased to retain public confidence, and that steps should be taken by the Minister to reconstitute the board.

Keane used extensive quotes from the book *The Tailor and Ansty* by Eric Cross, which had been banned in Ireland soon after its publication that year. The Editor of Oireachtas Debates excluded all quotations from the Official Report; which then read: 'The Senator quoted from the book'. Keane also taunted his fellow Taoiseach's nominee, William Magennis, for thinking that two men embracing in another book amounted to sodomy. It would be a further twenty years before Ireland's censorship laws would be liberalised.

Meantime, the Irish Farmers Federation (IFF), an organisation that was mainly Leinster based, decided to establish a political wing. This was to be the National Agricultural Party. Patrick Cogan, an independent TD who had been elected for Wicklow, was closely identified with the IFF and asked to pursue this project. Cogan, while supportive of the IFF, did not see the purpose of two agrarian parties existing. He pursued merger negotiations with Clann na Talmhan. These were successful and led to naming the merged party Clann na Talmhan – The National Agricultural Party. In theory the widened party now had a broader geographical base with the potential of appealing to more people in rural communities.

Emergency powers had extended the life of the Tenth Dáil. It would end up being the longest sitting Dáil. When a general election was held in June 1943, there would be four new parties contesting – Clann na Talmhan, Coras na Poblachta, Ailtirí na hAiséirghe and Monetary Reform.

Fianna Fáil had hit a high watermark in 1938, by winning a majority of seats and over 50 per cent of the vote. It was unlikely to achieve that again in 1943 and indeed failed to do so. Ten seats were lost and 10 per cent of the national vote. Fine Gael (including its Cumann na nGaedheal predecessor) lost votes and seats for the fifth successive general election. Labour had one of its more successful elections. It had won an additional eight seats, and yet the party had still to increase its support in two general elections in a row.

The biggest winner was Clann na Talmhan. In its first general election the party elected thirteenTDs, winning close on 10 per cent of the vote. Now nearly four years in existence, the party had organised well. Many of its organisers had had previous experience with other political parties. Clann na Talmhan had recruited many former Fianna Fáil activists, which also helped in its development.

The party ran thirty-nine candidates in twenty-three of the thirty-four constituencies. Its successes were Patrick O'Reilly in Cavan; Patrick Halliden in Cork North; Patrick O'Driscoll in Cork West; William Sheldon in Donegal East; party leader Michael Donnellan (who topped the poll) in Galway East; Patrick Finucane in Kerry North; John Meighan and John Beirne in the three-seat Roscommon constituency; Dominick Cafferky and Joseph Blowick in Mayo South, William O'Donnell in Tipperary; Denis Heskin in Waterford and Patrick Cogan in Wicklow. Parliamentary party meetings must have been interesting – five Patricks, two Williams and two Johns.

Oliver J. Flanagan secured election under the Monetary Reform banner. The other two new parties, Coras na Poblachta and Ailterí na hAiséirghe, fared less well in this election. Coras ran five candidates in four constituencies, polling under 4,000 votes. Ailterí ran four candidates in four constituencies accumulating just over 3,000 votes.

Eight independent TDs were elected in 1943, up from seven in 1938. John Cole was returned for another term in Cavan. Thomas Burke, again elected as an independent farmer in Clare, overcoming three Clann na Talmhan candidates in the constituency. Richard Anthony re-emerged from battle with Labour in Cork Borough. The Alfie Byrne dynasty, father and son, held firm in Dublin North East and North West constituencies.

In Leitrim Bernard Maguire was elected as an independent TD, topping the poll. Prior to this election he had been a Fianna Fáil TD, a party he had left in 1939. Another independent farmer, Philip O'Mahony, was elected in Kilkenny. Finally, having resigned from Fine Gael, James Dillon was again elected as an independent in Monaghan.

James Sproule Myles's long run of success came to an end in Donegal East. Joseph Hannigan was re-elected as an independent TD in 1938 but had joined Labour in 1939; he failed to hold the seat in 1943. The persistent Patrick Belton failed once again as an independent candidate in Dublin County.

Fianna Fáil was again short of a majority in the Dáil. On the vote for Taoiseach the Labour Party and Clann na Talmhan decided to abstain. One independent, Bernard Maguire (a former Fianna Fáil TD) supported de Valera. Supporting Fine Gael in opposing the nomination were John Cole, the two Byrnes and James Dillon.

The vote for Taoiseach took place on 1 July. Eight days later Oliver J. Flanagan made his maiden speech in a debate on the Emergency Powers Act. He did not obscure his opinions:

> How is it that we do not see any of these [Emergency Powers] Acts directed against the Jews, who crucified Our Saviour nineteen hundred years ago, and who are crucifying us every day in the week? How is it that we do not see them directed against the Masonic Order? How is it that the I.R.A. is considered an illegal organisation while the Masonic Order is not considered an illegal organisation?
>
> There is one thing that Germany did, and that was to rout the Jews out of their country. Until we rout the Jews out of this country it does not matter a hair's breadth what orders you make. Where the bees are there is the honey, and where the Jews are there is the money.

The Fourth Seanad first sat in September 1943. De Valera's eleven nominees were largely for Fianna Fáil Senators. He re-appointed the independent Senators John Keane and William Magennis. He also nominated a Labour Party Senator, Sean Campbell.

Outside of the three Dublin University Senators, others who were elected independent Senators included Joseph Hannigan, John Counihan and Michael Colgan. Hannigan, having been an independent TD, joined Labour but failed to get elected on its behalf. After the general election he resigned from Labour to stand as an independent to the Seanad where he was elected.

Also elected to the Fourth Seanad was former Farmers Party TD, Patrick Baxter. He had previously been elected as a Fine Gael Senator but on this occasion changed his affiliation to Clann na Talmhan, becoming that party's first member of Seanad Éireann.

The major political story of 1943 was of the discord within the Labour Party, timed to follow a successful election for the party. Elected on its behalf this time were James Larkin, senior and junior, and Roddy Connolly, son of party founder James. All had been involved in dalliances to form other socialist/communist parties. Conservative elements within Labour feared that a hardline reverse takeover might be taking place.

This was being informed by a long-standing, ongoing dispute between of the largest trade unions in the country, the ITGWU and the Workers Union of Ireland. At the heart of this dispute, which infected union and party politics, deep and bitter animosity existed between the leaders of the two unions in question, the ITGWU's William X. O'Brien, and Jim Larkin Senior, of the Workers Union of Ireland.

Both had distinguished pedigrees. O'Brien had served three terms as a TD, although he was unfortunate in the terms he did serve (1922-23, 1927-28, and 1937-38) which totalled to twenty-seven months of service. Larkin also had a fitful electoral record: elected in 1927 but immediately disqualified, then briefly an independent TD (1937–38).

Outside of the personal animosity, this was a battle for the soul of Irish social democracy. The Irish Labour Party had become far more conservative than many of its international counterparts. The dominance, in particular, of the Catholic Church of Irish public life, cast a shadow over all the institutions of the young State. There seemed no room for nuanced approaches. Irish/Catholic was deemed good; secular/atheist bad.

In this stilted atmosphere, the future of the Labour Party became an obsession for the President of University College Cork (and former Cumann na nGaedheal TD), Alfred O'Rahilly. In a series of articles for *The Standard* newspaper he excoriated the Labour Party for straying from Catholic values and for accommodating communistic interlopers.

The ITGWU, through O'Brien's instigation, sought to replace the Dublin executive of the party and by that to rescind Larkin senior's membership. On being rebuffed, the union disaffiliated itself from

Labour. It also sought to form an alternative umbrella grouping for Irish trade unions.

Eight Labour Party TDs were sponsored by the ITGWU. Five of these resigned from the parliamentary Labour party, claiming that Labour had left them. The five included Thomas Looney (Cork South East), Dan Spring (Kerry North), James Pattisson (Kilkenny), John O'Leary (Wexford) and the putative leader of the group, James Everett (Wicklow). With this breakaway a new party, National Labour, was born.

De Valera, sensing strife within an opposition party, decided he could improve the Dáil arithmetic in his favour. It would be the third occasion he would call a snap election in a year following a previous election. The election to the Twelfth Dáil took place on 30 May 1944.

The Taoiseach's third gamble was again successful. Fianna Fáil almost emulated its 1938 performance, winning a majority of seats and 49 per cent of the vote. The selection of new party leader (Richard Mulcahy) on the retirement of W.T. Cosgrave, did not improve Fine Gael's position. For the sixth successive election the party lost votes and seats.

Yet another poor Fine Gael performance was deflected by the damage Labour had done to itself. The combined vote of the two parties was lower than that won by Labour in 1943. Between them the two parties secured five fewer TDs than Labour had won in 1938. National Labour held most of the seats it was defending. Four of the five breakaway TDs were re-elected.

The electoral strategies of the two parties seemed more concerned with each other than with building a wider labour vote. In the Cork Borough constituency 'official' Labour did not run a candidate. In Dublin North East, National Labour ran two candidates (both of whom finished bottom of the poll) whose presence stopped the re-election of James Larkin senior. Likewise Labour ran two candidates in Cork South East, which spoiled the chances of breakaway TD Thomas Looney.

National Labour did not run a candidate against James Larkin junior (who held on to his seat) in Dublin South. No National Labour candidate stood against Roddy Connolly (in Louth) either, although he lost his seat. Only nine candidates stood for National Labour in these elections – the five breakaway TDs and four other candidates, two of whom were Larkin 'spoiler' candidates.

Clann na Talmhan failed to build on its momentum of the previous year. The party lost two seats, leaving eleven TDs. The implosion within Labour allowed Clann na Talmhan to become the third party in the new Dáil. Nevertheless, party leader Michael Donnellan felt obliged to resign because of the loss of seats. The reins were handed over to Joseph Blowick (of Mayo South, a constituency where the party had again elected two TDs).*

Ailterí na hAiséirghe stood seven candidates in this its second election. Each finished bottom of the poll in their respective constituencies. While the national share of the vote was marginally up, put into perspective that total was still less than half the number of spoilt votes that were recorded in the election.

Having chosen to paddle his own one-man canoe (apart from Ailterí), Oliver J. Flanagan increased his vote, to be elected again on a Monetary Reform ticket. Córas na Poblachta ceased to be politically active and did not contest the 1944 elections. Some of its principal activists would reappear later in other political parties.

Eight independent TDs were elected in 1944. Popular Gaelic footballer Thomas O'Reilly was elected in Cavan and Thomas Burke in Clare. Richard Anthony was returned in Cork Borough, where he was joined by William Dwyer (previously an unsuccessful Fine Gael candidate). William Sheldon was elected as an independent farmer in Donegal East (previously elected for Clann na Talmhan). Alfie Byrne retained his seat in Dublin North East but his son failed to do so in Dublin North West. Bernard Maguire was elected in Leitrim and James Dillon topped the poll in Monaghan.

John Cole's streak as an independent TD came to an end in Cavan, while Philip O'Mahony did not win a second term in Kilkenny. Patrick Belton still failed to be elected as an independent in Dublin County. It

---

*Others elected were Patrick O'Reilly in Cavan; Patrick Halliden in Cork North; Patrick O'Driscoll in Cork West; Patrick Finucane in Kerry North; Dominick Cafferky in Mayo South; John Beirne in Roscommon (John Meighan who had won a second seat there in 1943 was not successful that time); William O'Donnell in Tipperary; Denis Heskin in Waterford and Patrick Cogan in Wicklow..

should be noted that he had been consistently gaining significant first count tallies, but persistently seemed to be failing on transfers.

Also failing in Dublin South was Joseph Hannigan. He had been elected as an independent TD, was briefly a Labour TD, and then became an independent Senator. He died within months of his election, aged only 40.

Nine self-identified independent Senators were members of the Fifth Seanad. Two were again nominated by the Taoiseach – John Keane and William Magennis. Dublin University again elected three Senators, William Fearon, Joseph Johnston and T.C. Kingsmill-Moore. The National University elected a Senator called Michael Ryan. From the vocational panels John Counihan, Thomas Condon and James Douglas were elected.

Clann na Talmhan had three Senators elected, indicating that the party had acquired a considerable local authority base in the 1942 local elections. Patrick Baxter was joined by Edmund Horan and John Meighan.

A by-election was held in December for the Kerry South constituency. Clann na Talmhan presented a candidate along with Fianna Fáil and Fine Gael. Its candidate was Edmund Horan, who had recently been elected a Senator. While the by-election was won by Fianna Fáil, Horan beat Fine Gael into third place.

Political attention in 1945 was looking towards local elections and, for the first time, a contested Presidential election. Both were held in June 1945. There was still no national collation of local election results, making analysis impossible. It was later learned that Ailterí na hAiséirghe had a surprisingly strong showing, electing nine councillors, on a vote greater than it won in its previous two general election campaigns. Three of these were elected without a contest to Bandon Town Commissioners. The party also won seats on Louth County Council and Cork Corporation and two of its representatives were elected to Drogheda Borough Corporation. The remaining two councillors became members of urban district councils in Cobh and New Ross.

Fine Gael had been reluctant to run a candidate for the Presidency. Patrick McCartan (a member of the First and the Second Dáil) had been seeking support for an independent candidacy. There were two routes to such a nomination, one seeking the support of four City/ County Councils, the other being nominated by twenty members of the Oireachtas (Dáil or Seanad).

McCartan had failed to persuade four Councils. As a consequence Fine Gael nominated Seán MacÉoin. Twenty Oireachtas members, mainly Labour and Clann na Talmhan TDs, then indicated their willingness to nominate, leading the way for a three-cornered contest.

Sean T. O'Kelly, long-time lieutenant to de Valera and the Fianna Fáil party, was his party's candidate. On the first count he won shy of 50 per cent of the vote. MacÉoin won 30 per cent, with McCartan winning a very credible 20 per cent. What was significant about McCartan's transfers in the second count was the extent to which they broke down for the Fine Gael candidate. This seemed to indicate the existence of an 'anyone but Fianna Fáil' vote, that would prove significant in future elections.

In December 1945 a nnumber of by-elections were held on the same day, creating the effect of a mini general election. Five by-elections (in Clare, Dublin North West, Kerry South, Mayo South and Wexford) were caused by a series of deaths and resignations. Fine Gael contested only one of the by-elections, giving a sense of the condition of its organisational well-being. That was the Clare by-election, which was easily won by Fianna Fáil.

Dublin North West was a by-election caused by the election of Sean T. O'Kelly as Úachtarán na hÉireann. It was won by Éamon DeValera's son, Vivion, who was challenged only by a Labour candidate.

The Kerry South and Mayo South by-elections were two-party bun fights between Fianna Fáil and Clann na Talmhan. The Clann candidates performed very well, winning them over 25,000 votes. Fianna Fáil came out on top in Kerry South. In Mayo South, unsurprisingly, Clann na Talmhan was victorious. Its new TD, Bernard Commons, was the third Clann na Talmhan TD serving the Mayo South constituency.

The fifth by-election in Wexford was also complicated. It arose following the death of Richard Corish, the Labour Party TD for the constituency since the Third Dáil. Labour nominated his son, Brendan, for the vacancy. Wexford had traditionally been one of Labour's strongest constituencies. In the previous general election both Labour and

National Labour had elected TDs from the constituency, with National Labour outpolling its elder sibling.

In a pause in hostilities National Labour did not nominate a candidate for the by-election. This certainly helped the younger Corish, who was elected on the first count with a shade more than 50 per cent of the vote. If a general election had been held on those figures, under those trends, Clann na Talmhan would have been the second party, with Fine Gael the fourth.

A number of changes in 1946 was to give further consideration of those trends. Patrick Cogan resigned from Clann na Talmhan to sit again as an independent. He had expressed annoyance at a protest action undertaken by two of the party's TDs which saw each of them being imprisoned for one month. Cogan had been deputy leader of Clann na Talmhan. He was overlooked when party leader Michael Donnellan had resigned, which may also have been a factor.

The bigger earthquake factor was the emergence of a new party, Clann na Poblachta (Family of the Republic). The promoter of this new party was steeped in historical precedents. Seán MacBride ticked so many authentic republican boxes, the real wonder was why it had taken him so long to gain prominence.

The son of John and Maud Gonne MacBride, his father was killed during the 1916 Rising. His mother was the muse of poet W.B. Yeats. He had spent much of his childhood in France, which made him speak with a somewhat exotic accent. He had played with fringe radical republican politics and with Peadar O'Donnell had tried to establish Saor Eire in 1931. With that organisation proscribed by the then Cumann na nGaedheal government, he became more involved in the higher echelons of the anti-treaty IRA. By the mid 1930s he was the Chief of Staff of that organisation, albeit one who had an aversion to engage in military activity. On being replaced in that position he chose to become a barrister. He represented several prominent IRA prisoners, which helped increase his public profile.

MacBride's timing in setting up a new political party seemed impeccable. Fianna Fáil, after fourteen years of uninterrupted power, was coming across as tired. Fine Gael seemed in terminal decline. Labour was at war with itself. Clann na Talmhan showed no signs (or willingness) to expand beyond its rural bailiwicks. Clann na Poblachta could present itself as the alternative to Fianna Fáil, the party to replace Fianna Fáil, or even as the party the moribund post-treaty party Sinn Féin could have become.

Tapping into a sudden available fund of goodwill, the party also attracted a wide range of political activists. Like MacBride, Con Lehane had come from the republican movement. He had been involved in an earlier attempt at a political party, Córas na Poblachta. Peadar Cowan had been a member of the Labour Party's national executive and had several times been an unsuccessful Dáil candidate on its behalf. The party was also successful in attracting political neophytes like Dr Noel Browne, who wanted to work with the party in its campaigning on issues such as the tackling of tuberculosis.

The party had not even had its first meeting when a by-election was held in Cork Borough. This by-election had come about through the resignation of independent TD William Dwyer. The Fianna Fáil candidate, Patrick (Pa) McGrath, won without having to exert too much effort. What was interesting was the performance of others candidates. Running as an independent was the prominent War of Independence figure, Tom Barry. He won 2,574 votes – a respectable total.

Finishing ahead of him on the first count was Michael O'Riordan, standing under a Cork Socialist Party banner. This was a local variant of the Communist Party of Ireland. O'Riordan was not without his own prominence. He had fought for the International Brigade on behalf of the Republican Government is Spain in that country's civil war. In doing this he, and other Irish republicans, would have been in opposition to Eoin O'Duffy's Irish Brigade which supported Franco's nationalists. O'Riordan's 3,184 votes in the Cork by-election surprised many. In the years that followed, Michael O'Riordan would become the public face of Irish communism.

One sign of a government outstaying its welcome was the emergence of stories relating to sleaze. That summer one appeared around the activities of Dr Con Ward, a TD from 1932, and since that time he had been Parliamentary Secretary at the Department of Local Government and Public Health. In effect, he was the person responsible for health policy in the de Valera government.

Ward owned a bacon factory in Monaghan and had fired the factory manager. The manager's brother, Patrick McCarvill, was a former Fianna Fáil TD for Monaghan. He sent a list of allegations about Ward to the Taoiseach. As a result of these allegations a tribunal of inquiry reported in July 1946. Ward was cleared of all charges, except a charge of tax evasion on payments he received from the business. De Valera insisted he resign, which he did a week later.

Clann na Poblachta's first meeting was at Barry's Hotel Dublin, in July 1946. With its fresh-faced approach it was exciting much public attention. A national teachers' strike was taking place, which was symptomatic of growing public unhappiness with the government and its policies. Teachers and many other public servants were becoming attracted to Clann na Poblachta and its policies.

The first test of the electoral credibility of the new party took place in October 1947. Three by-elections were held in Dublin County, Tipperary and Waterford. They had been called due to the deaths of three TDs – two Fianna Fáil members and Clann na Talmhan's William O'Donnell.

Seán MacBride was Clann na Poblachta's candidate in Dublin County, with Patrick Kissane standing in Tipperary. Both performed well, finishing in second place in their respective first counts. Each still had a considerable job to meet the quota in either constituency. An interesting feature was the extent to which transfers broke heavily in favour of Clann na Poblachta against Fianna Fáil. The new party had achieved two stunning victories. The performance of its third candidate, Sean Feeny in Waterford, was not as inspiring, seeing him finishing fourth of the four standing.

De Valera, worried at the growing wind behind Clann na Poblachta, felt that the best way its impact could be lessened would be by calling an early general election. Before so doing he introduced the Electoral (Amendment) Act 1947 which increased the size of the Dáil from 138 to 147 TDs and increased the number of three-seat constituencies from fifteen to twenty-two. His intent was obvious – to make it more difficult to form an alternative government, and to make it harder for any new parties to make a breakthrough.

What de Valera could not control were accusations of corruption about the sale of Locke's Distillery in Kilbeggan, County Westmeath. This involved a syndicate that included a Swiss businessman called Eindiguer, a Clonmel solicitor named Morris, and an Englishman named Maximoe who was known to the authorities. These men had previously been involved in a scheme to introduce greyhound racing to Switzerland.

The goal of this syndicate was to acquire the distillery stocks of 60,000 gallons and to sell it on the British black market. Auctioneers Stokes and Quirke were hired to secure the deal. Quirke was a Fianna Fáil Senator and it was hoped that, through his influence on the governing party, an increase in the distillery's export quota might be secured.

Eindiguer claimed he was advised to give Taoiseach de Valera a Swiss gold watch to make this task easier. The management at Locke's were worried about the impending sale, fearing they would lose control of the distillery. They approached Oliver J. Flanagan (the Monetary Reform TD), who raised these allegations in the Dáil, under privilege. In November 1947 the Dáil approved the establishment of a tribunal of inquiry. The mud slung by Flanagan would embarrass Fianna Fáil and de Valera for several months. Seán MacBride made his maiden speech to the Dáil on this issue, in the course of the debate on a motion to establish a tribunal of inquiry.

The tribunal laid its report before the Dáil on 20 December 1947. The inquiry exonerated members of the government on allegations made against them, although it did judge that Oliver J. Flanagan had been 'reckless and irresponsible' in making the allegations. As the Dáil had already risen, no debate ensued. De Valera then proceeded to call a general election for 4 February 1948.

8

The Gathering of the Clanns

In running its first general election campaign Clann na Poblachta exhibited innovation, novelty, and a certain naivety. Under the innovation and novelty categories the party can be said to have developed the first party political broadcast in Irish politics. The party made the short film *Our Ireland* which was shown in a number of cinemas across the country. Directed by Liam O'Laoghaire, it was a five-minute 16mm film made in black and white. The film sought to draw attention to the fact that despite being in power since 1932, Fianna Fáil had failed to relieve poverty or remove Dublin's tenements. Seen in the film were Clann na Poblachta members Seán MacBride, its leader, Noel Browne, and Noel Hartnett who spoke to camera highlighting issues like the length of dole queues, emigration, food shortages, and the need to tackle the incidence of tuberculosis. The film warned against apathy on the part of the voting public by allowing Fianna Fáil to remain in power.

The naivety was shown in how the party organised its candidate selection. Ninety-three candidates were chosen to stand on behalf of Clann na Talmhan, standing multiple candidates in several constituencies. The party had only contested three by-elections, and had yet to contest any local elections. It possessed no intelligence as to where its electoral strength lay and knew nothing about what its candidates could, or would, transfer to each other.

While many of its candidates were first timers, the party did attempt to attract high-profile people to its banner. In Cork the party found itself turned down by the popular hurler and footballer, John (Jack) Lynch, who chose instead to stand for Fianna Fáil.

The results of the Thirteenth Dáil were far from conclusive. Even in a Dáil with nine additional seats, Fianna Fáil secured eight fewer seats, and 7 per cent less support from the electorate. Fine Gael reversed the trend of six previous elections by increasing its seat numbers by three, but its vote continued to decline, falling under 20 per cent for the first time. Clann na Poblachta won ten seats with the third highest amount of votes. Labour won a higher amount of seats, but even collectively with National Labour a lower level of support than Clann na Poblachta. Clann na Talmhan lost further ground, losing two seats. Twelve independents were elected.

Clann na Poblachta's ten seats were seen as a poor return. For a start, there were eighty-three disappointed candidates, among them key party activists like Noel Hartnett, who had narrated the party's publicity film. The party had won over 13 per cent of the vote, which should have brought better returns. Nevertheless, a significant Dáil presence had been achieved. Party leader Seán MacBride and fellow by-election victor Patrick Kinane were reappointed by their constituencies. John Tully was elected in Cavan and Peader Cowan became a TD for Dublin North East. Michael Fitzpatrick passed the winning post in Dublin North West. Con Lehane became the party's flag bearer in Dublin North Central and Dublin South East elected Noel Browne. Joseph Brennan became a TD for Dun Laoghaire and Rathdown. John McQuillan was elected in Roscommon, as was John Timoney in Tipperary South. The party won six seats in eight Dublin constituencies which somewhat undermined its hope to become a national party.

Clann na Talmhan returned with seven seats, representing the party's second general election of decline. Two of those seats again came from the Mayo South constituency, that of party leader Joseph Blowick, joined on that occasion by by-election winner Bernard Commons, at the expense of his colleague, Dominick Cafferky. Patrick Halliden was returned in Cork North. Patrick Lehane became a new TD for the party in Cork South. Former party leader, Michael Donnellan, was the first elected TD in Galway East, while another returnee was Patrick Finucane in Kerry. The seventh seat saw the party practising dynastic politics in Roscommon, with the son of the outgoing TD John Beirne (junior), being elected.

In Cavan its TD, Patrick O'Reilly, had left the party to be elected as an independent TD. The same was true of Patrick Cogan in Wicklow.

Patrick O'Driscoll did not stand again in Cork West and its new candidate did not regain the seat. With Tipperary now split into two smaller constituencies, William O'Donnell did not re-contest. The party did put up a candidate for Tipperary South but was unsuccessful. Denis Heskin was defeated in Waterford.

National Labour ran marginally more candidates (twelve) in this election. It succeeded in having one new TD elected, James Hickey in Cork Borough. Hickey had been elected in 1938 as a Labour TD, beating the independent labour TD Richard Anthony. Hickey had been a candidate a year previously when Anthony had beaten him. Anthony had been elected a Labour TD in both elections in 1927. He was successful as an independent in 1932, 1933 and 1937. He lost to Hickey in 1938 and beat him to win the seat in 1943, which he retained in 1944. In 1948 Hickey was the candidate of the breakaway National Labour party, Anthony (the five-term independent TD) was the official Labour Party candidate.

One Ailtirí na hAiséirghe candidate contested the 1948 general election. He was William Hargadon who stood in the Sligo/Leitrim constituency. He finished bottom of the poll with 323 votes. The potential of the 1945 local elections had since dissipated. Hargadon had been the party's only flag bearer. It seemed that the party had been more successful in selling pamphlets about the decline in Irish culture (written in Irish), than it had been in persuading voters to vote for its candidates.

Despite the criticism made of him by the Locke Tribunal Report (or maybe because of it), Oliver J. Flanagan saw a massive increase in his vote, to almost twice the quota needed. On this occasion he ran with a running mate.

Eleven independents were elected in 1948. Patrick O'Reilly fended off the frequently elected TD John Cole in Cavan. Thomas O'Reilly, who had been elected as an independent there in 1944, stood on this occasion for Fine Gael and was unsuccessful. Thomas Burke was again returned in Clare. Cork Borough produced another independent TD in the form of Michael Sheehan, then serving the third of a four-year term as Lord Mayor of Cork. William Dwyer was elected in 1944, resigned his seat to cause a by-election, stood again in 1948 but was unsuccessful.

William Sheldon was re-elected in Donegal East. The Byrne family dynasty was restored with Alfie the father winning in Dublin North East, and Alfie the son victorious in North West. Each topped the polls in their constituencies. John Flynn was elected as an independent in Kerry South. He had been a Fianna Fáil TD for Kerry and Kerry South constituencies between 1932 and 1943.

Former Fine Gael TD, Charles Fagan, was elected as an independent in Longford/Westmeath. James Dillon topped the poll in Monaghan. Bernard Maguire was again an independent TD for Sligo/Leitrim and Patrick Cogan, having left Clann na Talmhan, was returned in Wicklow.

Before the election, despite growing unhappiness with the performance of Fianna Fáil, there was little expectation that a change in government was possible. Fianna Fáil would remain, it was thought, too far ahead of the opposition, an opposition that was too diverse and far too divided on policy issues.

In 1947 some furtive attempts were made to present a more cohesive opposition. Roddy Connolly of Labour argued that co-operation between his party, Clann na Talmhan, and Clann na Poblachta could change public attitudes and facilitate progressive government. On the other side of the coin James Dillon was making back room proposals to form a new National party made up of Fine Gael and Clann na Talmhan. This proposal was not to the liking of Fine Gael leader Richard Mulcahy, even acknowledging the current weakness of his party.

This mood music seemed unlikely to change as the general election results slowly came in. It was nearly a week before the full results were known, after a marathon recount in Carlow/Kilkenny. When the results were announced it was Richard Mulcahy who took the initiative. He invited party leaders to a meeting in Leinster House on 13 February. All attended, other than James Everett of National Labour.

At this meeting the leader of the Labour Party, William Norton, proposed that no leader of any coalition party should be Taoiseach in any agreed government. This was politic on his part. Mulcahy, as well as being the initiator of the parties meeting to discuss the possibility of government, was also the elephant in the room. Amongst the former IRA members within Clann na Poblachta, Mulcahy continued to be a hate figure. In the middle of the Civil War, along with Kevin O'Higgins, he signed the death warrants of seventy-seven republican prisoners.

Mulcahy seemed to understand the difficulty that would be caused if he was nominated as Taoiseach. He proposed John A. Costello as a compromise, which was agreed by the other party leaders. The meeting went on to agree to a ten-point policy plan, general and anodyne in its description, which in effect would become a programme for government. Finally the meeting agreed how many cabinet positions should be held by each participating party.

Those ten points subsequently revealed were:

> Increased agricultural and industrial production
> Immediate all-out drive to provide housing for the working and middle classes at reasonable rates. Luxury building to be rigidly controlled
> Reduction in the cost of living
> Taxation of all unreasonable profit-making
> Introduction of a comprehensive social security plan to provide insurance against old age, illness, blindness, widowhood, employment etc.
> Removal of recent taxes on cigarettes, tobacco, beer and cinema seats
> Immediate steps to provide facilities for the treatment of sufferers of tuberculosis
> Establish a Council of Education
> Immediate steps to launch a National Drainage Plan, and
> Modification of means test as at present applied to old age, widows and orphans, and blind pensions.

The following day a number of meetings were held. Chief among these was a semi-formal grouping of six independent/other TDs – Alfie Byrne senior and junior, Charles Fagan, Patrick Cogan, James Dillon and Oliver J. Flanagan. These agreed to act as a cohesive group to support the formation of a government, nominating James Dillon as its Cabinet representative. At the same time the Labour and Clann na Talmhan parliamentary parties agreed to proceed.

The decision of Clann na Poblachta to enter government was far from certain. As a party with a strong republican component, the idea of voting for any Fine Gael Taoiseach, even John A. Costello, was always going to be a stretch. The party's national executive voted to proceed on a vote of eighteen for, sixteen against.

Later that evening the proposed likely cabinet members met at the Mansion House. Seán MacBride, on behalf of Clann na Poblachta, came on his own. He was seeking further information as to what portfolios would be available. At this meeting all present confirmed their commitment to attempt to form a government. John A. Costello would be told he was their preferred candidate to become Taoiseach, while the Labour and Clann na Poblachta leaders were insistent that no government could be formed should he choose not to accept.

This level of agreement put these opposition parties on a par with Fianna Fáil, but the decision of National Labour and other independents would still prove vital. On the day of these meetings, National Labour was meeting with its sponsors, the ITGWU. The ITGWU was instructing the National Labour TDs to support the re-election of de Valera as Taoiseach. It was an ill-tempered meeting, with James Everett informing the union officials that TDs were ultimately there to represent their constituents, constituents with whom they would insist on consulting.

The National Labour TDs came under a great deal of psychological pressure. Details of putative cabinets were circulating, mentioning individuals as possible Labour ministers, people whose names once mentioned would evoke negative responses from National Labour TDs.

On 17 February, after consultations with their constituents, the National Labour TDs came to a joint meeting of its National Executive with the Executive of the Congress of Irish Unions. They told this meeting that support did not exist, nor was it their intention to support Éamon de Valera as Taoiseach. The CIU/ITGWU made one last attempt, instructing the National Labour TDs to meet Fianna Fáil's Gerry Boland (De Valera's emissary) but the National Labour TDs refused to budge.

The new Dáil met for the first time on 18 February. First business was the election of the Ceann Comhairle. Frank Fahy was returned to the position, reducing Fianna Fáil's voting strength. For the nomination of the Taoiseach two nominations were taken – outgoing Taoiseach, Éamon de Valera and John A. Costello.

The de Valera vote was taken first. He was defeated by seventy votes to seventy-five. He received the votes of three independent TDs, Ben

Maguire and John Flynn (both who previously had been Fianna Fáil TDs) and Cork independent TD, Michael Sheehan. Ranged against him were the five other political parties, the newly assembled independent grouping and two other independents, Patrick O'Reilly and William Sheldon.

Those seventy-five TDs voted en bloc to elect John A. Costello. The country now had a new Taoiseach, the first non-Fianna Fáil Taoiseach in sixteen years. He was a reluctant Taoiseach, a man who had not sought that office ... a Taoiseach who had played little part in the government he would head.

Returning to Leinster House, having met the President, Taoiseach Costello announced the new cabinet. The Tánaiste (Deputy Prime Minister) was William Norton, leader of the Labour Party, who also became Minister for Social Welfare, while Minister for External Affairs was Seán MacBride, leader of Clann na Poblachta. Joseph Blowick, Clann na Talmhan's leader became Minister for Lands and The National Labour leader, James Everett received the Minister for Post and Telegraphs portfolio. James Dillion became Minister for Agriculture. Other Fine Gael ministers were party leader Richard Mulcahy as Minister for Education; Patrick McGilligan as Minister for Finance; Dan Morrissey as Minister for Industry and Commerce; Seán MacEoin as Minister for Justice and T.F. O'Higgins as Minister for Defence. Labour's Timothy Murphy held the party's second portfolio as Minister for Local Government. First time Clann na Poblachta TD Noel Browne became Minister for Health.

With thirteen members, this was the largest cabinet yet to be formed. Previous cabinets traditionally had eleven members. Portfolios were rejigged to placate all participants in the government. Up until 1947 the Department of Health had been coupled with the Department of Local Government, but later a Department of Health and Social Welfare was set up.

The new government made two stand-alone departments with cabinet ministers. Noel Browne would become the first dedicated Minister for Health. After sixteen years of Fianna Fáil being in office, this new cabinet would (unsurprisingly) be the least experienced government formed since the cabinets of 1922 and 1932 were formed. Only three members of the new cabinet had previous experience – Mulcahy and McGilligan as cabinet ministers and John A. Costello, who was a former Attorney General. Fine

Gael had last been in government under a Cumann na nGaedheal incarnation. All other parties were enjoying their first experience of government.

Ireland's first coalition government was reluctant to use the coalition. Even though throughout Europe coalition governments had become common, in Ireland this would be an inter-party government.

Within a week the secondary government positions (Parliamentary Secretaries) were announced. Liam Cosgrave (son of W.T. Cosgrave) was appointed Government Chief Whip. The Labour Party's Brendan Corish was appointed to the Department of Local Government, where a Labour Party colleague was the cabinet minister. The third appointment was Michael Donnellan of Clann na Talmhan (its former leader) to the Department of Finance.

By April 1948 the Sixth Seanad was elected. Included were three Clann na Talmhan Senators, two with Clann na Poblachta and fourteen declared independents. The three Clann na Talmhan Senators were directly elected. Existing Senators Patrick Baxter and John Meighan were joined by John Finan, an unsuccessful Dáil candidate in Roscommon (a constituency once represented by John Meighan).

Still to develop a local authority base, Clann na Poblachta depended on the Taoiseach's nominees to secure representation in the upper house. One of its nominees was Patrick McCartan, who had performed very credibly as an independent candidate in the 1945 Presidential election. McCartan had been a Clann na Poblachta candidate for Cork Borough, but had not secured a significant vote. He provided a link to the First Dáil having been elected in the 1918 Westminster election, and previously in a by-election some months before that. The second Clann na Poblachta nominee was Denis Ireland. He would have the distinction of being the first member of the Oireachtas, since 1921, to be a resident of Northern Ireland.

Eight independent Senators were elected to the Sixth Seanad. Three were elected, as they had been traditionally, for the University of Dublin. These were Joseph Bigger, William Fearon and William Stanford. George O'Brien was elected for the National University and he may have been the first qualified economist to have been elected to a House of the Oireachtas. O'Brien had been the president of the Statistical and Social Inquiry Society of Ireland, a forerunner of the Economic and Social Research Institute.

Elected from the vocational panels was John Counihan who was returned. Frederick Summerfield was also returned, although he had originally been elected in a by-election. Michael Colgan was elected back to the Seanad having been defeated in 1944, and Patrick Fitzsimons was a newly-elected Senator.

The Taoiseach nominated five independent Senators. Long-time Senator James Douglas was re-nominated and Edward McGuire, Séamus O'Farrell, Edward Richards-Orpen and Patrick Woulfe were all first-time Senators. The Taoiseach also nominated James McCrea as a Labour Party Senator. McCrae had been a Labour Party candidate for the Wicklow constituency, the same constituency as National Labour leader James Everett.

The first by-election of this Dáil occurred in December 1948 for the Donegal East constituency. It was brought about by the death of Fianna Fáil TD Neil Blaney. This was safely won by his son, also called Neil. The only significant element of this by-election was that in a three-cornered fight between Fianna Fáil, Fine Gael and Clann na Poblachta (there was no agreed government candidate), and the Clann na Poblachta candidate performed poorly.

The new government moved cautiously. It produced the least number of pieces of legislation in its first year of existence. The caution was necessary as a number of fault lines were developing. Many of these centred around Clann na Poblachta, whose enthusiasm, as a new party, was making an impact. Antipathy was growing between MacBride and McGilligan, with MacBride believing that funds were being released too slowly to meet the policy goals that had been agreed.

Antagonism also existed between Clann na Poblachta and Clann na Talmhan. MacBride developed a reputation for involving himself in every aspect of government. Joseph Blowick, as Clann na Talmhan leader, took offence at MacBride taking credit for the government's afforestation programme, a responsibility of his department. Later, after their experience of government, Clann na Poblachta TDs Noel Browne and Jack McQuillan revealed the contemptuous attitude their party had towards Joseph Blowick and its belief in his lack of competence. James Everett, the National Labour leader's contributions in cabinet were infrequent and limited, usually about issues he would define as having an impact in his constituency.

The relationship between the two Clann na Poblachta ministers MacBride and Browne was not as a deep as it could have been, although the pair did meet to coordinate their approach to cabinet. MacBride kept to himself the how and when of his strategic thinking. As party leader he would also have been aware that his surprise choice of Browne had created resentment in others within his parliamentary party, especially those who would have had expectations of ministerial office.

While that would be a continuing problem for the Clann na Poblachta leader, the new Taoiseach was also finding internal discipline difficult to maintain within his cabinet. It became clear quite quickly that the convention of collective cabinet responsibility would have to applied selectively. A number of incidents arose with different ministers from the various components within the government, whose public statements were at variance with accepted government positions. This required a nuanced approach. Generally, ministers could be said to be speaking in a personal capacity. Sometimes decisions made would have to be remade to keep particular ministers on board. The tolerance stretched to accepting a number of votes where cabinet members went into opposing lobbies.

Another factor in the new government establishing itself was the need to create appropriate levels of trust with the civil service. After sixteen years of Fianna Fáil government, there were concerns about whether civil servants could be thought of as neutral. Many new ministers fought a feeling that they were being managed by their officials. At the insistence of Seán MacBride, the Secretary at the Department of the Taoiseach did not attend cabinet meetings so minutes of those meetings were taken by the Government Chief Whip, Liam Cosgrave.

As Taoiseach, John A. Costello broadened and deepened the use of cabinet subcommittees. Thirty-two such committees were established. These became a more convenient mechanism to deal with conflicts and disagreements within the cabinet.

Two issues would exercise Costello's diplomatic skills, both relating to Clann na Poblachta's republican flank. Each one had the potential to challenge Fine Gael's law-and-order tendency. The first concerned the release of republican prisoners from Irish prisons, while the second was about allowing the reburial of republican prisoners who had been executed during the 'Emergency' years. Both issues were handled adroitly.

A flagship piece of legislation for the inter-party government came early in its life. The Republic of Ireland Act had a difficult genesis and a somewhat surreal announcement. Part of the bad feeling that existed between Fianna Fáil and Clann na Poblachta was a shared antipathy towards the External Relations Act, displaying acute divergence on how its existence should be challenged.

De Valera's government had drafted a bill that would address many of the criticisms of the 'independence light' option that was the Anglo-Irish Treaty. The bill de Valera left behind did not, however, address the question of Ireland becoming a republic. In the de Valerain mindset, becoming a republic was contingent on re-unification of the national territory.

More than a quarter of a century after the Treaty, the world was now a far different place. A further division of Europe was occurring and the countries of the colonised world were asserting their independence. Chief among the latter was India, now independent, now a republic, still a country within the Commonwealth. What Britain came to consider possible for India in 1947 was not possible for the Irish Free State in 1922.

De Valera's creeping republicanism, removing hated symbols imposed by the Treaty, before introducing an entire new Constitution, had fudged the status of the country. It may have been an effective republic, but it remained a member of the British Commonwealth.

The difficulty for many was the continued existence of the External Relations Act. MacBride as Minister for External Affairs, seemed to start his tenure by continuing with de Valera's creeping republicanism approach. When a new Argentinian ambassador presented his credentials addressed to the King, he was asked to represent himself with a new letter addressed to the President.

A second measure was to snub attending the Commonwealth Prime Ministers' conference that would be held in October 1948. In his correspondence with the British Government MacBride stated that Ireland did not consider itself a part of the Commonwealth, but would be prepared to be involved with this conference should the issue of partition be discussed.

MacBride's incremental approach was not even impressing some within his own party. Peadar Cowan (who had come to the party via Labour) had been pressing MacBride to take more comprehensive action. By July 1948 he had been expelled from the party for what was seen as his harassing treatment – the party's first casualty of its time in government.

The government's attention had become focused on a trip the Taoiseach was about to make to Canada in September 1948. The speech Costello was to deliver was made known to the cabinet, which approved of its contents. There was no recorded decision to repeal the External Relations Act, although it was understood, especially by the British Government, that action to abolish the act would be imminent.

Legend has it that Costello announced the decision to declare Ireland a republic after a fit of pique at perceived snubs received on the visit. One of these perceived snubs was the omission, deliberate or otherwise, of a toast to the President of Ireland. While the lack of such niceties had an effect on the tone of his announcement, Costello would have been confident that an understanding rather than an agreement had been reached on the decision within the inter-party government. A leaked newspaper story in the *Sunday Independent* may also have had the effect of encouraging Costello to go further than had been intended.

Having announced an intention to proceed, a further obligation rested on instigating, timetabling and implementing how this was to happen. On this there was yet to be a formal government agreement. MacBride submitted a draft bill to the cabinet (while Costello was still in Canada) – entitled the Powers and Functions of the President (External Relations) Bill. It would take a later cabinet meeting, after Costello's return, to formalise the decision to rescind the External Relations Act.

The instrument agreed to bring this about was initially entitled the Executive Powers of the State Bill. Within this legislation was a provision that the 'name of the State shall be the Republic of Ireland'. After further consideration it was felt that the bill should be referred to as the Republic of Ireland Bill, 1948. The new government had been in office for nine months, a gestation period that had produced a new name for the country.

When brought to the floor of the Dáil, an attempt was made by Alfie Byrne Jr, supported by his father, to prevent a second reading of the bill. When taken, a lengthy debate followed, at the end of which there was no division. The remaining stages went through the Dáil and then the Seanad, without controversy. The bill was signed into effect by Senator Sean T. O'Kelly on 21 December 1948.

Some collateral damage was suffered when the issue brought a negative view of the government and of Costello's actions. William Sheldon, a Donegal independent who had supported Costello's election as Taoiseach, withdrew his support for the government because of the intention to fully cut ties with the Commonwealth. Sheldon, like his independent predecessor James Sproule Myles, had the support of a large Protestant population in his constituency. Cutting ties with Britain in such a firm way was not an approved policy among his constituents.

Partition was the issue obsessing all Irish political parties at that time. This obsession impacted on the newly defined republic to assert its independent place in the world. An attempt in 1949 to join the United Nations was turned down due to the objections of a number of countries, most particularly Russia. The foundation of NATO as a military alliance produced a different dynamic. The assumption that having been neutral during the Second World War was not the dominant reason why Ireland did not join NATO. MacBride had made the issue of partition a precondition of Ireland joining, but one that other NATO members were not prepared to accept.

Ireland was offered an opportunity to become a founder member of the Council of Europe. It became one of the ten original members. Its attempts to use the new forum to persistently raise the issue of partition seemed to test the patience of its fellow members. As Minister for External Affairs, the Council of Europe provided Seán MacBride with a new platform to practise his interest in internationalism. It would see him being involved in the process that saw the drafting, and eventual agreement of the European Convention on Human Rights.

That year saw the inter-party government suffer an unexpected setback after the death of the Minister for Local Government, Timothy Murphy. As one of the Labour Party members of cabinet, Murphy had (with the help of Marshall Aid funding) helped put in place a significant increase in public housing. He was succeeded in that office by his party colleague Michael Keyes.

A by-election to fill the vacancy caused by Timothy Murphy's death was held quickly. His son William was the sole government candidate, holding off a Fianna Fáil challenge to become a new TD for Cork West.

November 1948 saw the third by-election of this Dáil. Fianna Fáil's Brian Brady had died. This necessitated a by-election in Donegal West. Both Fine Gael and Clann na Poblachta put forward candidates. The Clann candidate again performed poorly, but party transfers allowed Fine Gael surprise Fianna Fáil, making the position of the inter-party government that bit more secure.

Being in government together, the relationship between Labour and National Labour seemed to strengthen. Even before the 1948 election the sources of antagonism had been removed from their dispute. William X. O'Brien had retired from his stewardship of the ITGWU in 1946. James Larkin senior had passed away in 1947. Talks took place about reuniting what in effect were two wings of one party, rather than two separate parties. These saw the party being reunited in June 1950. With this the National Labour party was no more. The party had achieved little – its purpose merely to be an irritant and impediment to the Labour Party itself.

The largest impact of National Labour on this government may have been felt through a controversy surrounding its only leader, James Everett, the Minister for Post and Telegraphs. After reunification with Labour the issue caused its greatest impact, but its provenance rested solely with the personality of James Everett.

Known as the Battle of Baltinglass, part of Everett's Dáil constituency, the controversy related to an attempt to transfer the licence of a local post office from the long-standing postmistress to a younger man, with whom Everett had political connections. The decision led to a strong local boycott of the new licence holder.

The political effect of this was a reluctance by the Taoiseach or other prominent members of the government to criticise or censure James Everett in case it would destabilise the government. MacBride took the greatest heat on this from within his own party. In advance of the general election Clann na Poblachta was seen to have benefitted from growing public distaste at the perception of increasing political corruption. Not to have responded to this clear abuse of public office was to cause the next major breach within Clann na Poblachta's ranks. Senior member Noel Hartnett, who had narrowly missed being elected as TD (and had been the narrator on the party's publicity film), resigned from the party. He did so because he believed that a chance to highlight poor standards in public life had been missed. Expediency rather than political principle was determining Clann na Poblachta's participation in government.

Not that participation in government was in any way being shown to be electorally benefitting to Clann na Poblachta. When local elections were held in September 1950 the party found itself to be poorly organised and much less well supported. There were 153 candidates in those elections. When contrasted with the ninety-three candidates that sought election to the Dáil in 1948, the party was finding some difficulty in presenting candidates throughout the country.

Few of the unsuccessful Dáil candidates from 1948, especially those who had come close to winning seats, chose to contest these local elections. The important business of building and maintaining political bases was not being pursued with sufficient vigour. A similar lack of enthusiasm seemed to exist within the parliamentary party.

The common practice in Irish politics (up until the turn of the century) was for backbench TDs to also seek election to local authorities. This was considered important for TDs to maintain their voting base. Of the seven TDs in Clann na Poblachta who perhaps should have been standing, only one (Jack McQuillan in Roscommon) chose to do so.

Accessing nationally collated local election results remained difficult in 1950. However, Fine Gael's Richard Mulcahy did make notes of the results, which while comprehensive were not complete. What they do show is how difficult these elections were for Clann na Poblachta.

These notes showed that the national vote for Clann na Poblachta had more than halved since 1948 and stood at only 6 per cent. This put the party not only significantly below the newly reunified Labour Party, but also behind another of its partners in government – Clann na Talmhan (which had twenty-four elected county councillors). Indicative of the party's problems was its performance in the Dublin area. Six of the party's ten TDs were elected there in 1948. In 1950 the party had only four local government representatives in the same region – two members of Dublin County Council and two sitting as members of Dublin Corporation.

The inter-party government entered its third year of office, after what had been a number of incident packed years, to face what was to become the defining issue and ensuing crisis of its term.

Almost thirty years into the life of the State the influence of the Catholic Church on public life was pervasive. On being elected to government for the first time in 1932, de Valera had written to the Vatican offering the support of his government. In 1948 John A. Costello did the same, but with added obsequiousness. Several prominent Irish politicians of the time were members of a secretive society called the Knights of Columbanus.

Catholic social policy was a prime consideration in determining what legislation could be brought forward and considered. An area that had continued to be impeded was the introduction of legislation on adoption, legislation that would confer legal rights on adoptive parents and children. Touch kicking on this issue would continue throughout the life of this government. The phrase coined in a later era, 'an Irish solution to an Irish problem', could easily have been applied here. This was a government within a political system that was unwilling to legalise adoption in Ireland, but was willing to facilitate the export of Irish children to the United States for adoption.

It was legislation regarding maternity services, a Mother and Child scheme, that would provoke the worst political crisis experienced by the inter-party government. For most involved in political life, the Republic of Ireland continued to be a Catholic State for a Catholic People.

At the heart of this crisis was Dr Noel Browne, the second Clann na Poblachta member of the cabinet, and the first TD to have been made a dedicated Minister for Health. He had been appointed to cabinet ahead of other party colleagues who felt they may have had a better case for promotion. As party leader, Seán MacBride felt Browne made for a better fit as minister, best placed to deliver on the party's election commitment to tackle the tuberculosis crisis in the county.

The previous Fianna Fáil government had passed legislation and had put aside resources to tackle the issue. However, on leaving office those efforts had not shown material difference. On coming into office, Noel Browne had an additional advantage of securing funding from the Irish Hospital Sweepstakes.

There is no doubt that Browne threw considerable energy into seeking to achieve the eradication of tuberculosis. As minister, he was gaining a great deal of kudos for the perceptible improvement in infrastructure and the decreasing incidence of the disease. Through this effort Browne was becoming seen as one of the most effective and popular members of the government.

Within the civil service, Browne's frenetic activity was causing some concern, especially at the Department of Finance. The health budget was increasing significantly, admittedly from what had been a very low base. This expenditure was helping Browne to achieve innovations in several areas, outside of the issue of tuberculosis. A blood transfusion service was established, as was a National Rehabilitation Office. Inoculation and vaccination programmes were put in place. X-ray and radiography facilities were extended throughout the country.

As with tuberculosis, efforts had been made by the earlier Fianna Fáil government to provide an enhanced health service for women and children. Debate on a 1945 bill was strongly criticised by Fine Gael on the grounds that its provisions compromised individual liberties. The Parliamentary Secretary responsible for the introduction of the bill, Con Ward, ran into political difficulties of a different kind when adverse tribunal findings were made against him, forcing his resignation.

The bill was reintroduced in 1947, this time brought forward by Jim Ryan. It passed all stages in both houses, becoming an Act. One provision seemed to excite opposition that had not been vocal previously. The section sought to promote the concept of health education as one means to better improve maternal and children's health.

Within the Irish Medical Association (IMA), the representative body for Irish doctors, greater state involvement was seen as a threat to its members' economic standing. Those in the IMA, opposed to what was being suggested, sought support from the hierarchy of the Catholic Church, arguing that what was being suggested was far from being theologically sound.

This pressure led the Attorney General to declare the Act unconstitutional. The Council of State advised that the President should sign the Act, which he duly did. After the general election, but before the formation of a new government, James Dillon initiated a High Court action testing the constitutionality of the Act. In that election campaign, Clann na Poblachta seemed supportive of a Health Act that was consistent with Catholic teaching,

Once the government had been formed, Dillon withdrew his court action. The newly appointed Minister for Health had given assurances that the controversial aspects of the Act would be reviewed. The Act was then implemented in full, other than for two contentious sections.

Among the provisions that did proceed were measures allowing for specified services to be provided free of charge. As this would have been part of the original bill, Browne may have thought it then only required the publishing of regulations by his department to give effect to what the Act specified.

Still the IMA continued to oppose the free service aspect of the legislation. The drafting of the regulations was proceeding very slowly. In the summer of 1950 the newly elected President of the IMA, Dr P.T. O'Farrell articulated his organisation's continuing opposition, saying that the IMA opposed the Mother and Child scheme because it would be open to all, regardless of the ability to pay – a development which would lead to the disappearance of private practice.

In October 1950 the Catholic hierarchy expressed a desire to meet Noel Browne to express their reservations. The Minister went to Archbishop John McQuaid's Bishop's Palace in Drumcondra to meet a delegation. There he was read the text of a letter outlining the Church's concern. Browne responded in a way he felt addressed that concern. The following day McQuaid met the Taoiseach where he presented the same letter (it had been addressed to the Taoiseach). Subsequently it was seen that the Taoiseach and Noel Browne had different interpretations on whether the Archbishop was placated or not. (Browne, having graduated from Trinity College, (Dublin University), was looked at with suspicion by the Catholic hierarchy.)

In November Seán MacBride dined with Browne in an effort to keep him onside and in line. MacBride was gripped by a paranoia that

Browne was being manipulated by senior Clann na Poblachta member, Noel Harnett, a man he believed had constantly been trying to undermine his leadership since his perceived snub at not being nominated to the Seanad. According to MacBride, Browne told him he was dissatisfied with his leadership, with Clann na Poblachta, and with the government. He had long been considering resignation, waiting for an opportunity when it would have most effect. MacBride made the Taoiseach and other members aware of this threat. It was a threat that would remain unimplemented for several months.

An *Irish Times* report undermined MacBride's attempt to convey Clann na Poblachta cohesion on the issue. It reported that MacBride was being challenged by Browne and Hartnett, being charged with being more concerned with the stability of the government than the future of his party. The report further stated that it was Browne's belief that majority of the Dáil would be in favour of his scheme. He saw that majority as being composed of other Clann na Poblachta TDs, the Labour Party and Fianna Fáil (the party responsible for the original bill). The article included a telling point that MacBride had not, to date, publicly defended the Mother and Child scheme.

Having faced down the IMA, Noel Browne proceeded to issue regulations on the operation of the scheme. The Taoiseach complained that he had learned of their existence through a third party from outside of the government. Costello was also unhappy that the scheme had been issued without the approval of the cabinet. On this he was technically correct, although once the legislation had been passed there was no obligation for Noel Browne to do so.

Browne was to have one further meeting with Archbishop McQuaid. He had prepared for this meeting by seeking the advice of a theologian. He would argue to McQuaid that something not considered to be Catholic social teaching was a moral judgement by the Church. It was an argument for which McQuaid had no time. McQuaid later met the Taoiseach, who accepted unequivocally that being against Catholic social teaching meant that the scheme could not go ahead.

A subsequent cabinet meeting would oppose the scheme by twelve votes to the one vote of the Minister for Health. More significantly Browne had also lost support within his own party. On 11 April he sent a letter to the Taoiseach that he was complying with a request from Seán MacBride that he resign as minister.

Browne's resignation had placed the government in a precarious position. Jack McQuillan also resigned from Clann na Poblachta, in support of Browne. Three of the ten Clann na Poblachta TDs had now resigned. Towards the end of 1950 independent TD Patrick Cogan (once of the National Agricultural Party/Clann na Talmhan) announced he could no longer guarantee support for the government. He had been one of the group of six independent TDs who had secured a cabinet position for James Dillon. He had since regularly expressed unhappiness with Dillon's performance as Minister for Agriculture. The Baltinglass saga (within his constituency) seems to have been a final straw.

Patrick Lehane (who represented Cork South for Clann na Talmhan) also left his party, and with that general support for the government, because of overall dissatisfaction with its performance. Within a number of weeks, a number of other Clann na Talmhan colleagues removed themselves from their party. Patrick Finucane of Kerry North and Patrick Halliden of Cork North made themselves independents. With these actions Clann na Talmhan had returned to being solely a Connacht-based party.

This constant attrition made up Costello's mind that the only option that remained was to dissolve the Dáil and to call a general election. The Dáil was dissolved on 7 May with the election of the new Dáil to take place on 30 May 1951.

Several decades later when speaking at the launch of David McCullagh's authoritative book on the inter-party government, *A Makeshift Majority*, former Taoiseach Liam Cosgrave, Chief Whip in the inter-party government of 1948–51, underplayed the policy effectiveness of Clann na Poblachta. He was quoted as saying, 'I was privileged to be associated with men of the calibre that were in that government. I am talking particularly of our own party and of our colleagues in the Labour Party'.

These comments are somewhat unfair to Clann na Poblachta. The party undoubtedly created false expectations that could never have been met. It suffered because of its own internal contradictions. However, it provided the vital ingredients on which the inter-party government could be judged a success. It showed that governments other than those of Fianna Fáil could be formed. It proved that cohesive government could exist when made up from disparate, often conflicting, elements. Ultimately it provided nontraditional parties with a platform to influence and implement policy.

9

You Can't Keep a Long
Man Down

The shuffling of electoral cards in 1951 brought about a set of unexpected results. The main (and only) opposition party, Fianna Fáil, increased its vote but did not increase its number of seats. The principal victor was the largest party within the inter-party government, Fine Gael, which won an additional nine seats and an extra 6 per cent of the national vote. The Labour Party won fewer seats and votes than the two competing parties in 1948. Clann na Talmhan returned with one seat less, but its vote was almost halved. The party was winning less than one third of the vote it was winning eight years previously. It now only existed in its West of Ireland heartland.

The party most damaged in this election was Clann na Poblachta. It won less than one-third of the vote it had in 1948. This returned just two TDs, party leader Seán MacBride and John Tully in Cavan. It had made little attempt to emulate its 1948 performance. It ran twenty-six candidates in little over half the constituencies, a marked contrast to the previous election, where every constituency had been contested. In 1951 sixty-seven candidates – fewer candidates – stood for the party.

Those who remained with the party suffered many indignities. Con Lehane failed to be re-elected in Dublin South Central. Outgoing TD in Dublin North West, Michael Fitzpatrick, won 458 votes. The two seats won in the two Tipperary constituencies, which were held by Patrick Kinane and John Timoney, were both lost. Joseph Brennan, who had been a Clann na Poblachta TD for Dun Laoghaire, stood on this occasion as a Labour Party candidate, but did not retain the seat.

Adding insult to injury was the number of independents who had been elected, who previously had been Clann na Poblachta TDs. In this election Noel Browne, Jack McQuillan and Peadar Cowan were elected as independent TDs. In addition a former Clann na Poblachta councillor, Michael ffrench O'Carroll, was also elected as an independent TD, winning over twice the vote won by Seán MacBride in Dublin South West.

In Dublin South East, Noel Browne's constituency, the official Clann na Poblachta candidate was Patrick McCartan. McCartan had been the independent candidate in the 1945 presidential election where he won close to 20 per cent of the vote. In 1948 he was an unsuccessful candidate for Cork Borough. He subsequently was appointed to the Seanad by John A. Costello. However, in opposing Noel Browne in 1951 he was to finish bottom of the poll, winning 569 votes.

Clann na Talmhan may have retreated to Connacht, but in those constituencies the party was still managing to perform very well. The party again won two seats in Mayo South (almost winning three), two seats in Roscommon and a seat in both Mayo North and Galway East. Thomas O'Hara was their new TD in Mayo North (he had unsuccessfully stood twice previously as an independent). John Finan regained a previously held seat in Roscommon. In Mayo South, Dominick Cafferky and Bernard Commons once again swapped seats. In Munster, Patrick Lehane and Patrick Finucane were elected as independents in Cork South and Kerry North. Patrick Halliden did not stand again in Cork North. Added to former Clann na Talmhan TDs who had been elected as independents in 1948 – Patrick O'Reilly in Cavan and Patrick Cogan in Wicklow – the party could have had one of its best election performances.

The five National Labour TDs who had been elected in 1948 were all returned as Labour TDs in 1951. The Cork Borough soap opera had its last episode. James Hickey and Richard Anthony had crossed swords over a series of general elections, each wearing a different Labour affiliation. For this election both were official Labour Party candidates. Each polled significantly, but the 350 additional votes James Hickey had secured on the first count helped with his election.

On this occasion the Communist Party of Ireland made one of its infrequent appearances in Irish electoral politics, under the guise of the Irish Workers League. Its only candidate was Michael O'Riordan, who had performed so credibly in a by-election in Cork Borough in 1946. This time, standing in Dublin South West, he won less than 300 votes.

Fourteen independents were elected in 1951. Seven of these had been former TDs for Clann na Poblachta and Clann na Talmhan. The six TDs who had formed a grouping to participate in the inter-party government – Alfie Byrne senior and junior, Charles Fagan, Patrick Cogan, James Dillon and Oliver J. Flanagan – were all re-elected in 1951. William Sheldon of Donegal East, who had supported John A. Costello's election as Taoiseach, but was not formally part of the government, was elected again, as was John Flynn in Kerry South.

John Cole in Cavan, Thomas Burke in Clare and Bernard Maguire in Sligo/Leitrim all failed to be elected. Michael Sheehan who had been elected as an independent in 1948, stood in 1951 as a Fine Gael candidate in Cork Borough, but was not successful.

The new Dáil met on 13 June 1951. Patrick Hogan was chosen once again as Ceann Comhairle. The second item of business was expressions of sympathy on the death of the Papal Nuncio. Then came the taking of nominations for the position of Taoiseach. Outgoing Taoiseach John A. Costello was taken first. He was defeated by 72 votes to 74. The second nominee, Éamon de Valera, succeeded in being elected by 74 votes to 69. Supporting him were three former Clann na Poblachta members (Noel Browne, Peadar Cowan and Michael ffrench O'Carroll), while Jack McQuillan voted against. John Flynn, independent but also a former Fianna Fáil TD, was another supporter of de Valera. Also supporting his nomination was the independent TD (and former Clann na Talmhan TD) Patrick Cogan.

It could have been different if Costello had convinced the group of former Clann, now independent TDs. He had a meeting with Michael ffrench O'Carroll, an intermediary for Noel Browne, but Fine Gael failed to prove that it could bring about a Mother and Child scheme. Seán MacBride had tried to facilitate this support by declaring that while he would support Costello, he would not be seeking a position in government.

The election to the Seventh Seanad saw a number of independents consolidate their position in the upper house. Elected again were Patrick Fitzsimons, James McGee, James Douglas, Edward McGuire, Frederick Summerfield and Michael Colgan. Elected for the first time was Patrick Ághas, and James Johnston, who had been an independent Senator for Dublin University, became one of de Valera's eleven nominees.

Also elected for the first time was Noel Hartnett, once a Clann na Poblachta luminary. He was the fifth ex-Clann member to be elected to the houses of the Oireachtas in 1951. Clann na Talmhan had another successful Seanad election, electing three Senators – Patrick Baxter, Bernard Commons and John Meighan (all former TDs).

De Valera selected a cabinet that was little different from the one that had left office in 1948. It created a 'little has changed/business as usual' feel for the government. It was a cabinet that did not seem to possess an overbearing urge to innovate. There was some tidying up work to do. The new Minister for Health, Jim Ryan (who had also been Noel Browne's predecessor), implemented the remaining sections of the Health Bill, having secured agreement with the Hierarchy and the IMA on introducing a means test.

The presidential term of Seán T. O'Kelly was due to finish in 1952. There was little political enthusiasm for a contest. A Cork-based barrister and known satirist, Eoin 'The Pope' O'Mahony did try to secure nominations for an independent candidacy but was unsuccessful. Seán T. O'Kelly later gained automatic re-election as President.

Most political activity in the Fourteenth Dáil focused on the political direction of key individuals, decisions that would strengthen the position of Fianna Fáil and Fine Gael. In May 1952 James Dillon was approached by John A. Costello to rejoin Fine Gael. He accepted without hesitation. Within a week Oliver J. Flanagan had also joined Fine Gael. After another few days, Charles Fagan (who had originally been elected a Fine Gael TD) had increased Fine Gael's parliamentary party by three.

Three was the magic number of by-elections that were held in June 1952. These by-elections in Limerick East, Mayo North and Waterford were brought about by the deaths of two Fianna Fáil TDs, and the death of Bridget Redmond (wife of William). The Dáil numbers were unchanged by these elections as a Fine Gael gain in Limerick East was cancelled out by the loss of its seat in Waterford.

These by-elections did represent something of a sliver of light for Clann na Poblachta. Its candidates in Limerick East and Mayo North amassed close on 11,000 votes, 3,000 more than the party had won in those constituencies in the previous general election.

A fourth by-election followed in November, caused by the death of Alfie Byrne junior. He had followed his father in being elected to Dáil Éireann and had now predeceased him. His brother Thomas was chosen to contest the by-election. Fine Gael and Labour did not put forward candidates. Thomas Byrne outpolled the Fianna Fáil candidate by a two-to-one margin. Clann na Poblachta's candidate, The O'Rahilly, was a distant third with less than 1,700 votes.

Nine TDs died over the duration of that Dáil. A further five by-elections were then held. It was indicative of a generational change that was happening in Irish politics. Two of these by-elections took place in June 1953. They were for the constituencies of Cork East and Wicklow, caused by the deaths of a Labour and a Fianna Fáil TD. Fine Gael was the victorious party in both constituencies. The wind was very much at that party's back.

In October 1953, perhaps in an attempt to re-seize the initiative, Fianna Fáil announced it had signed up into its ranks three independent TDs who had supported de Valera's election as Taoiseach in 1951. The biggest catch was undoubtedly Noel Browne. He was dutifully followed by Michael ffrench O'Carroll, and Patrick Cogan, once Deputy Leader of Clann na Talmhan, completed the triumvirate. John Flynn, a former Fianna Fáil TD, also rejoined the party.

The other three by-elections took place in Galway South, Cork Borough and Louth. Each constituency remained in the hands of the party whose deputy's death had caused the vacancy. The by-election in Louth was particularly poignant. It was caused by the death of James Coburn, then of Fine Gael, but originally part of the group of National League TDs elected in June 1927. His death could be said to be the end of the Redmondite tradition in Irish politics.

After these by-elections de Valera's working majority had become tenuous to the point of non-existence. By the end of April the government had suffered defeat in a number of divisions on a Health Bill. Without new elections this would become a more frequent occurrence.

The last business of the Fourteenth Dáil was an adjournment debate secured by the independent TD (and former Clann na Poblachta TD), Peadar Cowan. It was on the subject of the mistreatment of a 14-year-old boy attending Artane Industrial School.

I gave notice this morning that, on the Adjournment of the Dáil, I would raise the matter of a boy who received injuries in Artane Industrial School on the 14th of this month. I want to state briefly to the Dáil the facts as they were reported to me. The boy concerned is aged 14½ years. He has been in Artane Industrial School for one and a half years, and, during his period there, his conduct has been satisfactory. On the 14th of this month he was punished for some boyish altercation with another boy. Apparently, as I am informed, before the punishment was inflicted, the doors were locked, the windows closed and the punishment, which was the normal punishment, was inflicted in the presence of all of his classmates. The punishment, I am informed, consisted of a number of slaps on the hand from the punishment leather that is generally used for that purpose, but on the completion of that punishment the boy was ordered to submit to further punishment with the edge of the strap and he refused to accept that punishment. The Brother in charge sent for another Brother to come in. Apparently the boy who was being punished felt that the Brother was being brought in for the purpose of compelling him to receive this additional punishment to which he objected. Whatever his boyish mind was, he ran from the place in which he was being punished, lifted a sweeping brush, which was apparently standing in a corner, and held it up as a protection. At this stage, the second Brother arrived and seeing the brush in the boy's hands, snatched it from him, struck him on the head injuring him, struck him on the back injuring him, struck him on the arm and broke his arm. That happened on the 14th and the boy was taken to hospital on the 16th instant when his arm was set in plaster and is still in plaster.

The mother of the boy, although she lives not too distant from the school, was not informed of the injury the boy had received, but she heard about it during the week-end.

She sought to see the Superior but was refused permission to do so. In regard to that, I should perhaps make it plain that, so far as I am informed, there was on that particular point apparently some misunderstanding but she sought the Superior during that week-end and did not see him. She saw him on the first occasion on Tuesday of this week when the Superior admitted to her that the boy had received the injuries I have mentioned and that he had been taken to hospital. She did not see the boy. Whether he was then in hospital or not, I am not in a position to say but she did not see the boy. She came to me about half past eight yesterday morning. I communicated by telephone with the Superior and she was then allowed to see her boy. She was shocked at the state in which she found him. Yesterday was the 22nd; the incident occurred on the 14th and eight days afterwards, on the 22nd, she saw the boy. I, immediately, having heard her story as to what had happened, sent a telegram to the Minister asking him to investigate the matter and I stated in that telegram that I would raise the matter on the Adjournment of the Dáil, and you, Sir, have kindly given me permission to raise it now.

These boys, who are sent to these schools by the courts, are all the responsibility of the Minister for Education, and the Minister for Education, as I understand it, must answer to this House and to the country for the conditions under which the boys sent there by the courts are kept, the conditions under which they live, the conditions of punishment and matters of that kind.

I think the House and the country will want to have from the Minister an assurance that an incident such as has occurred in this case will not be permitted to occur again. I am informed that the Brother who injured the boy was barely past 21 years of age, not much older than the little boy who was injured in the fashion I have described. I think the House will want an assurance from the Minister, and the country will want an assurance from him, that punishment, if it is to be inflicted on those sent to industrial schools, will be inflicted by some person of experience and responsibility. If punishment were to be imposed in a fit of hot temper, it would be exceptionally bad and, in fact, as in this case, it would be dangerous.

I regret very much that I have had to mention or raise this matter in this House. I have lived for many years convenient to Artane Schools. For many years, whenever I was asked, I have been a subscriber to the funds of the schools. I have seen their boys week after week passing my house, looking exceptionally fit, well clothed and happy. All of us have seen their magnificent band playing on big occasions in Croke Park and it would be regrettable that an incident, such as I have mentioned in this case, should be permitted

under any circumstances to occur in a school of that kind. I myself person-
ally am satisfied that it is an isolated instance. I am satisfied that the superiors
will take appropriate action against the Brother concerned. The very fact that
the incident did occur shows how necessary it is that this House, through
the machinery of the Department of Education and through the Minister
charged with that responsibility, should have the closest supervision of schools
such as this, where children, many of them without parents at all, are sent to
be brought up.

This incident, when I heard it yesterday morning and heard the details subsequently, profoundly shocked me. I am perfectly certain that the fact that it
has been raised in this House, that the Minister has investigated it, will ensure
that no similar incident will occur in the future. It will be a guarantee to the
parents and relatives of children who are in these industrial schools that this
House and the Minister and the staff of the Department will jealously guard
and protect those children while they are under the care of the State in these
institutions.

This was a significant contribution for a number of reasons. Firstly, it
countered a belief that such issues were not being raised contemporane-
ously. The corollary of this being that for a further sixty years, such issues
remained unaddressed. Secondly, it points to a challenging of the status
quo that was coming from a smaller party/independent perspective.

The election for the Fifteenth Dáil took place on 8 May 1954, when
the pendulum swung against Fianna Fáil. The party returned with four
fewer seats on a vote share reduced by three percentage points. The Fine
Gael vote increased by over 6 per cent, which helped the party win an
additional ten seats. The Labour Party's vote increased only marginally,
although there were now three extra Labour TDs. Clann na Talmhan's
vote increased slightly but its seat numbers were five seats, down from
six. Clann na Poblachta fell to a 3 per cent share of the national vote but
gained one new TD. The fourteen independent TDs were reduced to
five.

Clann na Talmhan lost its double seats in Mayo South (where
party leader Joseph Blowick was now the sole representative) and in
Roscommon. Part compensation was achieved when Patrick Finucane

won back a seat for the party (a party he had earlier resigned from) in Kerry North, restoring its Munster representation.

Clann na Poblachta almost doubled its representation in this election. The two TDs who had survived 1951 (Seán MacBride and John Tully) were again elected. A third seat was won by John Connor in Kerry North (a constituency that also elected a Clann na Talmhan TD). In Limerick East a fourth seat was almost won for the party by Steve Coughlan. He was in second position after the first count, in this four-seat constituency. Unfortunately he failed to gain sufficient transfers.

Five independents were elected in 1954. Two of these were Alfie Byrne and his second son, Thomas. William Sheldon retained, for a third time, a seat in Donegal East. Former Fianna Fáil TD, Bernard Maguire was elected after an absence in Sligo/Leitrim. The sole successful Provisional Clann na Poblachta TD was Jack McQuillan in Roscommon. Peadar Cowan was unsuccessful in Dublin North East.

Eight independents, elected in 1951, stood as party affiliated candidates in this election. Three of the independents who had joined Fine Gael (James Dillon, Charles Fagan and Oliver J. Flanagan) were each elected again under their new party banner. The Fianna Fáil newcomers (Noel Browne, Patrick Cogan and Michael ffrench O'Carroll) were not.

Half-hearted attempts were made in this election to increase diversity within the Irish political gene pool. Sinn Féin re-emerged in 1954. This 'Mark IV' version of the party raised its head with serious intent for the first time in twenty-seven years. It had fitfully participated in local elections, and had even lost its association with the anti-treaty IRA. High Court action aimed at securing dormant funding from the 1920s was challenged by the party, ending with the Court ruling this incarnation of Sinn Féin was not related to the original of the species. In 1954 this Sinn Féin party ran two candidates, in the Clare and Louth constituencies. Between them the two candidates won around 2,000 votes.

A political party named Young Ireland was formed in 1952. Calling for reduced public expenditure, accompanied by reduced taxation, along with a decentralised approach to industrialisation, the party stood three candidates in the 1954 election. Winning little over 1,000 votes between them, no real impact seems to have been made.

Two flags operations seems to have been put in place for this election. In the Dublin South West constituency, Myles Heffernan contested on behalf of the Cine Gael grouping. Advocating for restrictions on the foreign ownership of land in Ireland and for the office of President to be an unpaid one, the party through its single candidate secured 245 votes. Also in this constituency, contesting for the Irish Workers League was Michael O'Riordan. He had won 130 more votes than his Cine Gael opponent but he made no great advance.

The other one-man operation was National Action whose candidate Séamus Murphy contested the Dublin North East constituency. This party was committed to Catholic social teaching and to establishing a Christian state. These ideas secured a respectable 1,430 votes in that constituency.

None of these parties or their candidates would be involved in the selection of the next Taoiseach. The odds were very much in John A. Costello's favour. Throughout the term of the 1951-54 government, while Richard Mulcahy remained the leader of Fine Gael, Costello continued to be seen as the leader of the opposition – the alternative Taoiseach.

With Labour and Clann na Talmhan, Costello would already have a working majority. If Clann na Poblachta had been asked to participate the party would have been offered a cabinet position. The party's National Council chose not to participate, but was willing to support Costello's nomination as Taoiseach.

The putative programme was agreed between Fine Gael and Labour. Either Clann party were invited to join government on the basis of what had been agreed already. Others were there for their numbers, not their opinions.

When the Dáil reconvened on 2 June, both de Valera and Costello were nominated for the position of Taoiseach. De Valera could only secure the support of one independent, Ben Maguire of Sligo/Leitrim, who had once been a Fianna Fáil TD. Costello was easily elected again as Taoiseach, having gained the support of most of the rest.

A new government was formed with Joseph Blowick being appointed again as Minister for Lands. Soon his party colleague, Michael Donnellan, would again be selected as Parliamentary Secretary in the

Department for Finance, with responsibility for the Office for Public Works. Seán MacBride was offered a cabinet position but his party's National Council ruled that Clann na Poblachta, while supportive of the government, would not participate in it.

A programme for Government had been agreed between Fine Gael and Labour. Unlike the first inter-party government, this administration had a definite pecking order. The dynamic had a totally different feel from its 1948 equivalent. The parties who mattered were Fine Gael and Labour. In 1948 Clann na Talmhan had shown itself incapable of policy innovation. In this government, the party would show itself to be no different. Seán Mac Bride with his Clann na Poblachta compatriots would brood on the sidelines. Placating MacBride was again one of Costello's main tasks, but this time with MacBride not sitting in cabinet.

The Eighth Seanad was then elected. Since the introduction of the new Seanad in 1938, no government had held a technical majority. The upper house had never made life uncomfortable for any government because effective majorities seemed quite easy to achieve. Despite relatively large numbers of unaffiliated Senators, many would have had associations with the main parties of government. The number of actual independents, while still significant, would have less of an impact than they might have. [*]

The route into the Seanad for several independents was through Seanad by-elections. A practice was developing that when a vacancy arose within the main opposition party, the government would identify a suitable independent opponent to maximise support against its opposition.

In this Seanad, Clann na Talmhan again had three Senators. Two were elected (Patrick Baxter and Bernard Commons), indicative of a shrinking presence in local government, but still an impressive feat. Their third Senator, John Meighan (who was an outgoing Senator), was appointed by the Taoiseach, having failed to be elected. Patrick Baxter was elected as Cathaoirleach of the Eighth Seanad, an important office for the party to hold.

---

[*] The Oireachtas *Members Database* is poor at identifying the distinction between a Senator being an independent or being unaffiliated.

Clann na Poblachta did not succeed in having a Senator elected. Former member Noel Hartnett was successfully elected in 1951 but was unsuccessful in 1954. The election of independent Liam Kelly seemed to give Seán MacBride, at least, a presence in the Seanad. Kelly had been elected as an abstentionist to the Northern Ireland parliament in 1953. Having been active in the IRA, he was expelled in 1951. This led him to set a new paramilitary organisation Saor Uladh. Later a political wing, Fianna Uladh, was established. These organisations resolved to undermine government in Northern Ireland while recognising the legitimacy of the government in the Republic of Ireland.

Five of the six university seats were elected independents – Roger McHugh and George O'Brien for the National University of Ireland and William Fearon, William Stanford, and the already noted Owen Sheehy Skeffington for Dublin University. Among the Taoiseach's eleven nominees were James Douglas and Henry Guinness (of Guinness and Mahon).

A major political triumph for this government was Ireland's acceptance into membership of the United Nations. Ten years of patient diplomacy had paid off with this decision and the Republic of Ireland became a member on 14 December 1955. At a time of a considerable international tensions, the previous Minister for External Affairs, Seán MacBride, cannot have been too happy to have missed this limelight.

The local elections of 1955 produced many surprises. Fianna Fáil and Fine Gael finished well ahead of the rest, with close on 70 per cent of the poll. Independents were the next largest category. Labour had a poor election, finishing behind Clann na Talmhan and not much ahead of Clann na Poblachta. As with the general election, Sinn Féin had a small, though increased, presence in these elections. The party elected seven councillors.

At the end of 1955 a by-election took place in Limerick West. It involved Fianna Fáil, Fine Gael and Labour. Caused by a Fine Gael vacancy, it was won by Fianna Fáil. After this, a new electoral strategy was put in place by the parties participating in government and those who supported the government. In other by-elections that followed, if a vacancy occurred on the government side, a single candidate would contest the by-election on the government's behalf. To be opposed by Fianna Fáil.

The first use of this strategy occurred in Kerry North. John Connor, who had won the first new seat for Clann na Poblachta since the party's first general election in 1948, had died tragically after a car accident. His daughter Kathleen, only twenty-one years old, was selected to contest the by-election. There would be only two candidates, O'Connor for Clann na Poblachta and Daniel Moloney for Fianna Fáil. Government ministers from different parties even campaigned for O'Connor. The Taoiseach, John A. Costello, made a speech in Kerry on her behalf. The tactic worked, with O'Connor becoming the first Clann na Poblachta by-election victor since the party's breakthrough successes in 1947.

Within a month of this by-election Alfie Byrne, the undeniably popular but distinctly independent figure, died. The last of his kind, an Irish Party MP elected forty years earlier, he could have been swept into history's wake but chose to commit to the new state in a deep and abiding way. He was to serve thirty-four years in the Oireachtas, mostly in Dáil Éireann, although he also opted to become a member of the First Senate for three years.

The only election he had ever lost was the 1918 Westminster election. He never lost an election as an independent. His period in the Oireachtas was contiguous with serving as a member of Dublin Corporation. He became the first Lord Mayor of Dublin after the authority was re-established in 1930 (having been abolished in 1925). He held the office for a further eight years in a row, and then returned for a tenth year in the office in 1954–55.

He established a family dynasty in helping to get his son Alfie Jr elected. Alfie Jr predeceased his father in 1952 (he was 39 years of age). A second son, Thomas, entered the Dáil having won the subsequent by-election.

When the office of President of Ireland was created after the passage of the 1937 Constitution, Alfie Byrne had been considered as the most

---

* It should be noted that while Byrne campaigned in elections throughout as an independent, within the Dáil chamber he consistently lent his vote in support of Cumann na nGaedheal/Fine Gael governments.

suitable and most likely holder of that office. In the end, his candidacy was outmanoeuvred with the selection of Douglas Hyde.*

A third son, Patrick, was chosen to contest the by-election. Again there would be only two candidates. The Fianna Fáil candidate was the son-in-law of a senior party figure, Seán Lemass. This candidate, Charles J. Haughey, had been previously unsuccessful in the 1951 and 1954 general elections. This by-election would not be third time lucky for Haughey, the Byrne family brand being too difficult to overcome.

The third in this series of by-elections was in Laois/Offaly, a vacancy caused by the death of the Labour Party TD William Davin. His son Michael was chosen as the stand-alone government candidate. Despite the free field, and the benefit of the family name, he could not overcome the Fianna Fáil challenge.

The next two by-elections in Cork Borough and Carlow Kilkenny were brought about by the deaths of Fianna Fáil TDs. Fine Gael and Labour contested both as did a number of independents, but Fianna Fáil held both seats. The Fine Gael candidate in Cork Borough, Michael Sheehan, had been elected as an independent TD in 1948. This was his second time being unsuccessful as a Fine Gael candidate.

The final by-election during the term of the second inter-party government was held in the Dublin South West constituency, caused by the death of the Fine Gael TD Peadar Doyle. The gentleman's agreement of those supporting the government continued to hold, with Fine Gael on its own competing with Fianna Fáil, even though this was the constituency of Seán MacBride. The fourth use of this strategy saw its second failure when Fianna Fáil became the victors. Its candidate Noel Lemass, son of Seán, made more of an impact than his brother-in-law Haughey previously had.

The 1950s was a period of economic stagnation and mass emigration from Ireland. The economic and social policies of the leapfrogging governments differed little from each other. The big ideas were coming not from within the political system, but from within the higher echelons of the civil service. Big ideas were not, however, always good ideas. A 1956 memorandum from the Department of Finance was sent to a commission examining the future of public transport.

It stated 'that railways have outlived their economic utility (and that to invest in them) can no longer be seen as capital expenditure which could be properly met by borrowing, since the railways cannot be made solvent'. It went on to add that rail should be replaced by road transport as quickly as possible.

Within the cabinet the leader of the Labour Party, William Norton, made his displeasure known. The party regarded the establishment of CIE, and with that the nationalisation of public transport, as one of the achievements of its previous period in government. Outside of cabinet, Seán MacBride was also outlining his unhappiness.

The national debate needed to be directed towards new economic approaches. As the main party in government, Fine Gael sought, at least, to inform the debate. In October 1956 it produced a policy document, *Programme for Production*, which floated the idea of tax benefits for exports. It was the first shot in the salvo of new economic ideas that would lead the country into the next decade.

The more narrow political considerations in Irish politics had less to do with macroeconomics, and more to do with the re-igniting of a border campaign by the IRA. The renewed Sinn Féin presence sought to capitalise on this strengthened profile. This reached its height after a bungled raid on a police station in Brookeborough, County Fermanagh, which resulted in the deaths of Seán South and Fergal O'Hanlon. Their funerals reawakened republican sentiment.

The Dáil had risen in early December 1956. This New Year's Day incident would set alight national tension. Particular pressure was put upon Seán MacBride and Clann na Poblachta. Their claims to be the most republican party in Dáil Éireann were being tested. MacBride took these threats to heart. He announced the withdrawal of his party's support for the government.

Clann na Poblachta was not a direct participant in this government, but its three votes were vital in maintaining the government's working majority. Without it, John A. Costello was aware that continued government was not possible. Calling to the President, he sought that new elections should be called for 5 March 1957.

10

The Last Long Strides

In this election the pendulum swung firmly back in Fianna Fáil's favour. With a 5 per cent increase in its vote, the party won seventy-eight seats, a clear majority. Fine Gael's vote decreased by more than 5 per cent resulting in the loss of ten seats. Its parliamentary party was now almost half the size of Fianna Fáil's. The other parties of the previous government also suffered. Labour lost 3 per cent of its support and with that seven seats. Clann na Talmhan fell to under 3 per cent of the national poll, winning only three seats in adjoining Connacht constituencies. The party's front men, Joseph Blowick and Michael Donnellan, were again returned as was its Roscommon representative, John Beirne. Clann na Talmhan's Munster presence once again became detached when Patrick Finucane decided to stand in this election as an Independent Farmer, and not on Clann na Talmhan's behalf, and was subsequently elected.

There would be a new fourth party in the Dáil after this election, even if ignoring the Dáil was the essence of what this party was about. Thirty years after contesting its last general election with a major slate of candidates, Sinn Féin announced its return. In 1954 a toe had been dipped into the water when two candidates contested. This time, the publicity generated by the renewed IRA border campaign and republicanism awakened by the funerals of 'martyrs' made the party put forward twenty candidates.

Four of these candidates were successful – John Joe McGirl in Sligo/Leitrim; Eineachán O' hAnnluain in Monaghan; Rory Brady in Longford/Westmeath and John Rice in Kerry South. The abstentionist principle in the party remained absolute with the election of these four TDs, which gave an already majority Fianna Fáil government even greater security.

In retrospect, the level of Sinn Féin breakthrough in 1957 can be overstated. Thirty years later the party had won slightly more votes but fewer seats than it had in June 1927 despite the highest public profile it had received in decades.

Sinn Féin's breakthrough had been helped by the strategy deployed by Clann na Poblachta's leader, Seán MacBride. Having in effect brought down the government because of how the IRA border campaign was being dealt with, MacBride believed the election would have enhanced his party's republican credentials, but it proved to be the wrong strategy.

The party's vote almost halved from 1951 to under 2 per cent. The three seats held by the party were all under threat. Clann na Poblachta ran fifteen candidates, choosing not to stand candidates where it felt Sinn Féin was likely to be more successful. One of the Sinn Féin successes in 1957 was in the Kerry South constituency. This was the constituency where Clann na Poblachta had secured a successful by-election victory a little over twelve months previously, with a great deal of help from the parties of government. Its 22-year-old TD, Kathleen O'Connor chose not to contest the general election. The party decided it had no alternative candidate, so the seat was undefended.

It was Seán MacBride who ended up being the biggest victim of his poor choice of strategy. On the first count in his Dublin South West constituency he sat in fifth position for the five available seats. Four candidates challenged for that final seat. Only 235 votes separated Seán MacBride in fifth position and the Sinn Féin candidate in eighth. The transfers did not work to MacBride's advantage, allowing the Fianna Fáil candidate to pass him.

Clann na Poblachta clung tenuously to a Dáil presence. Its continuity was secured with the election of John Tully in Cavan, also in the face of a Sinn Féin challenge. Tully was now the only Clann na Poblachta survivor from the 1948 general election. In its eleven years of existence the party had gone from a high point of ten Dáil seats to almost a tenth of the vote it had received.

An interesting new entrant into electoral politics were candidates standing on behalf of the Irish Housewives Association (IHA). The IHA was a forerunner women's advocacy organisation. The decision to promote candidates in 1957 was an attempt to raise the issue of women in political representation. Three candidates stood in three Dublin constituencies, between them winning just under 5,000 votes. Many of these votes were won by Beatrice Dixon in Dublin South West. She was in the running for the fifth and final seat in that constituency and after the first count she was 190 votes behind outgoing TD, Seán MacBride and only fifty-five votes behind the eventual winner of that seat, Bernard Butler of Fianna Fáil.

Nine extra independent seats were won in this election, up from five in 1954. For the first time since 1938 the number of independents outnumbered the number of TDs elected by smaller parties. The trend could have been otherwise as this was the election where the first independent dynasty began to break up. Less than a year after Alfie Byrne's death, with election to the Dáil of a third son Patrick, the Byrne dynasty began to diverge. Patrick chose to contest this election as a Fine Gael candidate. His brother Thomas remained independent. Both were elected.

The independent farmer vote remained strong in Munster. In Kerry North, Patrick Finucane (who had alternated as a Clann na Talmhan TD) chose in this election to be an independent again. In Cork West, Florence Wycherley (almost elected in 1954) broke through in this election. William Sheldon continued to be elected in Donegal.

In Dublin South Central, standing on an Unemployed Action ticket (a group established a few short weeks before the election) a local carpenter, Jack Murphy, found himself elected. Dublin South East saw the re-emergence of Noel Browne, again as an independent. He had resigned from Fianna Fáil after he failed to gain its nomination for the Dublin South East constituency. It was a triumphant return, when he outpolled Fianna Fáil's Sean MacEntee. The hapless Clann na Poblachta candidate trailed in his wake, winning less than 400 votes.

A strong supporter of Noel Browne, Jack McQuillan was elected in Roscommon for a fourth consecutive term, his third as an independent. A third former Clann na Poblachta member was elected in Limerick East. Ted Russell had been an unsuccessful Clann candidate in 1948, 1951 and in a 1952 by-election (where he had polled well, with almost 6,500 votes). In 1950 he had been elected a Clann na Poblachta councillor as a member of Limerick Corporation.

In 1954, Clann ran Stephen Coughlan as its candidate, where he came close to winning a fourth seat for the party. In the 1957 election the two erstwhile Clann colleagues faced each other, with Coughlan as the official candidate. Rubbing further salt into Clann wounds, Russell emerged victorious.

In Dublin South West, winning the fourth seat and helping to ease out Seán MacBride, was the independent, James Carroll. A member of Dublin Corporation, he had previously been a candidate in 1954. Later in 1957 he was elected Lord Mayor of Dublin. An unsuccessful independent was Bernard Maguire in Sligo/Leitrim who failed to retain a seat he had first won thirty years earlier as a Fianna Fáil candidate.

The Sixteenth Dáil sat for the first time on 20 March 1957. De Valera's election as Taoiseach was to be a formality. The re-election of Labour's Patrick Hogan as Ceann Comhairle, combined with the abstentionism of the four Sinn Féin TDs, would further guarantee his election. Two independents supported his election – Will Sheldon and James Carroll. All other independents abstained in the vote.

In his new cabinet, in something of a departure, de Valera introduced a large infusion of new blood. Four new ministers were appointed. Seán Lemass was appointed Tánaiste and presumed heir apparent. A former minister Seán Moylan had failed to be elected. De Valera announced his intention to appoint him to the Seanad, and to then appoint him to the cabinet, making the first use of a constitutional provision to do so. He was duly appointed Minister for Agriculture. It was to prove a short-lived promotion, as he suddenly died in November 1957.

The elections to the Ninth Seanad produced few surprises. Ten independents could be identified as being part of this Seanad. Five of these were elected in the two university constituencies. New to their number was Patrick Quinlan, elected through the National University of Ireland. The three independents elected through the vocational panels were Patrick Fitzsimons, Edward McGuire and Joe Sheridan, who had previously been elected to the Eighth Seanad. De Valera, for his eleven nominees, selected two independents. In selecting long-term Cavan TD and Grandmaster of the Orange Order, John Cole, and the daughter of James Connolly, Nora Connolly O'Brien, de Valera was ticking two particular boxes.

An early by-election occurred in December 1957. The death of a Fianna Fáil TD brought about a contest in Dublin North Central. The beneficiary of this was the independent Frank Sherwin, who had finished third on the first count in this three-seat constituency in the general election, but despite winning 15 per cent of the vote, could not sustain that position when the final seats were allocated.

This heroic failure put him in pole position when the by-election was called. Despite the challenge of Fianna Fáil, Fine Gael, Labour and Sinn Féin, Sherwin became the next TD for Dublin North Central, and the tenth independent TD in the Sixteenth Dáil.

May 1958 was an interesting month in Irish politics. Noel Browne and Jack McQuillan announced their intention to set up a new left-of-centre political party, the National Progressive Democrats. Together they were to make their presence felt within Dáil Éireann. It was in their capacity as a functioning national party that would ask greater questions of them.

A greater surprise was the resignation of Jack Murphy, The Unemployment Action TD from Dublin South Central. Within the Dáil he had been treated less than respectfully. He had started to make something of an impact in national politics. In May 1957 after the new government introduced its first budget, another austere budget, Murphy announced his intention to go on hunger strike. While he did not spend too long on hunger strike, he was soon to address well-attended public meetings in Cork and Waterford.

His lack of welcome and support in the Dáil induced a crisis of confidence in the former IRA activist and carpenter. He did receive some support from Noel Browne, Jack McQuillan and Frank Sherwin (the independent elected at the Dublin North Central by-election). Where Murphy was most uncomfortable was within his own organisation, the Unemployed Action Committee. The involvement of several members of the Irish Workers League (effectively Ireland's communist party) had brought the organisation under scrutiny.

The IWL had been suffering from the anti-communist backlash that followed the Soviet invasion of Hungary in 1956. Protests held then in Dublin saw the party's office in Pearse Street being ransacked. As a result the party did not contest the 1957 general election. Instead its members involved themselves in the Unemployed Action Committee campaign which saw Jack Murphy being elected in Dublin South Central.

Once elected, Murphy found himself being advised by sources as diverse as Archbishop McQuaid and Noel Browne to rid himself of his communist allies. Feeling bereft of respect in Leinster House and suspicious of his allies, Murphy's tipping point seems to have been the changed perception he had gained within his own community.

Being taunted by James Dillon as a salaried representative of the unemployed must have seemed bad enough. Being thought of as a one-man welfare agency, solely because of his new status, was the strongest factor that made him turn his back on representative politics.

Before a Dublin South Central by-election there would be a by-election in Galway South. This was caused by the death of a Fianna Fáil TD. In a fight between Fianna Fáil, Fine Gael and Sinn Féin, Fianna Fáil held the seat.

The Dublin South Central by-election would throw up a whole different set of characters. There were five candidates, three of whom were Fianna Fáil, Fine Gael and Labour. The Unemployed Action Committee that had helped Jack Murphy in his election had removed itself from the scene. Seán MacBride saw the by-election as a possible means for making a comeback. It had not been the constituency where he had been a TD, but it was a constituency that had elected a Clann na Poblachta TD (Con Lehane in 1948) and had shown a persistent high level of support for the party. Out to spoil the party was Noel Hartnett, a Clann na Poblachta candidate in 1948 (in Dun Laoghaire/Rathdown). Here he was to be the first candidate for the newly established National Progressive Democrats.

After the first count the Fianna Fáil candidate Patrick Cummins was 3,000 votes ahead of the other four candidates, who were bunched with little more than 300 hundred votes between them. Transfers did not change the picture. Ultimately, Fianna Fáil had won what had been an opposition seat.

The Dáil electoral arithmetic was working in Fianna Fáil's favour. The policy agenda also seemed to be working to its advantage. In 1956, when still under 40 years of age, T.K. Whitaker was appointed as Secretary of the Department of Finance. He set to work on an economic programme that would encourage inward investment to the country. This he presented to the new government, who recast the document as a White Paper, citing his authorship. This became the *First Programme for Economic Expansion*.

It is possible that the healthy position of the government was inducing a false sense of confidence. This is when it thought it was a good idea to propose the changing of the voting system and the structure of constituencies – in effect to revert to the system that existed for Westminster elections up until 1918.

The government published the Third Amendment of the Constitution Bill, 1958. With its substantial Dáil majority, the bill quickly became an Act. This would be the first referendum to be held on a proposal to change the 1937 Constitution. A later piece of legislation, the Referendum (Amendment) Act, 1959, would define what the voters were going to decide on:

> At present, members of Dáil Éireann are elected on a system of proportional representation for constituencies returning at least three members, each voter having a single transferable vote. It is proposed in the Bill to abolish the system of proportional representation and to adopt, instead, a system of single-member constituencies, each voter having a single non-transferable vote. It is also proposed in the Bill to set up a Commission for the determination and revision of the constituencies, instead of having this done by the Oireachtas, as at present.

This was the time, and these were the circumstances, when Éamon de Valera decided to pass on the baton of being leader of Fianna Fáil. With Seán T. O'Kelly nearing the end of his second term as President, it was decided that de Valera should be his party's candidate. He was 76 years of age.

Fine Gael was not prepared to facilitate this accession. It again nominated Sean Mac Eoin (he had previously contested the 1945 election) as its candidate.

The Presidential Election and the Constitutional Referendum took place on the same day, 17 June1959. When the votes were counted there was a clear margin between de Valera and MacEoin, so de Valera was to be the third President of Ireland. There was a less clear margin of 35,000 votes in the referendum on the voting system. The additional votes were won by those campaigning against changing the Constitution. The government's proposal was lost on a 48–52 split.

De Valera's election saw Seán Lemass become leader of Fianna Fáil, and being nominated as Taoiseach, when the Dáil recovened on 23 June. Lemass was duly elected Taoiseach, supported by the same independents (Sheldon and Carroll) who had supported de Valera. Again all other independents (including the two NPD deputies) abstained on the vote. Lemass's first cabinet introduced two new ministers. Slowly Fianna Fáil was trying to re-invent itself.

Lemass becoming leader of Fianna Fáil was the second of the three changes in the leadership of the traditional parties. After the general election in 1957 Richard Mulcahy took the opportunity to step down as Fine Gael leader. He was replaced by James Dillion. His Labour counterpart, William Norton, stood down in 1960 after nearly thirty years at the helm. His two predecessors had lost seats in successive elections. He steadied the Labour ship, bringing Labour into government, as the party yo-yoed from election to election. It was to be his successor, Brendan Corish, who would try to introduce a greater level of consistency to the party.

July 1959 saw three by-elections being held on the same day. One, in Clare, was necessitated by de Valera being elected President. Other than a strong Sinn Féin showing, the result was a predictable Fianna Fáil victory. The second by-election held greater public curiosity. Bernard Butler had died. He was the Fianna Fáil candidate who had beaten Seán MacBride to win the fifth and final seat in Dublin South West in 1957.

Five candidates were to contest this by-election. Included was Seán MacBride contesting his second by-election in two separate constituencies in little over a year. Dublin South West was the constituency that had elected him three times to Dáil Éireann (in 1947 he won a by-election for the Dublin County constituency). Fianna Fáil, Fine Gael, Labour and Sinn Féin filled the slate.

MacBride polled well, winning over 5,000 votes. However, he found himself in third position after the first count, 1,400 votes behind Fine Gael's Richie Ryan. Whichever of these two would be ahead of the other on the second last count would win the seat, with the benefit of each other's transfers. That person would be Ryan. Seán MacBride had now lost his last three electoral contests, having won his previous four.

The third by-election was for the Meath constituency. That was a Fianna Fáil vacancy filled by a victorious Fianna Fáil candidate. It had been a four-way fight, with a Sinn Féin candidate finishing at the bottom of the poll with 7 per cent of the total.

A new decade loomed. Two further by-elections took place during the life of the Sixteenth Dáil. They were held in Carlow/Kilkenny and Sligo/Leitrim, but neither would involve smaller parties or independents. Fianna Fáil and Fine Gael divided the spoils. It seemed that two-and-a-half party politics were again beginning to dominate.

This trend was noticeable in the local elections of 1960. The decline in the smaller parties was becoming apparent at every level. Fewer candidates were being presented, meaning fewer votes were being contested, meaning that fewer seats were being won. In these elections Clann na Talmhan presented thirty candidates, down from forty-five in 1955. Thirteen seats were won, being five fewer councillors than the party had previously. Clann na Poblachta had twenty-one candidates, down from thirty-two. This elected ten councillors, down from eleven. A new party, the National Progressive Democrats, put forward only three candidates. Even though all three were elected, it does not seem to have been a strategy to broaden the reach of the party. Sinn Féin, seeking to benefit from its heightened profile, ran seventy-nine candidates, having run only nine in 1955. The party now had fifteen city and county councillors.

By the summer of 1961 Lemass had been Taoiseach for two years. The Sixteenth Dáil had sat for more than four years, longer than most of its predecessors. Lemass felt it was time to seek his own mandate. The general election was called for 4 October 1961.

11

The Swingeing Sixties

Lemass's appeal was less than de Valera's. The Fianna Fáil vote fell, with the party losing eight seats. Fine Gael and Labour were the main beneficiaries, Fine Gael going up by seven seats, Labour by four. The stories of the others were largely negative.

Sinn Féin again ran twenty candidates but lost about 40 per cent of the vote it had won in 1957. None of the four seats it had won were retained. Three of four who had been elected previously stood again but could not repeat their success. The party's candidates invariably finished bottom of the poll in many of the constituencies it contested.

The two Clann parties continued their slow and steady declines. Clann na Talmhan stood six candidates winning two seats – those of Joseph Blowick and Michael Donnellan. Clann na Poblachta put forward only five candidates. Seán MacBride made one last stab at returning for the Dáil. After the first count in Dublin South West he was seventh of fourteen candidates, but the fifth seat was beyond his reach. To make matters worse the winner of the party's only seat in the 1957 election, John Tully, failed to be elected in Cavan. The only sliver of light for the party was the election of Joseph Barron in Dublin South Central. Barron had previously been an unsuccessful candidate for the party in 1948, '51, '54 and '57. He would now be the sole flag carrier for the party.

After his fourth electoral defeat in succession, MacBride decided he would not repeat the experience of being party leader but without a seat in Dáil Éireann. He stood aside from the leadership of the party whose existence was so enwrapped with his personality. However, freed from the shackles of Irish politics, MacBride would achieve tremendous success in the field of international diplomacy.

In 1961 MacBride was a founding member of Amnesty International, becoming its International Chairman. He also helped establish the International Commission of Jurists, serving as its Secretary General. Later he would become President (1974–85) of the International Peace Bureau in Geneva.

He helped draft the constitution of the Organisation of African Unity (OAU) as well the first constitution of Ghana. Active in the United Nations, he held several prominent positions including Assistant Secretary-General; President of the General Assembly; High Commissioner for Refugees; High Commissioner for Human Rights and High Commissioner for Namibia.

Perhaps his finest achievement was his being awarded the Nobel Peace Prize in 1974. He shared the prize that year with the former Prime Minister of Japan, Eisaku Satō. In 1980 he was responsible for a UNESCO report examining global media trends such as concentration of ownership, and restrictions of information. It was controversially received, although some forty years later its findings still stand up to scrutiny. The links MacBride had established as Minister for External Affairs, more than a decade previously, would serve him well in these future roles.

Meanwhile in 1961 the bête noire of the Irish political establishment, Noel Browne, was now leader of his own political party, the National Progressive Democrats. The extent to which it was an actual political party was open to question. The effective partnership of Browne and Jack McQuillan were re-elected in their respective constituencies under their new banner. The party stood only one other candidate, Kathleen Brady in Carlow/Kilkenny. Noel Hartnett, who had stood on its behalf in the earlier Dublin South Central by-election, did not contest the general election.

Little effort seemed to have been expended. Within the party frustrations were being expressed. One person who resigned from the party as a result of these frustrations was future television presenter and Labour Party TD, David Thornley.

Browne and McQuillan had been two of nine independents elected in 1957. This number was further reduced with the ending of the independent Byrne dynasty, when Thomas failed to hold a seat in Dublin North West. His brother Patrick was again elected as a Fine Gael TD in Dublin North East.

Other independents elected in this election included previous by-election winner Frank Sherwin in Dublin North Central, as well as James Carroll in Dublin South West (once more beating Seán MacBride). Independent farmer, Patrick Finucane, was once again elected in Kerry North.

Three first-time independents were elected. In Dublin County, having previously been a Labour TD, Seán Dunne, stood as an independent against two of his former party colleagues, winning the seat. In Mayo North, Joseph Leneghan, who had twice been an unsuccessful Fine Gael candidate, was elected as an independent. Also with Fine Gael associations, although never having stood as a candidate for the party, was outgoing independent Senator Joe Sheridan, who was elected in Longford/Westmeath.

Three of the independents elected in 1957 did not return in this Dáil. William Sheldon did not stand again in Donegal North East. Florence Wycherley did not get re-elected in Cork West. In Limerick East, a constituency that had never returned a Clann na Poblachta TD (despite consistently high votes), the party continued to cast a shadow. Outgoing independent TD (and three-time Clann candidate) Ted Russell lost out to his former party colleague, now Labour candidate, Steve Coughlan.

There was little other alternative political activity in this election. Michael O'Riordan returned to the contest on behalf of the Irish Workers League. In his three outings as an IWL candidate he had received less than 1,000 votes, not even a third of the amount of votes he had won in the 1946 Cork Borough by-election. Another curiosity in the 1961 election was the first appearance of a candidate, Seán D. Loftus, who in this election was styling himself as a Christian Democrat.

To remain as Taoiseach Seán Lemass was at least two seats short of a bare working majority. This would be achieved by re-electing Labour's Patrick Hogan as Ceann Comhairle, and gaining the support of at least two independents. When a vote was taken he gained the support of

James Carroll and that of Frank Sherwin. Sixty-eight TDs opposed his elections. Ranged against him were the representatives of all the other political parties, with the addition of Patrick Finucane. Three other independents abstained on the vote.

The new cabinet was largely similar to the preceding one. Some portfolios were re-allocated. One new member was introduced to the cabinet table, the Taoiseach's son-in law – Charles J. Haughey.

The elections to the Tenth Seanad saw the traditional parties beginning to close their claws on the membership of the house. Nominally there were eleven independent members of the Seanad. Six of these were elected in the two university constituencies. Two of these were newly elected Senators – Dónall O'Conalláin for the National University and John Ross for Dublin University. The election of Ross would be the start of a mini dynasty that over fifty-five years later sees his son Shane sitting at an Irish cabinet table.

Lemass appointed two independents from his eleven nominees to the upper house. Both were former independent TDs seen to have represented Unionist traditions in border constituencies – John Cole from Cavan and William Sheldon from Donegal. Three independents were elected from the vocational panels. Previous Senators Patrick Fitzsimons and Edward McGuire were elected again. A newly elected independent Senator was Seán Brosnahan, the General Secretary of the Irish National Teachers Organisation (INTO).

Despite its bare working majority Lemass's government seemed blessed in its opposition. The main opposition party found little to differ with in terms of economic policy. Lemass would say, perhaps wanting to tease other parties, that the two-man National Progressive Democrats was the real opposition. Between them Noel Browne and Jack McQuillan were certainly industrious. Between 1958 and 1961, seven of the nine Private Member's motions had been proposed by either Browne, McQuillan or both. During 1961 and 1962, Browne and McQuillan asked 1,400 parliamentary questions, almost a fifth of the total number asked.

But Browne soon bored with the effect of this effort. In October 1963 he and Jack McQuillan became the Labour Party TDs. The National Progressive Democrats were no more, that is if they ever really existed.

Deprived of its real opposition, Lemass's government got on with the business of governing. A Second Programme for Economic Expansion in 1963 was brought forward. Minister for Justice Charles Haughey introduced a Succession Bill, which for the first time gave wives a legal right to their dead husband's estate. He also had a Criminal Justice Act passed which ended the use of capital punishment in Ireland.

The Succession Bill did not meet with universal approval. Independent TD (and former Fine Gael TD) Joseph Leneghan referred to the bill as 'petticoat legislation'. It did not seem to upset him enough not to later join Fianna Fáil.

Another interesting piece of legislation was an amendment of the Electoral Acts. This made the Clerk of the Dáil responsible for the new office of Registrar of Political Parties, making it a requirement for political parties seeking to contest local and general elections to register, in order to qualify for party names being used on ballot papers. The new register came into effect on 14 December 1963. On this register were Fianna Fáil, Fine Gael, Labour, Clann na Talmhan and Clann na Poblachta. One early attempt, made by Seán D. Loftus, to register a new party called the Christian Democrats was refused by the Registrar.

The by-elections held during the Seventeenth Dáil were largely three-sided affairs. The first of these was in Dublin North East, where Fine Gael's Jack Belton was succeeded, after his death, by his brother Paddy. Seán D. Loftus, again waving a Christian Democrat flag, won 2,500 votes. In Cork Borough, Fianna Fáil's John Galvin was replaced by his widow Sheila.

The family connection did not work for the Labour Party in the Kildare by-election, brought about brought about by the death of its former long-standing leader, William Norton, where his son Patrick failed to hold the seat. In Roscommon, after the death of Fine Gael's James Burke, the ensuing by-election would see him being replaced by the second widow to be elected in this Dáil term, Joan Burke. Pádraig O'Ceallaigh made up the numbers here for Sinn Féin.

The end of Clann na Talmhan's Michael Donnellan's career was captured in a moment of ecstasy and tragedy. In Croke Park for the All Ireland Football final, where his son John was captaining the Galway team, he died of a heart attack before his son raised the trophy. In the subsequent by-election in Galway East, John was to continue the family tradition. In an unusual twist he chose to stand as a Fine Gael candidate. Pádraig O'Ceallaigh once again flew a flag for Sinn Féin.

The final by-election of that Dáil term was in the Mid Cork constituency. The Labour Party better managed familial politics there when Dan Desmond was replaced by his widow Eileen. Sylvester Cotter stood there as a Christian Democrat candidate.

The day of the count for the Mid Cork by-election was the last sitting day of the Seventeenth Dáil. Despite having absorbed an independent TD and gained one seat in the by-elections, Sean Lemass felt Fianna Fáil's mathematical position in the Dáil had been too precarious for too long. He called a general election for 7 April 1965 to try and change that situation.

The movement brought up by this election between Fianna Fáil and Fine Gael was slight. Fianna Fáil won an additional two seats, giving the party half the available seats in the Dáil, but not an overall majority. There was no movement in the Fine Gael seat totals between the 1961 and 1965 elections.

The clear winner of this election was the Labour Party, which saw its Dáil presence increase to twenty-two seats, up six seats from the 1961 election. The collapse in support for other parties and independents saw Labour become the biggest beneficiary in the election. After the death of his colleague Michael Donnellan, Joseph Blowick chose not to contest the general election. There were no other Clann na Talmhan candidates.

The sole Clann na Poblachta representative, Joseph Barron, failed to hold a seat in Dublin South Central. He had been well positioned in fourth place for the four available seats. With three active Fianna Fáil candidates behind him that task became too difficult. Clann would be successful in having its previous sole Dáil representative, John Tully, re-elected in Cavan. In that election the party only presented four candidates.

The number of independent TDs in the Dáil was reduced to two, the lowest recorded level of any Dáil, other than the First and Second Dáils. The two survivors were independent farmer Patrick Finucane in Kerry North, successful in his eighth election (four as a Clann na Talmhan TD); the second successful independent was Joe Sheridan in Longford/Westmeath returned for a second term.

The two independent TDs (Frank Sherwin and James Carroll, both Dublin TDs) who had supported Seán Lemass's election as Taoiseach in 1961, failed to be re-elected. Joseph Leneghan, elected as an independent in 1961, after several unsuccessful attempts as a Fine Gael candidate, chose in that election to be a Fianna Fáil candidate. It was the wrong choice, as Seán Dunne won the seat. The former Labour, then independent TD, was re-elected as a Labour TD.

For Noel Browne and Jack McQuillan it was definitely the wrong choice. The former Clann na Poblachta, independent, National Progressive Democrats, and then Labour TDs, failed to be elected under Labour's colours. It was Browne's second failure having shifted affiliations (he had the added experience of a soujourn in Fianna Fáil). For McQuillan it was his first experience of defeat in six general elections.

A number of candidates of the unregistered Christian Democrats, led by Sean D. Loftus, polled insignificatly. In Dublin South Central, in his fifth election and fourth for the Irish Workers League (called the Irish Workers' Party since 1962, but still unregistered), Michael O'Riordan won less than 200 votes.

The immediate impact of the election was the resignation of James Dillon as Fine Gael leader. Liam Cosgrave, son of previous leader W. T. Cosgrave, was the unanimous choice of his party colleagues to become the new leader. Dillon, conservative both economically and in terms of social change, was being replaced by someone with a not too dissimilar outlook. The party had approached the general election suggesting a greater move towards liberalism and social democracy. Its manifesto, as much a treatise, entitled *Towards a Just Society*, had been authored by Declan Costello (son of John A.). The failure of the party itself to promote the principles being advocated would later be a source of frustration for him.

The secondary impact was the elimination of Clann na Poblachta as a political party. The party failed to re-register, its last TD choosing to complete his Dáil term as an independent. While it presented no candidates in the 1965 election, Clann na Talmhan continued to register as a political party.

The 1965 election represented a nadir for 'others' in Irish politics. With Clann na Poblachta removing itself from the political stage, there was now no fourth party in the Dáil for the first time since 1938. The three independents holding seats represented the lowest number since 1938. Between them the traditional parties of Fianna Fáil, Fine Gael and Labour had won 98 per cent of the vote. Political choice was at its most restrictive since the foundation of the State.

Clann na Poblachta had been the best opportunity of upsetting the dominance of the traditional parties. It had burst onto the political scene bringing with it the promise of being different and doing things differently. It grew an exaggerated sense of its potential, which saw it disappointing and being disappointed with its first general election. Nevertheless within a short time the party found itself in government. Within its parliamentary party were talented people, mercurial people who provided new energy to the business of government. This freshness, added with some innovation, helped create significant legislative achievements. The party's biggest problem was that the friction created by these talented individuals brought about creative tensions that made the party turn in on itself. The biggest lesson of its brief history was that big-bang politics, without the putting down of political roots, will struggle to bring about sustained political success.

Back in Dáil Éireann the election of the Taoiseach proceeded without a hitch. With the re-election of Labour's Patrick Hogan as Ceann Comhairle, Lemass had his effective working majority. The three independent TDs abstained from the vote. In his new cabinet Lemass named four new ministers. Only he and Frank Aiken remained from the first Fianna Fáil cabinet of 1932.

In the elections to the Eleventh Seanad eleven independents were elected or nominated. Only one of these was a new face, Denis Dalton for the National University of Ireland, and even he was the nephew of a long-time Dublin University Senator (and earlier TD), Ernest Dalton. On this occasion Dublin University saw a change in its representation with the return of Owen Sheehy Skeffington, winning back a seat John Ross had won in 1961.

There was some solace for those who had been defeated in the Dáil election. Jack McQuillan was elected as a Labour Senator. Joseph Leneghan was appointed by Sean Lemass as one of his eleven nominees, when he represented Fianna Fáil.

The following year, 1966, would be a year of bread and circuses in Irish politics. The fiftieth anniversary of the 1916 Rising was meant to rouse the populace with a proud retelling of the heroic struggle that helped bring the Nation into being. Active participants in The Rising remained significant actors in the political life of the country, none more significant than the Head of State and the Head of Government, Éamon de Valera. Street pageants, parades and television plays fed the hunger for nationalist fervour.

De Valera was coming to the end of his presidential term. At 83 years of age he was willing to seek a second term. The mood music from the anniversary made it seem that despite his age, he would be virtually assured of victory. Fine Gael felt obliged to bring an election into being. The party chose Tom O'Higgins, son of T.F. O'Higgins and nephew of Kevin. At 49 years of age he was thought of as a political teenager when compared to de Valera. As a candidate he was expected to be the sacrificial lamb.

One advantage of O'Higgins's relative youth was his ability to actively campaign, which contrasted with de Valera's tactic of resting on his laurels. The final election count on 2 June shocked many. De Valera had won with a margin of less than 1 per cent of the vote, just over 10,000 votes – an amount that was similar to the amount of spoiled votes cast.

Lemass took de Valera's near defeat as a sign that he too should move on; time to allow that final changeover to the following generation. When announcing his intention to go Lemass helped instigate the first contested leadership in the history of the party. Young turks Charles Haughey, George Colley and Neil Blaney indicated their intention to stand. None appealed sufficiently to senior members who searched and called for compromise candidates to come forward. The most likely of these was Jack Lynch, who continued to express reluctance.

Jack Lynch eventually announced his candidacy, an action that led Haughey and Blaney to withdraw as candidates and declared support for Lynch. Colley insisted on remaining a candidate. The ballot of Fianna Fáil TDs broke down fifty-two to nineteen in Lynch's favour. On 10 November 1966 he became Leader of Fianna Fáil and was then elected Taoiseach of the Irish government. Lynch chose to inherit

Lemass's cabinet, adding Sean Flanagan while reallocating certain port-folios.

The new Taoiseach faced an immediate political test in the form of two by-elections, held within a month of his election. The two by-elections in Kerry South (previously Fianna Fáil) and Waterford (previously Fine Gael) were contested by the three established parties. Fianna Fáil won both, giving Lynch an absolute majority at his first attempt.

Lynch, in most aspects, would come to be seen as a non-interventionist Taoiseach, allowing his ministers scope to portray initiatives as personal projects as much as government policies. It was an early cabinet meeting of the Lynch government that received and examined the memorandum received from the Department of Education on free secondary education – a policy that had been pre-emptorily announced a number of months previously by the Minister for Education, Donagh O'Malley.

In his first budget as Minister for Finance in April 1967, Charles Haughey introduced free travel for pensioners on public transport. He also allowed for the direct payment by the State of the standing charge on electricity for pensioners. Later he would introduce an artists' tax exemption. As Minister for Justice, Brian Lenihan was letting in some slight shafts of light in presenting a more liberal Censorship of Publications Act. In 1968, after steering Ireland's neutrally-led foreign policy, Frank Aiken was given the honour of being the first person to sign the Nuclear Non-Proliferation Treaty at the United Nations.

All political activity seemed to be centred around the government. In the Seanad Jack McQuillan had resigned the Labour whip to sit once again as an independent. Despite his commitment to radical causes, or maybe because of it, his membership of Labour had never seemed a good fit.

Twice-postponed local elections took place in 1967. Non-mainstream candidates won 12 per cent of the vote. Most of these were won by independents. Sinn Féin had seven candidates elected. The requirement to register as parties for local elections was availed of for the first time in these elections. Registered in 1967 was the Dun Laoghaire Borough Ratepayers Association, which seemed to have been a vehicle for a Cllr Ashmore, one of the listed officers. A sister organisation, the Dublin

Ratepayers Association, was also listed. The Donegal Progressive Party sought to represent the significant Protestant population living in the county, an electorate which had long been represented in Dáil Éireann through James Sproule Myles and later William Sheldon. The party secured continuous representation in Donegal County Council.

A brace of by-elections took place in November 1967. Held in Cork Borough and Limerick West because of the deaths of Labour's Sean Casey and Fianna Fáil's James Collins, Fianna Fáil won its third and fourth by-elections of the Eighteenth Dáil, further strengthening its majority. Future government minister Gerry Collins was elected in Limerick West, replacing his father James. The only other presence was Eoin (The Pope) O'Mahony who polled less than 900 votes in Cork Borough.

The next brace of by-elections took place in March 1968 in Clare and Wicklow. In Clare Fine Gael's William Murphy had passed away. In Wicklow an end to an era was marked after the death of James Everett, former leader of the short-lived National Labour party, former minister and instigator of the infamous Battle of Baltinglass. Fianna Fáil won its fifth by-election in Clare, again strengthening its majority. Fine Gael filled the Labour-created vacancy in Wicklow. Independents contested in both constituencies. Jean Grace won less than 300 votes. Standing as an independent republican socialist, Seamus Costello was a significant figure in Sinn Féin's debate on the future of that organisation. He polled a respectable 2,000 votes.

The second referendum to change the Constitution took place in October 1968. The Lynch government thought it might be able to succeed where de Valera and Lemass had failed in 1959. This time the approach was different. Two questions were asked. The first was to allow legislation to be framed to allow for a greater weighting in parliamentary representation for rural constituencies, to compensate for larger geographical areas.

Strategically it was hoped that winning more rural votes would make answering the second question positively that bit more palatable. The 1959 referendum on adopting a first past the post voting system had been unsuccessful, but not spectacularly so. Adding a second question in 1968 was seen as a cynical attempt by Fianna Fáil to peel away a valuable sector of the electorate. It would not prove to be a successful strategy as both questions were defeated with similar votes of 60 to 40 against.

The logic of Fianna Fáil's strategy seemed obvious, but its timing for both referenda seemed ludicrous. With support from 'others' declining and heading towards a historic low, Fianna Fáil governments chose to call these referenda. The electorate saw this as attempts to secure its political dominance in perpetuity.

The final by-election of the Eighteenth Dáil was also the least expected. At 47 years of age, the death occurred of the Minister of Education, Donagh O'Malley. He had been almost fourteen years a TD, but was less than three years a member of the Cabinet and had only been Minister for Education for a period of twenty months. Yet in that latter role he had helped bring into being one of most significant policy decisions in Irish politics in the form of free secondary education.

It was hoped that his widow Hilda would be the candidate for the by-election in the Limerick East constituency, but she was unwilling to stand. His nephew Des (who in his own right would create several more chapters of this story) was instead chosen as the candidate. Fianna Fáil duly held the seat. After the first count O'Malley was 6,500 votes ahead. The Labour and Fine Gael candidates were in dead heat for second place, each polling around 10,000 votes. An independent candidate, Michael Crowe, won 1,200 votes.

Despite the orgy of nostalgia that surrounded 1966, Northern Ireland had not figured largely in Irish politics in the decade that followed Sinn Féin's attempt to push voter buttons via the IRA border campaign. The international backdrop from the campaigns of Martin Luther King in the US to student protests in Paris were highlighting the absence of civil rights for many. In Northern Ireland the establishment of the Northern Ireland Civil Rights Association (NICRA), and the treatment meted out to its members, made the political establishment in the Republic look nervously at developments.

The election in April 1969 of 21-year-old Bernadette McAliskey at the Mid Ulster by-election for the British House of Commons, coupled with her stated intention to attend the parliament in Westminster, brought international attention to happenings in Northern Ireland. In the coming years no Irish government could afford to be indifferent.

It was two-and-a-half years since Jack Lynch had been elected Taoiseach. It felt time to seek a full mandate. It was also to be Liam Cosgrave's first general election as Fine Gael leader. For Brendan Corish it would be his third general election as Labour leader. For this election he sought to tread a more independent path for his party.

12

The Seventies Would Not Be Socialist

In the 1969 general election Labour campaigned using the slogan 'The Seventies will be Socialist'. The party stood more candidates than it ever had before and as a result the party's vote increased. Fianna Fáil countered with a 'Reds under the Bed' strategy. It turned out to be successful, if highly ironic, as it was a reprise of tactics used by Cumann na nGaedheal against Fianna Fáil in its early election campaigns.

In stressing its independence Labour also cut off possible transfer votes, particularly from Fine Gael, something vital for winning the final seat in constituencies. Labour won four fewer seats in this election. The party did see the election for the first time in its colours of the iconoclastic Noel Browne. Fianna Fáil and Fine Gael both lost votes but gained three seats each. Also squeezed into this election was support for 'others'. The three independents elected in 1965 was now reduced to a single independent.

No fourth party, of any description, contested this election. Independent farmer (and former Clann na Talmhan TD) Patrick Finucane chose not to contest. The last Clann na Poblachta TD to be elected, John Tully in Cavan, could not hold that seat as an independent. The sole independent in the Nineteenth Dail was Joseph Sheridan, who topped the poll in Longford/Westmeath.

Despite this reduction in numbers, the vote for independents increased marginally. After this election Fianna Fáil/Fine Gael/Labour only represented 97 per cent of the voting public. Jack Lynch had secured the first post-election absolute majority since 1957. His re-election as Taoiseach was assured. His new cabinet included two new members. Frank Aiken, the only link with the foundation of the party, chose not to be re-appointed.

The election for the Twelfth Seanad produced few surprises. One of the new and interesting Senators was a 25-year-old, Mary Robinson, elected for the Dublin University constituency. From the same constituency, a number of months later, the renowned Owen Sheehy Skeffington had died. His soujourn in the Seanad had seen him raise a number of social issues that otherwise would have been ignored. Issues like ending corporal punishment in schools and the abuse of children in institutions were first mentioned in the Seanad by Sheehy Skeffington. Neither issue was dealt with by the time of his death, though his contributions were to define their importance and significance.

Developments in Northern Ireland soon demanded an Irish government response. After a series of riots in August 1969 Jack Lynch declared that his government would not stand by and watch these developments (sometimes misquoted as 'not standing idly by'). A cabinet subcommittee was set up to examine how nationalist areas in Northern Ireland could be protected. As Minister for Finance, Charles Haughey was the key person on this subcommittee. He created a £100,000 fund for the relief of nationalist communities in Northern Ireland.

Slipping into a new decade it was clear that these issues were not going to go away. As difficult as these events were for the Lynch government, they were causing an existentialist crisis for Sinn Féin. Almost forty-four years after the party had torn itself apart on the issue of abstentionism, leading to the foundation of Fianna Fáil, the party leadership was again expressing a view that abstentionism was holding back political progress.

During the 1960s, despite the dual military and political leadership of the party, there was a move towards street politics from Sinn Féin activists. Involvement in issues like rent strikes was leading the party in a more leftward direction. Senior member Seán Garland was asked to produce a report considering the effects of ending abstentionism. Even asking the question was considered a heresy by many in Sinn Féin.

In the twilight world of a political party with a military wing, the initial decision to abandon abstentionism was taken at an IRA Army

Council in December 1969. This led to a cleavage in the military structure, with those who disagreed setting up a Provisional Army Council.

In January 1970 Sinn Féin held a special Ard Fheis to publicly endorse
the decision the abandon the policy of abstentionism. The relevant
motion did receive majority support but not the required two-thirds
majority. The party leadership sought to subvent this by asking the party
to support a motion supporting IRA policy. This precipitated a walkout
by those opposed to abstentionism. There would now be two Sinn Féin
parties, Official and Provisional. These parties would the Sinn Féin party,
'Marks Five and Six'.

Announcing their decision to detach from the broader organisation,
the abstentioners pledged allegiance to the Provisional Army Council,
declaring opposition to the ending of abstentionism, the drift towards
'extreme forms of socialism', the failure of the leadership to defend the
nationalist people of Belfast during the 1969 Northern Ireland riots,
and the expulsion of traditional republicans by the leadership during
the 1960s.

The turbulence of events in Northern Ireland was in stark contrast to
other mundane happenings in Irish politics. Seven days after the 1969
general election, Labour Party TD Seán Dunne died. The by-election
to fill the vacancy in the Dublin South Central constituency was held
in March 1970. Labour chose trade union leader Mattie Merrigan as its
candidate. This did not please the Dunne family as his wife Cora had
wanted to run. She chose to run as an independent. Another popular
local independent, Laurence Corcoran, also stood. Between the two
independent candidates 6,500 votes were won. This allowed Fianna
Fáil's Seán Sherwin to win the seat from Merrigan with a margin of
262 votes.

Sherwin was not related the former independent TD Frank Sherwin,
whose support had helped keep in office the minority Lemass government of 1961-65. In his autobiography, *Frank Sherwin: independent and
unrepentant*, Sherwin speaks of gladly accepting congratulations from all
of those, thinking Seán Sherwin was his son.

In April 1970 two further by-elections took place in Kildare and
in Longford/Westmeath. In Kildare, Gerard Sweetman (Minister for
Finance in the second inter-party government) had passed away. In

Longford/Westmeath it was the death of Paddy Lenihan (father of Cabinet Minister, Brian) that brought about the by-election. Fine Gael was victorious in both, eating into Fianna Fáil's Dáil majority.

Charles Haughey failed to appear in the Dáil to present his budget speech in 1970. He was suffering from injuries which may or may not have been the result of falling while riding a horse. It would soon be the least of his problems. Fine Gael leader, Liam Cosgrave, was given information that money from the cabinet subcommittee formed after the 1969 Northern Ireland riots, had been diverted to purchase guns to be used there.

Instead of raising the issue in the Dáil (maximising political benefit) Cosgrave went directly to the Taoiseach. Jack Lynch asked for the resignations of Haughey, Neil Blaney and the Minister for Justice, Mícheál O'Mórain. Haughey and Blaney refused to resign, obliging Lynch to sack them from the cabinet. Kevin Boland subsequently resigned as Minister in protest at Lynch's action.

Two court cases followed (the first collapsed) where competing testimonies shed little light on what truth was being told. The key conflict of evidence was between Haughey and the Minister for Defence, Jim Gibbons, whose accounts contradicted each other. The presiding judge stated that one of them had to be not telling the truth. The case against Haughey and others (Blaney was declared not to have a case to answer) found them not guilty. The damage done to Fianna Fáil was significant. It soon would give birth to significant political cleavage.

The descent into violence in Northern Ireland was being accompanied by the setting up of new political parties there. In April 1970 the Alliance Party was formed. A pro-union, anti-sectarian party, it sought to present a middle path. In August 1970 a party was established that sought to present a more cohesive approach towards representing the nationalist community – The Social, Democratic and Labour Party (SDLP).

August 1970 also saw the death of the last Clann na Talmhan TD and long-time leader of that party, Joseph Blowick. Despite not contesting any elections since 1961, the party had consistently placed an entry each year on the Register of Political Parties with the Clerk of the Dáil. This perhaps was in anticipation of a possibility of the party being revived. In these register entries Blowick was mentioned as the party's principal officer. It may have been an administrative error as this was some three months after his death..

On paper, the record of Clann na Talmhan reads as one of the more successful smaller parties in Irish politics. Over its quarter of a century lifespan the party had been in government twice. However, it is difficult to point to any particular initiative the party had been involved in while in government. Its most successful period seems to have been between 1943 and 1948 as an opposition party when it aspired to a political agenda outside of rural and agricultural issues. With seats in Munster as well as Leinster, the party made some attempts to establish itself as a national party. Slowly, in each subsequent election, the party lost one to two seats, or through defections until Blowick remained as it sole TD. Ultimately the party could never emerge from the straitjacket it had made for itself of being a rural party representing rural interests.

Kevin Boland's ministerial resignation in May of 1970 was later accompanied by his resignation from the Dáil itself. Six months later a by-election to fill this vacancy was held for the Dublin South County constituency. Boland himself was not a candidate. The Fianna Fáil candidate finished second to Fine Gael's Larry McMahon. An independent candidate, Joe MacAnthony, won more than 3,000 votes, similar to the Labour candidate. A second independent candidate won less than 500 votes. Another by-election was held on the same day in Donegal/Leitrim, resulting in a Fianna Fáil hold.

Boland would continue to be a fly in the ointment for the Lynch government. He was still a member of Fianna Fáil. It was in this context that he attended the party's Ard Fheis in February 1971. As Patrick Hillery, Minister for Foreign Affairs, was responding to the end of a debate, Boland took over another unused speaker's podium to goad the top platform. Shouting above the rising din, Hillery declared to Boland's supporters 'You can have Boland but you can't have Fianna Fáil', as Boland was being carried by his supporters after convention.

Later that year the Minister for Post and Telegraphs Gerry Collins brought forward a ministerial order under Section 31 of the Broadcasting Act which sought a prohibition on broadcasting 'any matter that could be calculated to promote the aims or activities of any organisation which engages in, promotes, encourages or advocates the attaining of any particular objectives by violent means'. While general in its drafting, the intent of the order was not to allow access to the airwaves of any political organisation which advocated, or made recourse to paramilitary activity.

Official Sinn Féin would have been seen as one such party. The 'Mark Five' Sinn Féin party, while clinging to its paramilitary ties, was also setting its face towards ending its policy of abstentionism. To this end, on 23 July 1971, the party placed itself on the Register of Political Parties. The first such Sinn Féin entry and the first 'new' entry of any national party since the register was opened in 1963.

A second new entry would soon follow. It seemed somewhat inevitable that Kevin Boland would cut his remaining ties with Fianna Fáil. In September 1971, at a gathering said to have been attended by 1,000 people, Boland announced his intention to form a new political party, Aontacht Éireann. Its unique selling point seems to have been that it considered itself more republican than Fianna Fáil.

Boland managed to persuade one TD to carry the new party's colours. He was Seán Sherwin, who had been elected in a 1969 by-election. This made Aontacht the first party to achieve Dáil representation since the National Progressive Democrats (which existed prior to the Register of Political Parties). Aontacht Éireann's own registration was far from plain sailing. Its initial application was not accepted in October 1971, before being accepted on appeal in November.

Still part of Fianna Fáil and continuing to cause difficulty for Jack Lynch was Neil Blaney. When the opposition placed a motion of no confidence in Jim Gibbons, Blaney felt unable to support it. After this action and a barrage of constant criticism, Lynch moved that Blaney be expelled from Fianna Fáil for 'conduct unbecoming'.

Approached by Kevin Boland to become part of Aontacht Éireann, Blaney instead chose to establish his own political organisation – Independent Fianna Fáil. While Blaney did not register his organisation it did exhibit many features of a political party. When in Fianna Fáil, Blaney was thought of as a wily campaigner. He would need those skills to ensure his political survival.

Northern Ireland, or its alternative formulation as the national question, loomed large in Irish politics, at this time on both parts of the island. The introduction of British troops in 1970 had first been looked at benignly, but poor community relations turned their presence sour. More than 100 political deaths had occurred by the middle of 1971. The Northern Ireland government response to this was to introduce internment without trial in August 1971. This disastrous policy intensified anger in republican areas.

On 30 January 1972 a protest was organised against internment in Derry. Twenty-six unarmed people were shot at by members of the Parachute Regiment of the British Army. Thirteen were killed on the day and a fourteenth would die months later from injuries received. The action led to protests across the island. In Dublin a crowd gathered, ending with the British Embassy in Merrion Square being set alight.

Despite these provocations there did not seem to be a shift in voter support to those urging direct action from the Irish government in Northern Ireland. While there was concern being expressed by official Ireland, little was being offered in terms of practical support. More political attention was being given to a referendum being held in May seeking approval for Ireland to join the European Economic Community (EEC). The text of that referendum read:

The State may become a member of the European Coal and Steel Community (established by Treaty signed at Paris on the 18th day of April, 1951), the European Economic Community (established by Treaty signed at Rome on the 25th day of March, 1957) and the European Atomic Energy Community (established by Treaty signed at Rome on 25th day of March, 1957). No provision of this Constitution invalidates laws enacted, acts done or measures adopted by the State necessitated by the obligations of membership of the Communities or prevents laws enacted, acts done or measures adopted by the Communities, or institutions thereof, from having the force of law in the State. The purpose of the proposal is to allow the State to become a member of the Communities commonly known as European Communities.

Those seeking approval included Fianna Fáil, Fine Gael, employer and farmer organisations. Opposed were the Labour Party, Official Sinn Féin and the trade union movement. It was an emphatic victory – 83 per cent to 17 per cent. Fifty years after the signing of the Anglo Irish Treaty (an event that had not been officially marked) Ireland had wholeheartedly decided to become part of a new treaty arrangement.

Fine Gael provided some slight light relief in 1972. Leaders of Fine Gael had never been known for their charisma. Liam Cosgrave would never have claimed to possess any. Some of his behaviour that year could be considered bizarre. When Fianna Fáil introduced stringent new security legislation in the form of the Offences Against The State Bill, Cosgrave voted with the government rather than support the position than had been advocated by his party. Then, during his leader's speech at his party's Ard Fheis, he rounded on his internal critics by making extremely strange fox hunting analogies. It did not convey affinity with ordinary people.

The last by-election of the Nineteenth Dáil was in the Mid Cork constituency in August 1972. It marked the first appearance of Aontacht Éireann in an electoral contest. Its candidate, Patrick O'Callaghan, finished last of the four candidates, winning 1,172 votes and 3 per cent of the poll. The by-election was won by Gene Fitzgerald of Fianna Fáil who was twenty-two votes short of the quota on the first count.

Voters were invited to cast their votes once more in December 1972, when the government put forward two constitutional amendments for consideration. The first related to a reduction in the legal age to vote from 21 to 18 years of age. The second was about replacing the provision recognising the special position of the Catholic Church, with new provisions protecting freedom of religion and specifying other religious denominations. Both measures were strongly approved with 84 to 85 per cent majorities.

Within a number of weeks Jack Lynch had called a general election. One of the factors that was said to have influenced him was the uncertainly of the voting intention of new voters (aged between 18 and 21), thought more likely to vote against the government, making it preferable to hold an election before such voters became registered. A court case was taken to postpone the election, in which a 20-year-old litigant (represented by Seán MacBride) sought the right to vindicate his vote. He did not succeed but was awarded costs on a public interest basis.

This general election realised a number of other firsts. Fine Gael and Labour produced a joint programme of what they would do together in government should they be elected. Official Sinn Féin contested its first election as a non-abstentionist party. And, of course, this was the first test for Kevin Boland's Aontacht Éireann.

The quirks of the proportional representation system saw Fianna Fáil marginally increase its vote but it lost six seats. The Labour Party vote dropped by three percentage points, yet the party won two additional seats. The Fine Gael seat total was up by three. Neil Blaney succeeded in joining Joe Sheridan as an independent member of the house. Between them, Fine Gael and Labour would have a working majority.

With the participation of Official Sinn Féin and Aontacht Éireann, the votes for 'others' began to creep upwards, now standing at 5 per cent of the electorate. Neither party was successful in winning a seat, although Official Sinn Féin performed better. Its ten candidates averaged about 1,500 votes each. The thirteen Aontacht Éireann candidates averaged less than 1,000 votes. It was a disappointing election for the new party. Only two of its candidates passed 2,000 votes – Kevin Boland in Dublin South County, and James Kelly (a former Irish Army intelligence officer implicated in the Arms Trial) in Cavan.

Michael O'Riordan stood in Dublin Central constituency for the newly named, but as yet unregistered, Communist Party of Ireland. He secured some additional votes over previous election performances, but still totalled less than 500. In Dublin North Central, appearing on the ballot paper as Seán D. Christian Democrat Dublin Bay Loftus, the dogged independent did not perform much better.

13

A Coalition of All Talents

This was a government that chose to call itself something that no other inter-party government would. This was a two-party coalition, a National Coalition government, dependent neither on the other parties nor on independent members. While consisting of only two parties, those parties were of themselves coalitions. Liam Cosgrave had to balance his party between its Christian Democrat and Liberal wings. As leader of the Labour Party, Brendan Corish had to balance his party's traditional and celebrity wings.

Cosgrave brought into the cabinet his strongest internal party critic, Garrett FitzGerald. It was not as Minister for Finance, which as an economist he would have hoped for, but as Minister for Foreign Affairs. Labour's 1969 intake included Conor Cruise O'Brien (famed for his work for the United Nations in The Congo) along with Justin Keating and David Thornley (once of the National Progressive Democrats) who had both achieved public attention as television presenters. O'Brien and Keating were made ministers, while Thornley was not.

In the Seanad Elections the most interesting elections were again for the university constituencies. In the National University constituency, Augustine 'Gus' Martin (UCD Professor of Anglo-Irish Literature and editor of the school text books *Exploring English* and *Soundings*) was elected as an independent. For the Dublin University constituency Mary Robinson was joined by Noel Browne, standing again as an independent. Browne had failed to secure a Labour nomination for the previous general election. Within months any remaining formal ties with Labour ended with Browne's expulsuion from the party.

In making his eleven nominations to the Seanad, Liam Cosgrave broke with precedent by failing to appoint any independent Senators. All eleven appointed were members either of Fine Gael or Labour.

Also in May 1973 the third public election and fourth constitutional process had happened in a five-month period. The second presidential term of Éamon de Valera was coming to an end. He had passed his ninetieth birthday. He remained concerned with his legacy and the need for Fianna Fáil to provide a viable candidate. His initial preference was for his long-time cabinet colleague, Frank Aiken, who felt he had made his commitment. Attention then turned to the previous Tánaiste and longest serving, still active, Fianna Fáil minister, Erskine Childers.

Given how close he had come to unseating de Valera in 1966, T.F. O'Higgins was considered the favourite to be the first candidate (outside of Douglas Hyde) to become President, not having been associated with Fianna Fáil. Childers carried some associations that made him stand out. His father had owned the yacht, *The Asgard*, that had been associated with the 1914 Howth Gun Running. As a Protestant, he caused a problem for many within that community who traditionally had supported Fine Gael.

This election also saw some American campaign techniques being used for the first time. The end result was that a Fianna Fáil candidate was elected as President, although he was not the favourite.

Some manner of revenge was gained by Fine Gael in the ensuing by-election, caused by Erskine Childers's elevation. The party won the Monaghan by-election. Also contesting was an Aontacht Éireann candidate (who had not contested the general election), polling slightly over 2,000 votes. Another candidate who claimed to be Communist (Marxist/Leninist) polled under 200 votes.

The new government, despite all its talents, entered office just as a global economic recession (caused by an increase in world oil prices) was beginning. This would shadow all of its activities throughout its term of office.

One area where initiatives were beginning to bear fruit was in Northern Ireland. Stand-alone government had been suspended in Stormont. The British Government, working with the Irish

Government, brought various parties around a table. In the first instance this led to elections to a Northern Ireland Assembly being held in June 1973. There followed further discussions which resulted in the signing in December of the Sunningdale Agreement. Through this, power-sharing devolved government was to be introduced. The agreement did not meet with universal approval, but it did introduce a note of hope into what had become an increasingly intractable problem.

The new Northern Ireland Executive came into being on 1 January 1974. It consisted of eleven ministers, six of whom were from the Ulster Unionist Party, four from the SDLP, and a single minister from the Alliance Party. What had been the office of Prime Minister was now referred to as the Chief Executive.

The Executive faced strong opposition from the start. The Ulster Workers' Council was set up to oppose its existence. This was formed by unionist political parties opposed to the Sunningdale Agreement – The Democratic Unionist Party (led by Ian Paisley) and the Vanguard Unionist Party (led by William Craig), while Harry West led discontented Ulster Unionist Party Assembly members. Also within this group were shadowy loyalist paramilitary organisations – the Ulster Defence Association (UDA) and the Ulster Volunteer Force (UVF).

On 15 May 1974 a strike of unionist workers was called which brought Northern Ireland to a standstill. Within a fortnight the strike achieved its effect, by forcing the resignation of Brian Faulkner as Chief Executive and the collapse of the Executive.

The Cosgrave government was obviously disappointed at this turn of events, but other events were bringing ongoing violence in Northern Ireland into sharper focus. In the midst of the Ulster Workers' Strike, loyalist paramilitaries planted bombs in Dublin and Monaghan, actions that resulted in thirty-three deaths. These were the first large-scale violent events that had occurred in the Republic since the onset of The Troubles in Northern Ireland.

Two months previously a Fine Gael Senator, Billy Fox from Monaghan, had been murdered. While a number of men were arrested and convicted for this, the reasons why he was targeted and murdered remained clouded in confusion. Allied to the bombings, the Cosgrave government feared an escalation of violence throughout the island.

Many within Fine Gael were arguing for a more confrontational approach with the IRA. In this they were joined by the Labour minister, Conor Cruise O'Brien. This influenced a more loose approach to policing, where a freer hand or a collective blind eye was given to the existence of a group within the Gardaí, who came to be known as the 'Heavy Gang'.

At the same time social policy was not progressing very smoothly under the National Coalition. At the end of 1973 the Supreme Court had declared unconstitutional the ban on married people having access to contraception. The coalition government brought forward enabling legislation. This came to the floor of the Dáil where deputies were given a free vote. As Taoiseach, Liam Cosgrave voted against his own government's legislation.

However, some socially progressive legislation was introduced, largely dependent of the country's membership of the European Economic Community (EEC). The civil service marriage ban was brought to an end in 1973. Equal status and equal pay bills were to follow.

Local elections took place in 1974. Very little movement was evidenced in the voting percentages. Seventy-five independent councillors were elected. In the mini league contest between Official Sinn Féin and its Provisional counterpart, the provisionals' had seven councillors elected to the officials' six. Aontacht Éireann put forward fourteen candidates, none of whom was elected. That party had established no local authority base, although it previously had a presence through a member of Cork Corporation.

In 1968 a new party registered for local elections purposes – The Cork City Ratepayers Party. Prior to the registration of parties, a Cork Civic Party had contested local elections, electing a significant number of councillors. The new party was a vehicle of Noel Collins, once a Fine Gael councillor, who was elected to Cork County Council. Another example of a local party, prior to registration would have been the Limerick-based Gluais Linn, which would have been represented on Limerick Corporation in the 1940s by Ted Russell before he joined Clann na Poblachta.

Back in 1974 a by-election in Cork North East saw a Fianna Fáil hold. A significant feature of this by-election was the performance of the Official Sinn Féin candidate, Joe Sherlock, who polled over 5,000 votes.

Meanwhile, Official Sinn Féin was facing a second separation from its ranks within a few short years, with the formation of the Irish Republican Socialist Party (IRSP) in December 1974. At the heart of this dispute was an ongoing argument about whether the Official IRA was right to announce its ceasefire from military activities in 1972. Chief among those who disagreed with this and who thought it important that a republican party should maintain a parallel military infrastructure it was prepared to put to use, was one of Official Sinn Féin's more charismatic members, Seamus Costello.

At its foundation meeting, a military wing, the Irish National Liberation Army (INLA), was surreptitiously set up. Within the first executive of the IRSP was Bernadette McAliskey, now no longer a Westminster MP. Her sojourn in the party was short. Its first internal argument centred around what should be the reporting mechanism between the party and its military wing. As a new party the IRSP had one advantage. Since 1967, Seamus Costello had been an elected public representative at town council and at county council level.

Irish politics ended unhappily in 1974 with the unexpected death of President Childers. He had been in office for fewer than eighteenth months. His plans to expand the scope of the presidency had been constantly stymied by Liam Cosgrave as Taoiseach, to the extent that he had considered resignation. His death created considerable problems for the government. Since 1972 the country had had three constitutional referenda, a general election, a presidential election and local elections. Outside of voter fatigue, within Fine Gael and Fianna Fáil there was little appetite to undergo the cost of another campaign.

Efforts were made to secure an agreed candidate, and with that being able to avoid an election. The candidate chosen was Cearbhall Ó Dálaigh, who as Carroll Daly had been appointed by Éamon de Valera as Attorney General in 1946, serving until 1948, appointed again in 1951 until 1953. In 1948 he had been an unsuccessful Dáil candidate. In 1951 he failed to secure election to Seanad Éireann.

In 1953 he was appointed by de Valera as the youngest member of the Supreme Court. Within a decade he would be made Chief Justice by the government of Seán Lemass. From this office he served as a member of the European Court of Justice. There could be no denying that

O'Dálaigh was eminently qualified as a guarantor for the Constitution – a significant role of the President.

Two by-elections took place in March in two Galway constituencies, Galway North East and Galway West. Both had been caused by the deaths of two Fianna Fáil members. The successful candidates were the children of the former TDs Michael Kitt in North East and Geoghegan Quinn in West. In North East an independent candidate won 400 votes. In West, a Gaeltacht activist, Pól O'Foighil, polled over 2,000 votes, while a Sinn Féin candidate had fewer than 700 votes.

The final by-election of 1975 was in Mayo West. There, Fine Gael repeated the formula that had worked so well for Fianna Fáil in Galway. Enda Kenny replaced his late father, Henry as a TD for the constituency. A third candidate was an independent called Basil Morahan, who came close to 1,500 votes.

Two new entries were included in the Register of Political Parties in 1975. The IRSP followed Official Sinn Féin in registering. Later in the year the Communist Party of Ireland was registered.

As the seventies moved into its second half Northern Ireland still loomed large over the politics of the island. The plug was finally pulled on the Northern Ireland Assembly, which never reconvened. Horror attacks, such as the Miami Showband massacre, continued to appal.

In the summer of 1976 this would reach a crisis with the assassination in Dublin of the British Ambassador to Ireland, Christopher Ewart-Biggs. This inspired the government to introduce an Emergency Powers Bill. Much to the government's chagrin President O'Dálaigh referred the bill to the Supreme Court, where it was found to be constitutional.

The death of a member of the Garda Siochana, while this was happening, added to the bad feeling that existed. At an army passing out parade in Mullingar, the Minister for Defence, Paddy Donegan, was reported as criticising President O'Dálaigh as a 'thundering disgrace' for practising his constitutional role, although, anecdotally, the phrase used was believed to be more colourful in nature.

O'Dálaigh took these comments, spoken to army personnel, as an affront to his role as the titular Commander-in-Chief of the armed forces. Donegan offered his resignation but it was refused by Liam Cosgrave. Instead he was moved sideways in a mini cabinet reshuffle.

This left O'Dálaigh with little option but to resign, less than two years in his office. With this resignation the government was now required to oversee the selection of a third President of Ireland during its term of office. Given the controversy brought about by O'Dálaigh's resignation, the government was happy to accede to Fianna Fáil's suggestion of an agreed candidate, the former Minister for Foreign Affairs Patrick Hillery.

The final by-elections of the Twentieth Dáil took place in June 1976 for the Donegal North East and Dublin South West constituencies. Donegal North East was the constituency of the now independent TD Neil Blaney. The by-election would pit his Independent Fianna Fáil organisation against the party from which he had been expelled.

Blaney's candidate, Paddy Keaveney, found himself 121 votes ahead of his Fianna Fáil rival. The near perfect split of the once Fianna Fáil party allowed the Fine Gael candidate to top the poll, but only by a margin of 202 votes. Also contesting was an independent candidate, Tony Gill, who won more than 2,000 votes. These transfers were to prove vital in deciding the eventual winner of the by-election. The candidate to benefit most was Paddy Keaveney.

The Dublin South West by-election also brought together an interesting gathering of individuals and political circumstances. Noel Lemass, son of Seán Lemass, had died. His widow, Eileen, had been chosen as Fianna Fáil's candidate. It was a formula that proved itself over and over again. It seemed to be working again when Lemass found herself nearly 3,000 votes ahead after the first count. Her nearest challenger was the General Secretary of the Labour Party, Senator Brendan Halligan. He in turn was 1,700 votes ahead of Fine Gael's Jim Mitchell.

Making up the rest of the ballot were Tómas Mac Giolla, leader of Official Sinn Féin (1,679 votes); Kevin Boland flying his Aontacht Éireann flag (1,186 votes); Ite Ni Chionnaith, the first official IRSP candidate (287 votes) and independent Blathnaid Ni Chinneide (113 votes). Halligan succeeded in winning enough transfers to overturn Lemass's first count lead.

The manner of Halligan's victory gave the national coalition government confidence that it could – and would – be re-elected at the following general election. To help it on its way the Minister for Local Government James Tully had produced a revision of Dáil constituencies in 1974 designed to give the outgoing government an advantage. This legislation became known as the 'Tullymander'.

The thinking behind the redrawing of constituencies was the belief that with Fianna Fáil support weaker in the area Dublin area, creating a number of three-seat constituencies would most likely break down Fianna Fáil, Fine Gael and Labour. It presumed a not very significant change in voting patterns.

Presumptions were very much to the fore as the general election approached. Liam Cosgrave called the election for June 1977. The months of campaigning preceding the elections made it a general election like no other previously experienced in Ireland. Using the template of the 1973 Presidential election, Fianna Fáil General Secretary Seamus Brennan added even more American gloss to the campaign. There was more colour, battle buses and campaign songs. The hoopla was new but so would be the greater take-up of auction politics.

Manifestos, previously known as election programmes or platforms, had never been given the attention, or received the public traction, in Ireland that seemed to exist in other jurisdictions. The Fianna Fáil manifesto for the 1977 General Election would change forever how such documents were viewed in the future.

Mixing pump-priming economics with a series of giveaways, it was presented by its author (Fianna Fáil's economics guru, Martin O'Donoghue) as a series of stimuli to increase spending and restore consumer confidence. The giveaways were eye-catching – domestic rates on dwellings were to be abolished, as was the annual payment of motor tax, the cost of these partially being met by increased taxation elsewhere. These proposals seemed to catch the coalition parties off guard, although by the time election day approached those parties were beginning to match several of those promises.

14

Jack is Back

As the dust settled on the various election counts on 17 June 1977, it was clear that the giveaways had been received enthusiastically and that the redrawing of the constituencies had failed spectacularly. For only the second election in the history of the state, Fianna Fáil had won more than 50 per cent of the vote, delivering a then record twenty-seat majority in Dáil Éireann. In a Dáil that now had four additional members, Fine Gael had lost eleven seats, Labour two, with two additional independents being elected.

There was a significant upswing in the votes received by 'others' in this election. It now stood at almost 7.5 per cent of the vote. The bulk of this vote was for independent candidates. Joining Joe Sheridan and Neil Blaney in the Twenty-first Dáil would be the prodigal Noel Browne (now standing in the north side Dáil constituency of Dublin Artane and not his traditional constituency of Dublin South East), and a newly elected TD from Limerick East, also with a Labour background, Mick Lipper.

Like the man he deposed, sitting TD and Labour Party candidate Steve Coughlan, Lipper had been an elected Clann na Poblachta member of Limerick Corporation. On joining Labour he became an unsuccessful Dáil candidate on its behalf in a by-election and for two general elections. In 1977 his boat came in, but as an independent candidate.

Official Sinn Féin (now Sinn Féin – the Workers' Party (SFWP) since February 1977) ran seventeen candidates in this election, up from ten in 1973. This saw the party win an additional 10,000 votes but again no seats. Joe Sherlock, who had performed quite creditably in the Cork

North East by-election in 1974, saw his vote drop by 1,000. Finishing fifth for the four available seats in the Waterford constituency was Paddy Gallagher who was SFWP's best vote getter.

Former partners in Official Sinn Féin, the IRSP stood only one candidate in this election. It was the founder of the party, Seamus Costello, who polled less than a 1,000 votes, 300 votes fewer than those won by the Official Sinn Féin candidate in the Wicklow constituency.

The Communist Party of Ireland participated in its first official election. The party put forward two candidates, neither of whom was party leader Michael O'Riordan. Between the two candidates the party won just over 500 votes.

Aontacht Éireann did not put forward any candidates. Kevin Boland's outing in the Dublin South West by-election would be the last time the party would contest an Irish election. Shortly after that he and other founding members resigned their membership of the party, after an influx of far right-minded individuals. The party continued its registration for several more years, but never again actively participated in Irish politics. In its short active life the party had never really gained any traction.

Neil Blaney, with whom Kevin Boland had resigned in sympathy over the Arms Trial, was having greater success with his non-party bid. Defending two seats in Donegal North East, Independent Fianna Fáil amassed an impressive almost 14,000 votes. However with Neil Blaney winning three times the votes won by his 'party' colleague, Paddy Keaveney, only one of those seats could be retained.

Another non-party party was the Community grouping in Dublin that came close to winning 10,000 votes. This was a loose affiliation of candidates (not formally registered as a party), who did not share political philosophies or policy coherence, but were committed to working on behalf of Dublin.

With a twenty-seat majority there would be no uncertainty about Jack Lynch being elected as Taoiseach for a third time. In selecting his cabinet he sprang one surprise – Charles Haughey returned from the wilderness to become Minister for Health and Social Welfare.

Meanwhile the coalition parties were licking their wounds. Among the factors they felt had prevented their return to government was a constant, though mild, lampooning that government had received from the popular TV programme *Hall's Pictorial Weekly*. Liam Cosgrave resigned as leader of Fine Gael, being replaced by his *bête noir*, Dr Garret FitzGerald. A similar exercise occurred within Labour, with Frank Cluskey replacing Brendan Corish.

The Fourteenth Seanad election saw no independent or third-party candidate emerging from the vocational panels. The National University of Ireland elected two new Senators – Gemma Hussey and John A. Murphy. The 'new' Senator for Dublin University was the recently deposed minister of the previous government, Conor Cruise O'Brien, who contested as an independent.

Mary Robinson had been the independent Senator for Dublin University, but in 1975 she chose to join the Labour Party. She contested the Dáil election for the party in the constituency of Dublin Rathmines, where she finished fourth for the three available seats. She was re-elected to the Seanad under the Labour Party's banner.

In his eleven nominees for the Seanad Jack Lynch chose two independents – businessman and art collector, Gordon Lambert, of the Jacobs Biscuits Company and former Secretary of the Department of Finance (and author of the two Programmes for Economic Expansion), T.K. Whitaker.

In October 1977 the leader of the IRSP and Wicklow county councillor, Seamus Costello, was assassinated. It was believed to be part of the feud brought about by the Official IRA calling a military ceasefire in 1972. The guns remained to be used on each other. It was another reminder that spill-over violence from the 'Troubles' was always likely to erupt in the Republic, even though government policy on Northern Ireland seemed more talked about than acted on.

Charles Haughey was relishing his return to government. He threw himself into several health awareness campaigns such as anti-smoking and dental health, having toothbrushes distributed to every primary school pupil in the country. It was Haughey's first time sitting around a cabinet table with Des O'Malley, who was Minister for Industry and Commerce and given responsibility for a flagship policy of the government.

In 1971 a Nuclear Energy Board was established to define policy and bring about the location and construction of nuclear power plants in Ireland. Carnsore Point in County Wexford was chosen as the first location for such a plant. As the government minister responsible, Des O'Malley was enthusiastic for the policy and adamant that it be pursued. The proposal excited a considerable amount of public disquiet, leading to the establishment of a strong protest movement. In this movement there were high-profile musicians and other artists and many young people. The campaign culminated with a concert cum rally at Carnsore Point in the summer of 1978. For some who attended, this was a seminal moment that would inform future political developments in the country.

An attempt to develop the tinge of radicalism that was seeping into Irish politics was made with the forming of a Socialist Labour Party (SLP) in 1977 (registered in 1978). Formed by Matt Merrigan (former Labour candidate and prominent in the ATGWU) and Noel Browne TD, the party positioned itself very much to the left of Labour. Long-standing colleagues and supporters of Noel Browne, Jack McQuillan and David Thornley were loosely associated with the SLP. This was the fifth political party in whose interests Browne had sat as a member of the Dáil.

Also in 1978, a registration was made for a Socialist Party of Ireland (SPI). This was the name used by Roddy Connolly for a prototype communist party in the 1920s. This version does not seem to have been particularly active and the registration was not renewed in 1979.

So 1979 was a year to be politically active. Many political triggers were pulled, several in relation to events in Northern Ireland. In London, in the car park of the House of Commons, the Conservative party spokesman on Northern Ireland Airey Neave was assassinated, an action for which the Irish National Liberation Army later claimed responsibility.

Local elections were scheduled that year, and new elections were to take place for the European Parliament. Since 1973 Ireland's members to this assembly had been appointed. This would be the first European Community-wide poll to elect members to the parliament.

Legislation was amended to allow for political parties to register participation in European elections. Before the first election one such registration was made by the Community Democrats of Ireland, a group associated with the Liberal grouping in the European Parliament.

Before those elections were held Irish politics tied itself in knots on a matter of social policy. The Supreme Court decision on McGee versus The Attorney General was made in 1974. It found that married women were having their rights and health compromised by not having legal access to contraception. The Coalition government failed spectacularly in passing enabling legislation, when with a free vote the then Taoiseach, Liam Cosgrave, voted against the proposed bill.

In 1979 the responsibility then fell to Charles Haughey as Minister for Health. In tabling a bill that he referred to as 'an Irish solution to an Irish problem', he proposed that married couples could access contraceptives (medical and non-medical) but only with a prescription received from a doctor. Doctors and pharmacists were allowed to opt out from prescribing or honouring prescriptions on moral grounds.

Greater trouble existed for the government in the form of public protests at the high level of personal taxation and the extent to which income was affecting lower paid workers. In March 1979 trade unions organised a number of marches throughout the country on the issue, with the predominant march taking place in Dublin, where over 100,000 people took part.

Forty-six candidates presented for the European elections in the Republic. Technically these elections represented the first time the entire island had voted since the 1920 local elections. The slate of candidates in Northern Ireland and their party affiliations was not replicated anywhere else on the island, although Sinn Féin the Workers' Party was the only party to contest all five Irish constituencies, trading in Northern Ireland as Republican Clubs Workers' Party.

Three of these candidates were independents. Two of these (Neil Blaney and T.J. Maher) secured the highest votes achieved in these elections, winning two of the available fifteen seats. The third candidate (Seán Dublin Bay Rockall Loftus – the Rockall being a new addition) received close to 22,000 votes in his constituency, outpolling several Fianna Fáil and Fine Gael candidates. In secondary elections, voters were becoming emboldened to vote against traditional parties.

The small number of smaller party candidates could be put down to a number of reasons. The Euro-constituencies were geographically large, making them difficult in which to campaign. Election deposits required to have candidates' names placed on the ballot were proportionately larger for these elections, discouraging many from putting themselves forward.

T.J. Maher was the surprise package of that election. He had been a high-profile person, and was believed to have been a highly effective President of the Irish Farmers Association. He has been elected to that office by a large, but selective electorate. This was his first attempt at seeking election to public office. Not only was he successful, he succeeded in winning the largest vote (86,000) of any candidate in the Republic. Impressive as that vote was, it was little more than half the vote won by the most successful candidate on the island of Ireland, the 170,000 votes won by the Rev. Ian Paisley in Northern Ireland – the highest vote of any individual candidate anywhere in the European Community.

In retrospect, the performance of T.J. Maher should not have seemed so surprising. A significant interest group, benefitting most from transfer payments from the European Community, gravitated towards his candidacy. The performance of Neil Blaney in the far-flung Connaught Ulster constituency was equally impressive. It was a performance that certainly would have been noted by his former colleagues in Fianna Fáil.

For Fianna Fáil these elections were an eye opener. Winning little more that one-third the support of the electorate, the party had gained its lowest share in a national election since its first Dáil election in June 1927. Fine Gael had come within 1.6 per cent of the Fianna Fáil vote. 'Others' and independents secured almost a fifth of the available votes.

Sinn Féin – The Workers' Party stood six candidates in these elections, with two candidates in two of the four constituencies. For that party it was a profile-raising exercise. Nevertheless, it was the highest level of vote the party had achieved since it abandoned abstentionism. The Community Democrats fared less well. Its three candidates between them won less than 4,000 votes.

The European elections were held on the same day as the local elections. In those elections Fianna Fáil fared better, winning under 40 per cent, with about a 5 per cent lead over Fine Gael. Independents and smaller parties performed less well, polling under 15 per cent of the vote. For 'others' to perform better in the European rather the local elections, despite the presence of candidates and parties which did not contest the former, showed the value of known, prominent candidates in the winning of votes.

Local elections were where the two Sinn Féin parties competed with each other. Sinn Féin the Workers' Party stood more candidates and won the greater amount of votes, (31,000 votes with sixty-nine candidates) but Provisional Sinn Féin, still an unregistered party, had more councillors elected (ten to seven for SFWP).

The Socialist Labour Party ran twenty-eight candidates, largely in the Dublin city and county area, winning 9,290 votes. None of the party's candidates came close to winning a seat. With a similar, although more concentrated vote, Neil Blaney's Independent Fianna Fáil elected four councillors in Donegal. Not contesting these elections, seemingly lacking direction since the assassination of its leader, Seamus Costello, was the IRSP.

In July 1979, only a month after the local and European elections, two constitutional referenda were held. Less than 30 per cent of the electorate came out to vote. One referendum was held on the issue of adoption and sought to remove legal uncertainty and so confirm that adoptions sanctioned by the Adoption Board, had the same legal standing as if approved by a court. The second referendum was an attempt at Seanad Reform, expanding the franchise to include degree holders from third-level institutions outside of the National University of Ireland and Dublin University (Trinity College Dublin). Both referenda were passed with overwhelming support,

On 27 August 1979 the Provisional IRA raised the ante with two shocking actions. In Warrenpoint, County Down, a number of bombs killed eighteen British soldiers. Off Mullaghmore, County Sligo, a bomb in a boat killed Queen Elizabeth's first cousin, Lord Mountbatten, his friend Lady Brabourne, and two fifteen-year-old boys – Mountbatten's grandson, Nicholas, and a local boy called Paul Maxwell.

September and October saw the first-ever Papal visit to the country. Colossal crowds attended events and venues visited by Pope John Paul II. While the visit was meant to mark the fealty of a grateful people to its dominant religion, it subsequently came to be seen as the beginning of the questioning of the nature of that relationship.

The Papal visit should have offered the government some relief from a deteriorating economic situation. Industrial relations were at an historic low. Almost one-and-half-million working days were lost through strikes that year. A postal strike lasted for four months. A bus strike resulted in the Army being brought out to provide services. The long-standing personal popularity of Jack Lynch as Taoiseach could not keep growing public discontent at bay.

Within Fianna Fáil this discontent expressed itself in an unlikely form. Síle de Valera (MEP for Dublin; TD for Dublin Mid County and a member of Dublin County Council) the granddaughter of party founder Éamon, made a speech in Fermoy County Cork calling on Lynch to 'demonstrate his republicanism'. Fermoy was situated in the Cork North East constituency, one of two Cork constituencies scheduled to hold by-elections, the other being the Taoiseach's own constituency of Cork City.

The Cork North East by-election came about because of the death of the Fianna Fáil deputy Seán Brosnan. It was the death of Labour's Pat Kerrigan that brought about the Cork City by-election. In Cork North East Myra Barry, daughter of sitting TD Dick Barry, won through for Fine Gael. Former TD Liam Burke made it a double for Fine Gael. The Fianna Fáil vote in both constituencies was 35–36 per cent. Both its candidates were a distant second.

Sinn Féin the Workers' Party could take great encouragement from these by-elections. Joe Sherlock won a historic 9,000 votes in Cork North East. In Cork City, Ted Tynan passed 3,000 votes.

As Taoiseach, Jack Lynch could take no solace in these results. He realised that if he could not deliver in Cork, he was unlikely to ever deliver again in the rest of the country. Within weeks he resigned as Taoiseach and as leader of Fianna Fáil. Lynch, who had been the compromise candidate in 1966, had been leader of Fianna Fáil for thirteen turbulent years, while leading the country's government for nine of those years.

His resignation on 5 December was intended to catch some by surprise. Ireland was holding the Presidency of the European Community. Lynch had just hosted a European Council meeting in Dublin, and while another month remained in the Presidency, Lynch felt that this was the time to stand aside. A meeting of the Fianna Fáil Parliamentary Party was arranged for two days later to choose his successor.

15

A Right Charlie

The two contenders to replace Lynch had been the two young turks who had sought to replace Seán Lemass in 1966. George Colley was seen as the candidate who represented continuity. Charlie Haughey, who had spent his years in the political wilderness cultivating party grassroots on the 'chicken supper' circuit, was seen as a person who would take the party in a different direction.

Colley, by most commentators' opinions and in his own assessment, was the favourite to win. It was something of a surprise when Haughey emerged victorious on a vote of 44 to 38. A new era in Irish politics had begun.

Haughey would not find the Irish political establishment particularly accommodating towards him. A substantial group within his party was opposed to his elevation and so would remain. In the debate on his election for Taoiseach, Haughey had to bear the leader of the opposition, Garret FitzGerald, refer to him in the most bitter of terms, a person with a 'flawed pedigree'.

Nevertheless, Haughey came through this vote, and introduced his first cabinet. His selections tried to keep prominent Lynchites onside while he also tried to settle scores. There would be no place for Jim Gibbons in the new government. George Colley, no longer Minister for Finance, would remain as Tánaiste, with an agreed but not public veto on the appointments of ministers for the Departments of Justice and Defence. One significant departure in Haughey's cabinet appointments was assigning Máire Geoghegan Quinn as Minister for the Gaeltacht, the first woman to be appointed to an Irish cabinet since Constance Markievicz in the government of the First Dáil.

Within a month of taking office Haughey addressed the nation in a special broadcast. Seeking to create a greater awareness of the deteriorating economic situation in the country, Haughey told a national audience: 'As a community we are living way beyond our means.' Throughout his career in public life Haughey had faced questions about how his lifestyle could be squared with a State salary, so making this the opening theme of his term as Taoiseach was greeted by many as something of an irony overload.

Haughey embarked on a charm offensive with the newly elected British Prime Minister, Margaret Thatcher, presenting her with a silver teapot and at first they seemed to get on well, but events in Northern Ireland would soon place a strain on that relationship. Prisoners at the Maze Prison had been looking for special-category status that was once held, but had been removed by the British Government.

For several years prisoners had engaged in dirty protests, called *On The Blanket*, to highlight their campaign. This seemed to be achieving little. It was felt that the campaign should be extended, so seven prisoners took part in a hunger strike. This was called off after fifty-three days in the belief that their demands had been met.

At the end of 1980 Charles Haughey faced his first electoral test. Fianna Fáil TD Joe Brennan died and Clem Coughlan as the Fianna Fáil electoral candidate performed impressively, outpolling Independent Fianna Fáil candidate, Patrick Kelly (who polled 14,000 votes). Sinn Féin the Workers' Party candidate Seamus Rodgers scored more than 2,600 votes.

After a year in office, Haughey had been mulling over whether or not he should call a general election. A Fianna Fáil Ard Fheis was organised for the middle of February 1981. Haughey had intended to announce a general election there. However, tragedy struck on Valentine's Night when a tragic fire occurred at the Stardust nightclub in Artane, Dublin, which took the lives of forty-eight young people. The fire occurred in the heart of Haughey's Dáil constituency and all election plans were put on hold.

The decision to postpone was correct, but if Haughey had been able to hold the election when he intended, he would have been able to avoid the impact of a second hunger strike at the Maze Prison, which began on 1 March. The organisers of this second hunger strike took a different strategic approach. Instead of a group of hunger strikers beginning their strike together, individuals began refusing food at staggered times. First to refuse food was a republican prisoner called Bobby Sands.

The initial reaction to this hunger strike was low key. A greater focus would arrive after the death of an independent republican MP, Frank Maguire. This created a vacancy in the ever-closely contested Fermanagh South Tyrone constituency. Each of the nationalist and republican parties and several prominent individuals expressed an interest in contesting. Through various means of persuasion Bobby Sands was to stand alone as a H Block candidate. Against him was the high-profile Ulster Unionist Harry West. In a poll of 60,000 voters Sands emerged victorious with a majority of 1,500 votes. Within a month, the newly elected MP had died on the sixty-sixth day of his hunger strike.

When Charles Haughey finally decided to call an Irish general election, this was the surrounding mood music. The election was called for 11 June. Nine Northern Ireland prisoners (not all hunger strikers) would contest as H Block candidates. During the election campaign a further three hunger strikers would die.

None of this was helpful to Charles Haughey whose Fianna Fáil party squandered the largest ever Dáil majority. In a new Dáil, with eighteen additional seats, Fianna Fáil lost six seats to return seventy-eight TDs. Fine Gael had an excellent campaign, the first in which it was led by Garret FitzGerald. The party won an extra twenty seats, and was now only thirteen seats away from Fianna Fáil's total. For Labour it was a disappointing campaign. It too was under a new leader, Frank Cluskey. The party polled under 10 per cent of the national vote, losing two seats in the process, one of which was the seat that had been held by Frank Cluskey himself.

The H Block campaign succeeded in having two candidates elected, and came close to electing a third. The successful candidates were Kieran Doherty in Cavan Monaghan and Paddy Agnew (not a hunger striker) in Louth. Both remained incarcerated. The IRSP did not put forward candidates in this election, although three of the ten hunger strikers that would eventually die were members of the INLA, the military wing of the party.

Putting aside its paramilitary past seemed, at last, to be paying dividends for Sinn Féin the Workers' Party. The party made its breakthough with the election of Joe Sherlock in Cork East. Sherlock had impressed in several by-elections and was now seen to have gained his reward. The breakthrough was achieved with only a slight increase in the party's voice.

The Socialist Labour Party raised its flag for the first time in a Dáil election. The party ran six candidates in five Dublin constituencies. Its actual status was exposed through Noel Browne winning a seat on the party's behalf. Browne's vote was more than three times the combined vote of all five other SLP candidates combined. None of the party's other candidates broke four figures. One of its candidates, in Dublin West, received one of the lowest votes in the country (63). This was behind one of the two Communist Party of Ireland candidates, who along with his party colleague, won 360 votes. The CPI was outpolled by the Socialist Party, a newly registered party that was linked to the previously, and briefly registered Socialist Party of Ireland. This variant of the Socialist Party ran two candidates in two Dublin constituencies, winning 570 votes. Organised in 1976 prior to registering as a party, a candidate stood on its behalf in the 1977 general election winning over 2,000 votes – Eammon O'Brien in Dublin North County.

Neil Blaney's Independent Fianna Fáil ran two candidates in county Donegal, now divided into two constituencies. Blaney topped the poll in Donegal North East, comfortably being elected. His colleague Patrick Kelly polled well, but not well enough, in Donegal South West. Three other independents were elected. Seán Dublin Bay Rockall Loftus finally made the breaththrough in Dublin North Central. In the musical chairs that was the left-wing politics of Limerick, Jim Kemmy, as an independent socialist, dethroned the Labour Party's Mick Lipper. Kemmy, had resigned as a member of Labour a decade earlier (he had been a member of the party's national executive) after a dispute with the party's then Limerick TD, Stephen (Stevie) Coughlan.

The fourth independent was John O'Connell who had been elected for the Labour Party since 1965. When he refused to stand in another constituency to allow his party leader Frank Cluskey a clear run, he chose instead to stand as an independent in Dublin South Central, consigning Cluskey to defeat.

Joe Sheridan chose not to re-contest in Longford Westmeath. Kevin Boland tried one last time in Dublin South West. Making his first appearance in Dublin South East, in what would be a recurring role, was

William Fitzsimon, Abbey of the Holy Cross. Three candidates stood on a community platform in Dublin constituencies. They won over 5,600 votes between them, more than half of them going to the candidate who stood in the Dublin Central constituency and had come close to winning the final seat there. His name was Tony Gregory.

The lure of Leinster House remained greater than that emanating from Brussels. Independent MEP T.J. Maher, sought election to the Dáil in the Tippeary South constituency, but was not successful.

With six different political groupings, this would be the most diverse Dáil since 1961. Others were responsible for 8 per cent of the national vote. For the first time since 1965 the votes of others would determine who would form the government. Neither Fianna Fáil nor Fine Gael Labour would have a majority of seats needed. It this new Dáil eighty-three seats would be the magic. With the inability and unwillingness of the H Block TDs to attend, eighty-two seats would suffice. Fine Gael and Labour together made up eighty seats.

On 30 June, when the Dáil reconvened, John O'Connell was selected as the new Ceann Comhairle. The votes of five other TDs were the most valued and sought. A vote for Haughey secured only the additional support of Neil Blaney, while the rest of the House voted against. FitzGerald only won one extra vote with Jim Kemmy. He was opposed by Fianna Fáil but all others abstained. His election was secured although it was a government that would be without security. FitzGerald appointed as his Tánaiste the new leader of the Labour Party, Michael O'Leary, who had been a high profile minister in the 1973–77 coalition government.

The H Block campaign had a parallel objective. Behind the general election campaign, and that for the Fermanagh South Tyrone by-election, Provisional Sinn Féin was testing the political system. At its 1981 Ard Fheis, the party's Director of Publicity, Danny Morrisson, speaking to delegates said:

> Who here really believes we can win the war through the ballot box? But will anyone here object if, with a ballot paper in one hand and an Armalite in this hand, we take power in Ireland?

This became known as the Armalite and the Ballot Box strategy.

Its next chapter was the Westminster by-election, brought about by the death of Bobby Sands, in Fermanagh South Tyrone. His campaign manager Owen Carron was the chosen successor. Choosing another prisoner was not an option, as the British Government had passed legislation prohibiting this. Carron's election machine was Provisional Sinn Féin and he was elected with an enhanced majority.

The new independents who came into the Fifteenth Seanad were Liam Ryan in the National University of Ireland and Shane Ross (winning a seat his father had once held) in the Dublin University constituency. Also in that constituency, Mary Robinson reverted to being an independent again. She had unsuccessfully contested two general elections, and had been elected to Dublin Corporation on its behalf of the Labour Party. With the party once again in government, she chose again to be an independent.

Gemma Hussey had been elected as an independent to the previous Seanad for the National University. She subsequently joined Fine Gael and was an unsuccessful general election candidate on its behalf. She was re-elected to this Seanad as a Fine Gael Senator.

In December 1981 a meeting was held at the Central Hotel in Dublin. It had been called by Christopher Fettes, an Englishman who had been living and working in Ireland for a number of decades. He called the meeting because of what he had felt was an absense in Ireland of a political organisation that was liberal in outlook and gave attention to environmental issues. About forty people attended the meeting. The discussion was on whether to form an organisation that would campaign outside the political system or whether a political party should be formed.

A majority believed that a party, similar to those beginning to take root in Germany, particularly in West Germany, a Green Party should be formed. There was a reluctance to use the word 'green' because the word and the colour were seen to have particular connotations in Irish politics. This would be the first meeting of the Ecology Party of Ireland.

The coalition government was by now six months in office and was about to present its first budget. The Minister for Finance, John Bruton, would have little good news to deliver. One of his proposals was to impose value-added tax on children's shoes. This would be a step too far for Jim Kemmy to support. Last-minute efforts were made to persuade him. It was a necessary measure, he was told, as women with small feet were able to avoid this tax. Unable to pass a budget, the government had no option but to go again to the country. The second general election in eight months was called for 18 February 1982.

This election resulted in only slight changes between Fianna Fáil and Fine Gael. Fianna Fáil gained three seats with Fine Gael losing two. The votes received by both parties increased slightly. The Labour Party's level of representation remained unchanged. Sinn Féin the Workers' Party made a considerable advance, going from one seat to three.

The number of independents remained at four. John O'Connell was automatically returned as Ceann Comhairle. Jim Kemmy was re-elected in Limerick East. Neil Blaney was also returned but not as the customary poll topper in Donegal North East. He won the third of the three available seats. Independent Fianna Fáil's vote in Donegal South West also slipped significantly. Seán Dublin Bay Rockall Loftus would enjoy only the briefest of soujorns in the Dáil. His place as prominent Dublin-based independent would be taken by Tony Gregory, elected in Dublin Central. He would become the story of this election.

Having been elected in 1979 to Dublin Corporation as an independent councillor, Gregory had already spent much of that decade being active on the fringes of Irish left-wing politics. Originally a member of Official Sinn Féin, Gregory was encouraged by his friend, Seamus Costello, to join the IRSP, although Gregory would later state he played no active part in the party. He left the party after Costello's murder. He followed that association by a brief flirtation with the Socialist Labour Party, a link Gregory brought to an end by standing as an independent in the 1979 local elections.

Given these associations, there were ironic counterpoints with Tony Gregory's rise as a national politician, and the fate of those parties with which he was associated. The Socialist Labour Party had imploded in 1981 with the resignation of Noel Browne from the party. Browne spent his final months in Dáil Éireann once again sitting as an independent TD. He did not contest the general election and neither did the Socialist Labour Party.

The IRSP, having been politically inactive since Costello's death, did contest this general election. Six candidates were put forward but none performed particularly well. None of the candidates broke three figures in the votes they achieved, collectively winning less than 3,000 votes. Put into perspective, as a single candidate standing in one constituency, Tony Gregory equalled the combined IRSP vote and then surpassed it by a further 2,000 votes.

Provisional Sinn Féin was also involved in electoral experimentation. As a follow-up to the H Block campaign the party contested this election under its, still unregistered, name. Around 17,000 votes were amassed without any of its candidates being in contention. With far more modest expectations the two Communist Party candidates won 462 votes.

Those 462 votes were votes that were not won by the Ecology Party. With the election coming only two months after the party's initial meeting, the party was not prepared. A press release was distributed among the media outlining the party's policy priorities. Without candidates and any indication of a support base, those ideas were not given much of an airing.

The seduction of Tony Gregory began. The odds always seemed to favour Charles Haughey. His willingness to meet Gregory on his own turf won Haughey credit from the Gregory camp. It contrasted well with a lack of empathy that seemed to emanate from FitzGerald. From Haughey there also seemed to be a greater willingness to meet Gregory's demands and to see that state resources were to be made available to have those demands met.

Gregory insisted that any agreement to support the incoming government had to have its details made public. It was to be witnessed by the leader of the ITGWU union, Michael Mullen. Pejoratively referred to as the *Gregory Deal*, critics condemned it as an exercise in vote buying. In reality it was a mini programme for government, made with a deputy who represented some of the poorest communities in the country. It operated on several levels, primarily for the Dublin Central constituency. Among it commitments were 500 jobs to be created immediately in Dublin's inner city, with several thousand more to follow over a three-year period. It stipulated that 440 social housing units were to be built in the area, with a further 1,600 to be provided in the wider Dublin region. Broader commitments were sought for the State to take a specified large site in

Dublin Port, and to nationalise threatened paper mills in Clondalkin. A £100 million price tag was put on these commitments.

There were some in Fianna Fáil who did not want Charles Haughey's name to go forward for nomination as Taoiseach. Haughey tried to pre-empt any challenge by insisting on the full loyalty of his front bench, also stating the any parliamentary party vote would be a rollcall vote, so that constituency organisations know how their representatives voted for or against the party leader. His opponents circled around Des O'Malley, as the alternative to Haughey as leader of Fianna Fáil and the next Taoiseach. Their campaign was marked by different conspirators following different strategies. As the vital parliamentary party meeting approached, Haughey was outmanouevering his opponents at every opportunity. By the time the meeting happened, the O'Malley campaign was shrouded in confusion. O'Malley announced the withdrawal of his interest. No vote was taken and Haughey remained in control of Fianna Fáil.

On seeing off his internal critics and securing an agreement with Tony Gregory, Haughey's election again as Taoiseach was now more comfortable than had been originally anticipated. He had the support of Neil Blaney and Tony Gregory. He was also to win the support of the three Sinn Féin the Workers' Party TDs. Joe Sherlock, now joined by Proinsias De Rossa and Paddy Gallagher, explained why in the debate on the nomination of Taoiseach:

> On behalf of my party, Sinn Féin The Workers Party, I wish to say that my party decided to support the nomination of Deputy Charles J. Haughey. The factors considered by us in arriving at that decision are that it appears to us to be the choice of the voters that there should be a Fianna Fáil Government, and that the proposals but forward in the economic and industrial package by Fianna Fáil seem to be what the country needs at this time. I make this point with as much emphasis as I can. The lack of cohesion on the Coalition side was not conductive to convincing us that the Coalition were worthy of our support. Also, everybody will agree that at this time the country needs continuity of government. Our support is unconditional and we have made no deal or pact. One consideration only will guide our judgment in Opposition, and that is the interests of the working class of this entire island. Every action,

every word, every deed, every piece of legislation coming from Government will be judged in that light and we will vote accordingly. We are, in fact, the workers' party and have as our goal the establishment of a democratic, secular, socialist and unitary State. We have declared our total opposition to terror-ism and violence in Northern Ireland and we say here today to the people of Northern Ireland that we will resist any attempt in word or deed of the Government to coerce or to assist in the coercion of the people in the North.

Finally, I repeat that what the country needs is a Government who will give continuity, so that issues important to the people can be tackled. We will judge each issue on its merits and will vote accordingly.

While their votes were not technically needed, the three SFWP TDs almost found themselves not participating. Having a conflab outside the Dáil chamber the three TDs were unable to gain access when the doors of the chambers were locked, as per tradition, to allow for a vote to take place. A journalist then motioned the three TDs through to the press gallery, where the three vaulted into the Dáil chamber.

Installed back in office, Haughey set about shaping a cabinet more in his image. He informed George Colley that his veto on certain cabinet appointments no longer applied. Colley was also told that Ray McSharry was to be made Tánaiste. Colley indicated he would not serve in cabinet under those conditions.

The Sixteenth Seanad had one new independent elected – Brendan Ryan for the National University. No independents were elected from the vocational panels. It was among the Taoiseach's nominees that new and interesting members to Seanad Éireann were to be found. Independent Fianna Fáil had its first Senator, James Larkin (not related to the trade unionist) nominated, a quid pro quo for Dáil support. Two Senators were nominated to reflect different traditions in Northern Ireland. One was the Deputy Leader of the SDLP, Seamus Mallon, the other John Robb, known for encouraging cross-community dialogue.

The precariousness of the government's position was clearly shown when a Finance Bill amendment (on the width of a tax band) required the casting vote of the Ceann Comhairle. The Workers Party TDs had opposed the government's position and without Tony Gregory's support the government would have fallen then.

The invasion by the Argentine junta led the government of the Falkland/Malvinas islands in March 1982 to put the Irish Government under an international diplomacy spotlight and threatened Anglo-Irish relations. Ireland at that time was a temporary member of the United Nations Security Council, where the Irish delegation voted for Security Council Resolution 502 which condemned the hostilities and demanded an immediate Argentine withdrawal from the islands. Ireland would later supported European Community economic sanctions against Argentina. However, with sinking of the Argentinian ship *General Belgrano*, in an act that many viewed as a war crime, the Irish position changed, looking for the removal of sanctions, leading to a chill in relations with the government of Margaret Thatcher in London.

In April 1982 a number of changes occurred in the Register of Political Parties that sought to redefine left-wing politics in Ireland. The first change saw Jim Kemmy cease to be an independent TD, now choosing to sit for a party he helped to form – the Democratic Socialist Party. The party was a joining together of Kemmy's Limerick Socialists with the largely Dublin-based Socialist Party that had run a handful of candidates in 1977 and 1981. The party promoted the principle of consent and a continued unionist veto on the question of a United Ireland. On social issues the party argued for a decidedly secularist approach.

The second alteration of the Register saw Sinn Féin the Workers' Party drop Sinn Féin from its title. From here on in the there would be no further need to make a distinction between Official and Provisional, or on the location of party offices (Gardiner Place or Kevin Street). Only one Sinn Féin now existed – a grouping that represented the minority of the minority from the divisions that carved up the original organisation. This variant of Sinn Féin, Sinn Féin 'Mark VI', had inherited the sole interest in the title. It remained a title that was unregistered.

Next part in implementing his masterplan was for Haughey to strengthen his Dáil majority. The incoming government had within its gift the ability to appoint an Irish member of the European Commission. This was usually awarded to a senior member of the government party. Haughey decided to inveigle Fine Gael's Richard Burke, a former government minister, to accept the appointment. This caused a by-election in the Dublin West constituency.

This by-election pitted Eileen Lemass, the widowed daughter-in-law of Sean Lemass (and sister-in-law of Haughey's wife, Maureen) against Fine Gael newcomer Liam Skelly. Lemass had unsuccessfully contested in 1976 a by-election in Dublin South West, held after the death of her husband Noel. After the first count Lemass was 300 votes ahead of Skelly. There were over 8,000 votes still to distribute.

Most of these votes had been won by Tomás Mac Giolla, leader of the newly entitled Workers' Party, the first time that designation had been used in an Irish election. Another party making its full debut, was the Democratic Socialist Party. Its candidate, Michael Conaghan, won 667 votes. At the other end of the historical cycle, Mattie Merrigan was flying a flag one last time for the soon to be defunct Socialist Labour Party. He won 334 votes. These votes should be set against the extremely poor performance of the Labour candidate who won 703 votes. Four other independent candidates won about 1,000 votes together. These votes transferred heavily to Skelly, who ended up being the surprise winner. Haughey's gamble had failed.

A second by-election was held in July 1982. It was for the Galway East constituency after the death of sitting TD, John Callanan. It was a straight fight between Fianna Fáil and Fine Gael, and Noel Treacy held the seat for Fianna Fáil.

In Northern Ireland a new attempt was being made to bring about a return to devolved government. Elections were held for a new Assembly in October 1982. Sinn Féin was contesting its first parliamentary election in Northern Ireland and won five seats, while the Workers Party won 16,000 votes. The Deputy Leader of the SDLP had his election successfully challenged on the basis of his membership of the Seanad. These elections also saw the first time a candidate on the island of Ireland contested an election on an ecological or green platform – Malcolm Samuels in Antrim North.

During the summer of 1982 politics in the Republic of Ireland took several bizarre turns. A man suspected for a double murder, Malcolm MacArthur, was found to have stayed in the home of the Attorney General, Patrick Connolly, who subsequently resigned. In seeking to explain the events Haughey was quoted as saying that what had happened was 'a bizarre happening, an unprecedented situation, a grotesque situation, an almost unbelievable mischance'. Conor Cruise O'Brien, by then editor at the British newspaper *The Observer*, re-arranged and initialised these adjectives to spell GUBU, a phrase that would be applied to several other crises that would occur during this period. The Minister of Justice Seán Doherty, appointed in February, had become associated with a number of unsavoury incidents that would, eventually, be added to this catalogue.

The business of governing had almost been seen as a sideshow to these soap opera incidents. Haughey was trying to face two ways at once, spending public money in attempts to ingratiate a sceptical voting public, while talking tough on the need for spending control. The former behaviour led to Fianna Fáil back-bencher Charlie McCreevey moving a vote of no confidence against his leader.

McCreevey, and those working with him, were attempting to re-organise those whose push against Haughey had failed so miserably eight months previously. Des O'Malley was not centrally involved in this attempt, not learning of the motion of no confidence until he had returned from abroad. It was the hope of McCreevey and others that O'Malley would still be a central part of this new move against Haughey. What had been a front bench in February was a cabinet in October. Resignation from cabinet, serial resignations from cabinet, would create a momentum against Haughey. Des O'Malley and Martin O'Donoghue resigned, seeking to create such momentum.

A meeting on 4 October was a lengthy one. Parallel debates were occuring on procedure, on Haughey's character. The issue of a secret ballot was determined by a show of hands. The twenty-seven who wanted a secret ballot were outvoted. The alphabetical rollcall vote that followed saw fifty-eight TDs in support of Haughey, with twenty-two against. A 'Club of 22' had been formed. The meeting ended in acrimony with Haughey supporters waiting outside jostling and verbally abusing Haughey objectors. Jim Gibbons, a Haughey nemesis since the Arms Trial, was assaulted in the melee.

The death of Bill Loughnane, a TD from Clare, weakened the Dáil position of Haughey's government. Jim Gibbons then suffered a heart attack. He may not have had the inclination, but he now would be physically incapable of attending Dáil votes. The release of a long-term economic strategy, *The Way Forward*, outlining a more austere approach to public expenditure, did not meet with the approval of the Workers Party or from Tony Gregory.

The Labour Party held its party convention at the of October 1982. The party's ongoing debate on coalition or not, attracted heated comment. The preferred position of party leader Michael O'Leary was to agree a pre-election pact with Fine Gael, as had happened in 1973. The convention agreed, after the intervention of former leader Frank Cluskey, that any decision on coalition would follow a general election.

Unhappy with this decision, O'Leary resigned not only his leadership but also his membership of the Labour Party. On 1 November O'Leary was replaced by thirty-two-year-old, Dick Spring, as leader of the Labour Party. Spring had followed his father Dan (a TD from 1943 to 1981, seven of those as part of the breakaway National Labour Party) as a TD for Kerry North. On 2 November Michael O'Leary announced he had become a member of Fine Gael.

On 3 November Garret FitzGerald tabled a motion of no confidence, which the government countered with a motion of confidence. With confidence votes the convention had been to have pairing arrangements, cancelling out the votes of deputies who would be mutually incapacitated. Oliver J. Flanagan also had a heart attack. It was hoped that he could pair with Jim Gibbons, but no pairing was forthcoming. Consideration was given to bringing Jim Gibbons to Dublin in a heart ambulance.

At the end of a two-day debate the consideration of various voting combinations proved moot. Oliver J. Flanagan did come to the House to vote against Haughey, as did the three Workers' Party TDs. Jim Gibbons was not stretchered into the chamber. Tony Gregory abstained, not voting against the government, although his vote would not have changed the result. Having lost the confidence of the Dáil, Haughey went to the President to have a general election called. This was set for 24 November and was the third general election to be held within eighteen months.

16

Garret the Good

The election did not result in a collapse in Fianna Fáil support. The fall in national vote share of 2 per cent resulted in a loss of six Dáil seats. The Fine Gael vote share increased by a similar amount, allowing the party to gain seven seats. Fine Gael had won its highest ever level of votes and seats. In the Dáil chamber the party was now within five seats of Fianna Fáil, the closest the two parties had ever been.

The Labour Party won an additional seat while its votes remained static, still under 10 per cent. The Workers' Party won it highest ever share of the vote, winning over 55,000 votes, but lost one of three seats it had held. Three independents were elected, which was also one less than had existed before. Together Fine Gael and Labour has a workable majority.

It was a bitter-sweet election for the Workers' Party. After several attempts, party leader Tomás Mac Giolla succeeded in being elected in Dublin West, while Proinsias De Rossa was re-elected in Dublin North West. However, despite the party's overall increase in vote, the seats of Joe Sherlock in Cork East and Paddy Gallagher in Waterford were lost.

For the independents, John O'Connell, who had been the outgoing Ceann Comhairle in the outgoing Dáil, was returned automatically. Neil Blaney's Independent Fianna Fáil stood only himself in this election. He won the second of the three available seats in Donegal North East. Meanwhile Tony Gregory had by now established himself in Dublin Central.

There was a squeezing of 'others' in this election. Three elections in eight months had drained the resources necessary to be politically competitive. Jim Kemmy, running now as leader of the Democratic Socialist Party, lost out to to the Labour Party's Frank Prendergast, having one more turn on the roundabout politics that was Limerick East. His party ran seven candidiates who together won more than 7,000 votes, although most of those votes had been won by Jim Kemmy. Only one other of the party's candidates, John de Courcey Ireland, broke four figures, which he did while standing as the party's candidate in Dun Laoghaire. De Courcey Ireland (now a national treasure through his expertise on maritime history) had already played a role on the fringes of Irish politics. In the 1940s he had been accused of orchestrating entryism into the Labour Party in the dispute that led to establishment of National Labour.

Stand alone Sinn Féin ('Mark VI' version) decided to sit out this election. Eyes were set on elections in Northern Ireland that were to take place in the near future. The Ecology Party, still unregistered, stood seven candidates. Its seven candidates averaged between 500 and 600 votes each. The highest vote was won by Owen Casey with more than 1,300 votes in the Cork South Central constituency. Owen was the son of a popular former Labour TD and Lord Mayor of Cork, Seán Casey. Owen had been active in local environmental and anti-nuclear groups, which also had enhanced his profile. The only other Ecology Party candidate to come close to four figures in this vote was Roger Garland, who won 950 votes.

The IRSP stood a single candidate, Jim Lane in Cork South Central. Jim ran a well-known left-wing book shop in Cork. He was heavily involved in social activism in the city. He polled 398 votes. Flying the flag for the Communist Party in Dublin West was John Montgomery, who polled 259 votes.

When the Dáil reconvened the Fine Gael and Labour coalition had a working majority of six. This gave the incoming government the confidence to choose a Ceann Comhairle from among its own number. They chose Fine Gael's Tom Fitzpatrick. There would be two votes on the nomination for Taoiseach. The two Workers' Party TDs and Tony Gregory voted against both nominees. Neil Blaney voted for Haughey and against FitzGerald. John O'Connell voted for Haughey but then abstained on the vote on FitzGerald.

Fianna Fáil's failure to hold office created a presumption that Haughey's resignation would be imminent. Several candidates were being identified, or were in the process of identifying themselves. The party had been under siege since the new Minister for Justice, Michael Noonan, had revealed that his predecessor had authorised the tapping of the phones of several well-known journalists – Geraldine Kennedy, Bruce Arnold and Vincent Browne. Also revealed was the bugging of a phone conversation by the former Tánaiste, Ray McSharry against his former cabinet colleague, Martin O'Donoghue.

Haughey was not going too quietly or quickly. His supporters organised a rally outside the party's headquarters on Mount Street, where several hundred placard-waving supporters loudly expressed their loyalty to the leader. Haughey's opponents saw that rally as another act of intimidation.

The Seanad election helped Fine Gael create an Oireachtas party that was larger than Fianna Fáil. Few other changes occurred about new independent members entering the Seanad. Bríd Rodgers of the SDLP was one of the Taoiseach's nominees to the Seanad, a nomination that had been held by her party colleague, Seamus Mallon. Most attention was given to those who were elected for Fianna Fáil to see who could be identified as pro- or anti-Haughey.

On the day that counting for the Seanad elections was taking place a tragic traffic accident happened in County Westmeath. This took the life of Fianna Fáil Donegal South West TD Clem Coughlan. He had been a Haughey supporter but was by then believing that Haughey needed to go. He was travelling at the time to Dublin, where a parliamentary party meeting was due to take place, when it was hoped the issue of the leadership could be addressed. The chairman of the Fianna Fáil parliamentary party Jim Tunney opened that meeting with a vote of sympathy for Clem Coughlan, and then promptly adjourned proceedings, catching those opposing Haughey off guard.

A petition to call a special parliamentary meeting was signed by fifty-one TDs, a majority of the parliamentary party. Haughey countered with a circulated statement to party members arguing that he would be prepared to take the question of his leadership to the party's Ard Fheis. The statement encouraged Ben Briscoe to table a motion calling on Haughey to resign. The parliamentary party meeting took place on 7 February. After a lengthy debate a vote was taken (this time by secret ballot). When the votes were counted, to the surprise of many, Haughey emerged victorious by 40 votes to 33, thereby surviving a third challenge to his leadership.

The by-election caused by the death of Clem Coughlan took place in Donegal South West in May 1982. It was easily won by his brother Cathal. Amongst the other candidates, Seamus Rodgers of the Workers' Party came close to winning 3,000 votes.

A new unit of local government was established that summer. Shannon Town Commission, as with such commissions, had the fewest functions and least amount of decision-making of any political body in the country. What was significant about its first election was the success of Brigid Makowski of the IRSP, the first public representative to have been elected directly under its banner.

Restored to office, Garret FitzGerald gave renewed focus on his much-vaunted *Constitutional Crusade*, which he had first raised in 1981. The purpose of this crusade was to modernise Ireland and to make it more attractive to those in Northern Ireland who might want to participate in a united Ireland. The difficulty caused by his call for a crusade was that it was creating an expectation for any grouping intent on having the Constitution changed and to have it changed in ways that could be unpredictable.

In the run-in to the 1981 general election both FitzGerald and Haughey gave commitments to a group, PLAC, seeking the insertion of a pro-life (anti-abortion) clause in the Irish Constitution. FitzGerald promised he would make this insertion in the context of general changes he felt were necessary. Haughey promised he would do this as a stand-alone commitment. Seeking to own the issue Haughey, while still in government, had produced a wording in October 1982. This wording read:

> The State acknowledges the right to life of the unborn and, with due regard to the equal right to life of the mother, guarantees in its laws to respect, and, as far as practicable, by its laws to defend and vindicate that right.

Fitzgerald had misgivings about this wording, despite his being enthusiastic prior to the election. The newly appointed Attorney General

Peter Sutherland advised the wording was so flawed that it could lead to abortion becoming legal in Ireland. As a referendum bill was proceeding through the Dáil, Fine Gael introduced, at the last minute, an alternative wording. This wording was defeated by eighty-seven votes to sixty-five. There were eight Fine Gael abstentions. Labour largely voted against but a small number supported this wording.

When it came to the Fianna Fáil wording, the vote was eighty-seven for and eleven against. Fine Gael officially abstained on the vote. Eight of its TDs voted with Fianna Fáil. These included Liam T. Cosgrave, the son of the former Taoiseach and Leader of Fine Gael. Among the eleven who voted against this wording were six Labour TDs led by Dick Spring, two Fine Gael TDs (Monica Barnes and Alan Shatter), the two Workers' Party TDs and Tony Gregory.

There followed a bitter and divisive referendum campaign, which ended with an emphatic two-to-one victory for the Pro Life forces, on a turnout of 54 per cent.

Thwarted on the abortion issue, FitzGerald moved to forward other aspects of his crusade. In March 1983 a New Ireland Forum was formed, meant to outline a shared nationalist approach to the development of political structures throughout Ireland. It would meet for a year before reporting. Criticisms of the body included the fact that it was limited in its membership, involving only delegations from Fianna Fáil, Fine Gael, Labour and the SDLP.

Elections to the British House of Commons in June 1983 gave some indication of the extent to which the New Ireland Forum may have been an empty vessel. In the next phase of its 'Armalite and the Ballot Box' strategy, Sinn Féin shook Northern Ireland politics with Gerry Adams winning the Belfast West seat from the former leader of the SDLP, Gerry Fitt. The IRA bombing in October at the Grand Hotel in Brighton during the Conservative Party conference, killing five and almost assassinating the British Prime Minister Margaret Thatcher, indicated that peace was not coming soon.

Ten days after the Abortion referendum, it was learned that George Colley had died at 57 years of age. The nearly man of Irish politics, his opposition to Charles Haughey defined him. Two months later, a by-election was held in his former Dublin Central constituency. This was easily retained by Fianna Fáil. Among the 'others', for the Workers' Party Michael White did well with 4,342 votes. For the still-unregistered Sinn Féin, Christy Burke won 2,304 votes. The Ecology Party (also still unregistered) ran Tony Ryan who won 458 votes. Edward Glackin for the Communist Party of Ireland won 243 votes.

Fianna Fáil had already extended its parliamentary party in 1983. John O'Connell, former Ceann Comhairle, Labour Party TD and sub-sequently independent TD, had been persuaded to join – a journey that had once been made by Noel Browne.

The now one and only Sinn Féin party experienced a significant change of its own that year. At the party's Ard Fheis the leadership of the party passed from one-time abstentionist TD Ruairí O'Brádaigh, to the rising star of the movement – West Belfast-based Gerry Adams. Much of the leadership moved northwards at that Ard Fheis.

The year 1983 saw the end of the presidential term of Patrick Hillery. Seán Mac Bride had made it known he would be available for the office and, given his enhanced international status, this would not have been the most unfair of expectations. But neither the government nor Fianna Fáil were prepared to offer him a nomination. Not enough other nomi-nators existed in the Oireachtas. Mac Bride seemed uninterested in pursuing the County Council route. The government and Fianna Fáil already seemed intent on reappointing Hillery, so that Patrick Hillery was re-elected unopposed as President of Ireland.

The government, only a year in office, experienced a resignation when the former leader of the Labour Party, then Minister for Trade, Commerce and Tourism, resigned his place at the cabinet in a dispute on the government's approach to the Dublin Gas Company.

Early in 1984 the Sinn Féin MP for West Belfast, Gerry Adams, was shot and wounded. The seemingly hopeless situation in Northern Ireland was in desperate need of a new approach. The New Ireland Forum reported in May 1984. It suggested three possible options: a uni-tary state, a federal or confederal state, or joint British and Irish authority. In reacting to the report, British Prime Minister Margaret Thatcher made her famous 'that is out, that is out, that is out' speech. It seemed the Forum's work had been scuppered before it could bring any change to the stilted debate that was the constitutional status of Northern Ireland.

Neither was it helped by a breach of unanimity on the Forum side. Fianna Fáil leader Charles Haughey declared that a United Ireland was the only option. Within Fianna Fáil he was challenged on this stance by Des O'Malley, who accused Haughey of stifling debate. For this challenge O'Malley had the Fianna Fáil whip removed from him. He, while still a member of Fianna Fáil, had in effect become an independent TD.

Local Elections were due in 1984. Once again they had been postponed under the pretext of promised local government reform. It was not possible, however, to postpone the European Elections, the second public iteration of which took place in June. For a second-order election, where the votes of others tended to become maximised, this was an enormous victory for the established political order in Ireland. Fianna Fáil and Fine Gael won fourteen of the fifteen available seats. Labour lost all four of the seats it had held.

T.J. Maher was the only shaft of light for 'others' in this election. He was safely elected again in the Munster Euro-constituency, even though he dropped 30,000 from his previous performance. Neil Blaney missed re-election while dropping 50,000 votes. The Workers' Party upped its vote again. Its satisfaction was somewhat tempered by the first appearance of Sinn Féin in these elections. Winning 55,000 votes, Sinn Féin outpolled the Workers' Party by 7,000 votes.

The Ecology Party had now registered as the Green Alliance. This would be its first time contesting the European elections. Its candidate was Christopher Fettes, the party's founder, contesting the Dublin Euro-constituency. He won over 5,000 votes, finishing marginally behind John de Courcey Ireland of the Democratic Socialist Party.

Held on the same day as the European elections was a by-election for the Laois Offaly constituency, brought about by the death of Fianna Fáil's Ber Cowen, aged 52 years of age. His 24-year-old son, Brian, was selected as his preferred replacement. He cruised to a first count victory. An independent candidate called Joseph McCormack won 1,471 votes. For the Communist Party of Ireland, Eóin O'Murchú won 120 votes.

Holding up the tally was the mysterious James Tallon. He had first stood in the 1981 general election for the Wicklow constituency. He subsequently had stood in one further general election, and four by-elections. His cumulative vote to date was little over 400 votes, an average of about 70 votes per election.

Also held on that day was a constitutional referendum on extending voting rights in for British citizens living in Ireland. It passed on a three-to-one margin.

Early in 1985 Minister for Health Barry Desmond introduced the Health (Family Planning) (Amendment) Bill, designed to make the availability of condoms and spermicides open to all adults, without the need for a doctor's prescription. Fianna Fáil opposed the bill, which was intended to dismantle the earlier legislation introduced by Charles Haughey. Des O'Malley, now without the Fianna Fáil whip, announced his intention not to vote against the bill. In his contribution to the debate he described his stance as 'standing by The Republic' saying:

> The politics of this would be very easy. The politics would be, to be one of the lads, the safest way in Ireland. But I do not believe that the interests of this State, or our Constitution and of this Republic, would be served by putting politics before conscience in regard to this. There is a choice of a kind that can only be answered by saying that I stand by the Republic and accordingly I will not oppose this Bill.

Haughey moved to have O'Malley expelled entirely from Fianna Fáil. A meeting of the party's national executive was convened. On a rollcall vote a motion that O'Malley be expelled from the party for 'Conduct Unbecoming' was overwhelmingly passed. In every respect now, O'Malley was an independent TD.

For the Labour Party there would be collateral damage from the moving of this bill. Its deeply conservative TD from Tipperary South, Seán Treacy (who had been Ceann Comhairle during the Twentieth Dáil, 1973-77) voted against the bill, an action that resulted in his immediate suspension from Labour's parliamentary party. Treacy would confirm the divorce by resigning from the Labour Party.

Postponed local elections were held in June 1985. These were successful elections for Fianna Fáil. The party's share of the vote finished far above the combined vote for Fine Gael and Labour, governments rarely succeeding in mid-term elections.

The Workers' Party did very well, by adopting a more targeted approach. It almost trebled the amount of seats it had (twenty as against seven in 1979) while not especially increasing its vote. On Dublin Corporation the party won six seats, three times the representation of Labour on that council. Sinn Féin won more votes than the Workers' Party but won only half the number of seats.

In its first election the Democratic Socialist Party ran about a dozen candidates in Dublin and in Limerick. In Dublin its candidates made little impact. In Limerick, stronghold of party leader Jim Kemmy, the party performed extraordinarily well, winning three seats on Limerick Corporation – Kemmy himself, Tim O'Driscoll and future government minister, Jan O'Sullivan.

The Green Alliance was also contesting its first set of local elections. Running more than thirty candidates, mainly in Dublin but also with a sprinkling of people in Munster. The party won more than 7,000 votes. This was an upward trajectory even if still relatively small beer. The good news was that the party made an electoral breakthough – its candidate in Killarney, Marcus Counihan, who had campaigned mostly on the issue of the National Park there, found himself elected to Killarney Urban District Council. An unusual feature of this election for the Green Alliance was that a majority of its candidates had been female. Many had been reluctant candidates, several only being convinced when told that the likelihood of election was remote.

Independent Fianna Fáil increased its membership of Donegal County Council from four councillors to six. The Community grouping again performed well in the elections to Dublin Corporation. An unregistered local political party, the Waterford People's Party, elected a councillor to Waterford Corporation. An independent socialist organisation helped elect Declan Bree to Sligo County Council and Sligo County Council.

Local politics indulged, the national political priorities turned again towards Northern Ireland. Despite the poor reception given to the report of the New Ireland Forum, it seemed at least to create some momentum for further discussion between Irish and British government officials. These talks, which had largely gone unrecorded, resulted in the signing of the Anglo Irish Agreement at Hillsborough Castle, County Down on 15 November 1985. The agreement gave the Irish Government an advisory role in the governance of Northern Ireland, while re-affirming Northern Ireland's position within the United Kingdom subject to those living there deciding otherwise. Charles Haughey led Fianna Fáil's opposition to the Agreement, claiming it was against Articles Two and Three of the Irish Constitution. When the Agreement was put forward to Dáil Éireann one Fianna Fáil politician indicated she did not share her leader's opposition. Mary Harney voted with the government, an act that led to her being expelled from Fianna Fáil.

Her next move might have been to become a member of Fine Gael. Garret FitzGerald later reported that Harney had approached him about that prospect. They talked about when a good opportunity for that to happen would be, but somehow the deal was never sealed.

She instead joined Des O'Malley in the political wilderness. Sensing this, and probably not seeking a political future with Fianna Fáil, consideration turned to forming a new political party. Encouraging them in thinking of such an endeavour was Michael MacDowell, who had been chairman of Garrett FitzGerald's constituency party in Dublin South East, leaving that post, and the Fine Gael party, with a sense of frustration. His family lineage also saw him being the grandnephew of Eoin MacNeill, head of the Irish Volunteers in 1916. At a press conference held on 15 December 1985, these three sat at the top table as a new party announced its arrival on to the Irish political scene. Thus the Progressive Democrats were born.

O'Malley and Harney were soon joined by others. First to join was Pearse Wyse from Cork, who had shared a Dáil constituency with Jack Lynch. He was followed by former government minister and fellow 'Club of 22' member, Bobby Molloy from Galway. The fledgling party received perhaps its biggest fillip with the first defection from Fine Gael – Michael Keating, who represented Dublin Central.

O'Malley embarked on a nationwide recruitment tour, where he spoke to large crowds. Opinion polls indicated that the party could win up to 25 per cent of the vote in a national election. Over twenty local representatives elected in the local elections in June 1985 declared themselves Progressive Democrats. This gave the new party a significant local authority base. While many of these councillors had been elected as independents, others came from Fianna Fáil, Fine Gael and even Labour.

The party achieved a presence in the Seanad through the defections of two Labour Senators, Timmy Conway and Helena McAuliffe-Ennis.

The party began to define itself as a liberal party, liberal on social issues such as contraception and divorce, but also economically liberal, seeking to promote low taxation, public expenditure control (particularly social welfare spending) and the privatisation of state companies. In announcing its policy agenda, the party crystallised its support base. Despite appropriating the name of the earlier Noel Browne vehicle, it was clear that in policy terms these two parties had not a lot in common. Another interesting feature emerging from opinion polls was that support for the Progressive Democrats seemed to be affecting Fine Gael more than it was hurting Fianna Fáil.

As the Progressive Democrats set about establishing a foothold for itself, much political energy in 1986 was being directed towards a key part of the liberal agenda, the removal of the prohibition on divorce in Ireland. The forming of the Divorce Action Group followed by the publication of a private members bill in the name of Michael O'Leary, Fine Gael TD and former leader of the Labour Party, put pressure on the government to take action on the issue.

A referendum was called for 24 June 1986. Fianna Fáil opposed removing the prohibition. The near two-to-one margin in favour of maintaining the prohibition, reflected the Ireland of that time. In that regard, Charles Haughey (regardless of personal standards or behaviour) and Fianna Fáil seemed closer to the pulse of where the country was.

Three days before that referendum, a second tragedy struck the Coughlan family in Donegal. Less than three years after he replaced his brother Clem, who had been killed in a car crash, Fianna Fáil TD Cathal Coughlan died suddenly. He was only 50 years of age. His 21-year-old daughter was selected to be a candidate when next the voters of the constituency would vote.

Another significant event was the 1986 Sinn Féin Ard Fheis (held at the Mansion House in Dublin) that debated a motion on ending abstentionism in relation to election to the Houses of the Oireachtas. This was a motion that had been debated by its predecessor parties in 1926 and again in 1970. On the third day of the Ard Fheis (2 November) a lengthy debate ensued. The key arguments, for and against, were made on behalf of the leadership by Martin McGuinness and against by former party leader, Ruairí O'Brádaigh. Delegates supported the motion, voting 429 in favour and 161 against. The obvious side effect of this debate was an unhappy minority grouping which remained committed to the policy of abstentionism. This group styled itself Republican Sinn Féin. It would remain unregistered but would contest local elections.

On 21 January 1987 Sinn Féin made its first entry in the Register of Political Parties at Leinster House. The day before this the Labour Party had withdrawn from government. Discussions on the impending budget had not been going well. Fine Gael's insistence that deep public spending cuts needed to be made was being met with Labour's refusal to accept such priorities. An election was inevitable. Garret FitzGerald decided on a four-week campaign, reallocating portfolios held by Labour TDs to other Fine Gael ministers, in effect for the course of the campaign creating a Fine Gael government. Nor would there be any pre-election pact with Labour. The die, indeed several dice, had been cast.

17

To Hell or to Tallaght?

The results of the election were not kind to the parties of the previous government. From its high watermark of November 1982, Fine Gael had won nineteen seats less. Labour sank to its lowest ever share in a national election, 6.4 per cent, although despite the lack of a pre-election pact transfers helped the party hold on to twelve of the sixteen seats it had previously won. Fianna Fáil, which had lost four of its TDs through the formation of the Progressive Democrats, won an additional six seats in this election (a net gain of ten). Even so, the party had not won an overall majority.

In its first election, the Progressive Democrats performed very well. The party had failed to realise the perhaps unrealistic expectations of the opinion polls that accompanied the foundation of the party. The PD performance did not better the vote won by Clann na Poblachta in 1948, nor that of the Farmers Party in 1923. In 1923 the Farmers Party also won more seats than the PDs had in 1987.

Nevertheless there would be fourteen PD TDs in the Twenty-Fifth Dáil. The five breakaway TDs – O'Malley, Harney, Wyse, Molloy, and Keating – were all safely elected. Joining them was instigator Michael Mac Dowell (elected in Garett FitzGerald's constituency of Dublin South East); Martin Gibbons (son of former Fianna Fáil minister, Jim Gibbons, in Carlow/Kilkenny); Mairín Quill (twice previously a Fianna Fáil candidate for the Dáil, and an acolyte of Jack Lynch, in Cork North Central); Anne Colley (daughter of former Tánaiste, George, in Dublin South); Pat O'Malley (a cousin of Des, in Dublin West); Geraldine Kennedy (political journalist whose phone had been tapped by Sean Doherty, as Minister for Justice) in Dun Laoghaire; Peadar Clohessy (another former Fianna Fáil Dáil candidate, elected with Des O'Malley in Limerick East); John McCoy (making it three PD seats in Limerick in Limerick West); and Martin Cullen (who came from an independent political bachground). His father and grandfather had been mayors of Waterford.

The Workers' Party continued its upwards trend, electing four TDs in this election. Joe Sherolock returned to the Dail, being elected again in Cork East. A new Workers' Party TD was elected in Dublin North East. He was the yacht-owning solicitor, Pat McCartan. Another new party would be represented in this Dáil, even if its representative was not a new TD. Jim Kemmy regained a seat in Limerick East, this time as leader of the Democratic Socialist Party. The party ran three other candidates, all in Dublin constituencies, none of whom broke three figures in their vote totals.

The now independent Sean Tracey in Tipperary South joined Tony Gregory and Neil Blaney to make up the independent contingent. Once again Independent Fianna Fáil restricted its activity to Donegal North East.

Putting aside its policy of abstentionism did not seem to pay any immediate benefit for Sinn Féin. There was little change in the vote received by the party than it had received in its previous electoral outing.

The Green Alliance ran nine candidates in this election and collectively these candidates won about 7,000 votes, not even a constituency quota but nearly double what the party had received in November 1982. Three of the party's candidates won over 1,000 votes – Roger Garland in Dublin South; Máire Mullarney in Dublin South East and Trevor Sargent in Dublin North.

An unregistered party styling itself the Tax Reform League stood four candidates, polling less than 4,000 votes. The Communist Party of Ireland ran five candidates, consisting of four candidates in two constituencies. Together, its candidates still won less than 800 votes.

When the Dáil reconvened on 10 March, the now independent TD Seán Treacy was selected for a second time as Ceann Comhairle. A number of nominations were received for the position of Taoiseach. First vote was for the incumbent, Charles Haughey. Garret FitzGerald lost the position on a vote of fifty-one votes for 114 votes against. Attention then turned to a vote on Charles Haughey. This vote was tied at 82 votes each. The missing vote was that of Tony Gregory. Perhaps he was informed by the unimplemented approaches of the deal that had not been implemented in 1982. Maybe his antipathy to the Anglo Irish Agreement made Gregory favour Haughey over FitzGerald, but not enough to directly vote for Haughey. That decision was left to the new Ceann Comharile, Sean Treacy, who chose Haughey.

This now decided, the next choice for the Fine Gael parliamentary party was to choose a successor for Garret Fitzgerald. The party's most successful leader would now step aside to be replaced by someone unknown. The expected successor was Peter Barry from Cork. A contemporary to and as patrician as FitzGerald, the closeness in age was seen to be a disadvantage. He was 58 years of age, the same age as Mikhail Gorbachev, leader of the Soviet Union.

Two other candidates were to emerge. Forty-year-old John Bruton had been a TD since 1969, and was by now a two-time Minister for Finance. Two years his senior was Alan Dukes, someone who was less rooted in Fine Gael. Having originally worked as an economist with the Irish Farmers' Association (IFA), Dukes stood as an unsuccessful European Parliament candidate for the party in 1979. He was first elected as a TD in 1981, finding himself a member of the cabinet on his first day in the Dáil.

The wider Fine Gael parliamentary party, including Senators and MEPs, met in Leinster House on 21 March. The chosen method of voting was single transferable vote – secret ballot, with only the final vote revealed. This saw the announcement of Alan Dukes as the new leader of Fine Gael.

The new Seanad brought several new and returning Senators. In the vocational panels, as had been the case for several Seanad elections, there was no 'others' present. A new Senator was elected in the Dublin University constituency. David Norris had achieved prominence having taken a 1983 Supreme Court action against the Irish State over its laws against homosexuality. The action was lost on a three-two split decision. On being elected to the Seanad he was continuing his action to the European Court of Human Rights. Leading his legal team was his now Seanad colleague, Mary Robinson.

In the National University constituency John A. Murphy returned to the Seanad. Newly elected was the General Secretary of the Irish

National Teachers Organisation (INTO), Joe O'Toole. Five of the eleven nominees made by Charles Haughey were independents. The nominations seemed to be made with an eye to his legacy, his desire to be seen as an erudite man of art and culture. From Northern Ireland, John Robb was once again appointed. Joining him was the playwright, Brian Friel, the naturalist Éamon de Buitléar, the archaeologist, George Eogan, and the horse breeder John Magnier.

Another one-time independent, John O'Connell, was also one of the Taoiseach's nominees. He had failed to be elected at the general election after having become a member of Fianna Fáil in 1983.

In 1987 the first changes were agreed to be made to the foundation treaties that brought about the European Community. It was the view of the Irish Government that ratification of these changes only required a parliamentary vote. In this the government was challenged in the Supreme Court by an agricultural economist, Raymond Crotty. Crotty argued successfully that the Single European Act (the legal instrument that contained the proposed changes) impacted on the Irish Constitution, and could only be approved through a vote of the Irish people in a referendum. This referendum was held in May 1987. The changes were approved on a 70 to 30 margin.

In domestic politics, the minority Haughey government was given some comfort from a speech made by Fine Gael leader, Alan Dukes, to the Tallaght Chamber of Commerce. There he said:

> When the Government is moving in the right direction, I will not oppose the central thrust of its policy. If it is going in the right direction, I do not believe that it should be deviated from its course, or tripped up on macro-economic issues.

When followed through, this meant that Fine Gael would abstain from voting on issues where it believed the government was going in the right direction. This became known as the Tallaght Strategy.

The only electoral activity in the Republic in 1988 was the initial election for the Leixlip Town Commission. What was significant about this was the first electoral success of Catherine Murphy, who stood on behalf of the Workers' Party. Her subsequent career would involve several other manifestations of others in Irish politics. She would, at this time, have been acknowledging a change of leadership in her party with Prionsias De Rossa replacing Tomás MacGiolla. Another significant change occurred with the Green Alliance. The party had changed its entry on the Register of Political Parties. This now read – The Green Party – Comhaontas Glas.

Events associated with Northern Ireland continued to horrify the world. November 1987 had seen the slaughter of eleven people after a Remembrance Day bombing at the Centopath in Enniskillen. March 1988 would be a murderous month. Beginning in Gibraltar, a British Army shoot-to-kill action killed three IRA activists on a reconnaissance mission. Their burials at Milltown Cemetary in Belfast led to the deaths of three more people, killed by the loyalist paramilitary Michael Stone. At the funeral of these victims, two plain clothes undercover British Army personnel were recognised, dragged out of their car, beaten, then later shot dead. It all seemed so relentless. Initiatives to alleviate this situation seemed to be running into sand.

The Progressive Democrats sought to raise the tone of political debate by going a step further than Garret FitzGerald had with his constitutional crusade. The party produced a draft for a new Constitution. The lack of references to God in the draft upset some, relegating media interest in other proposals from the document, one of which was to discard the Seanad.

Otherwise, politics as usual was consumed with efforts to tackle the national debt. One of the more controversial and audacious measures to act on this was the introduction of a tax amnesty on undeclared income. For a period between March and October 1988, anyone declaring any such income would face a one-off payment at a rate lower that the then standard rate of tax. The amnesty brought in a sum of money (£500 million) far in access of what had been anticipated. The new money was the equivalent of 2 per cent of the then GNP of the country. Shortly after this amnesty was ended the Minister for Finance, Ray McSharry, left the government when he was appointed as Ireland's European Commissioner, holding the Agriculture portfolio.

Internationally the government experienced considerable embarrassment when the European Court of Human Rights in Strasbourg delivered its judgement on the case of *Norris versus Ireland*. It found in the litigant's favour, that Irish laws on homosexuality were repugnant to human rights.

As the decade fell into its final year, improved opinion poll ratings were encouraging Charles Haughey to consider whether he should seek to improve his mandate. An opportunity was created by the government's defeat in April on a private members motion calling on additional resources to be provided for haemophiliacs, infected by the HIV virus through tainted blood products provided by a State agency. As a private members motion, the vote was not strictly binding on the government. It certainly represented an embarrassment. Haughey could justifiably argue that the vote undermined the stability of the government. Nevertheless, he waited another month before seeking a dissolution of the Dáil. This allowed the holding of a general election on the same day as European Elections, which were due.

Haughey's gamble failed. He and Fianna Fáil came back with four fewer seats. This matched the gain achieved by Fine Gael, in its first outing under new leader Alan Dukes. This represented a modest rise in support, still far removed from the party's November 1982 peak.

The Labour Party won an additional three seats, while the party continued to remain under 10 per cent of the national vote. At its 1989 party convention it had undergone some spring cleaning. Repeating the purge that had occurred in British Labour, the Irish party passed a motion that membership of the 'militant' faction was incompatible with that of the Labour Party. This facilitated the effective expulsion from Labour of militant members, the most prominent of whom was Joe Higgins.

The biggest losers of the election were the Progressive Democrats. In falling from fourteen seats in 1987 to six in 1989, the party had slid from the third largest group in the Dáil to the fifth. Its survivors were Des O'Malley and Peadar Clohessy in Limerick East; Bobby Molloy in Galway West; Mairín Quill in Cork North Central and Pearse Wyse in Cork South Central. Mary Harney in Dublin South West won the only Dublin seat for the party in a region that had returned six PD TDs in 1987. In the twenty-eight-month period between the elections, the party's vote had more than halved.

By entering into a pre-election pact with Fine Gael, in an attempt to stop Fianna Fáil re-entering government, the Progressive Democrats had caused itself tremendous damage. On the one hand, the party re-lent votes it had taken from Fine Gael in 1987. On the other hand, the very existence of the pact cut off many potential transfers from Fianna Fáil to the PDs.

Leapfrogging over the PDs was the Workers' Party (under its new leader Prionsias De Rossa), which had its best ever election. The party almost doubled its number of Dáil seats, now standing at seven TDs. Its new TDs were Pat Rabbitte in Dublin South West and Éamon Gilmore in Dun Laoghaire (both trade union officials and former luminaries in student politics). The seventh Workers' Party TD was Eric Byrne in Dublin South Central. Six of the seven Workers' Party TDs were elected in Dublin city or county.

The leader of the Democratic Socialist Party, Jim Kemmy, was re-elected in Limerick East, winning over 9,000 votes. He was one of only two candidates put forward by the party, the other being Michael Conaghan, whose vote did not take the party's national vote over the 10,000 figure.

A name change also seemed to work for The Green Party. Standing eleven candidates, the party came close to quadrupling its vote. The chief beneficiary of this was the party's candidate in Dublin South, Roger Garland, who saw his strong first count allied to a strong transfer pattern, making him the first elected Green Party TD. There were several strong performances for the party. First-time candidate in Dublin South East, John Gormley, almost spoiled the Fine Gael plan to unseat Michael Mac Dowell by diverting votes from Garret FitzGerald. On the final count only a couple of hundred votes separated FitzGerald and Gormley. In Dublin North Trevor Sargent recorded just under 3,000 votes. In Dun Laoghaire the Greens recorded another significant vote.

Four independents were elected to this Dáil. Sean Treacy, as Ceann Comhairle was returned automatically. Tony Gregory and Neil Blaney had seemingly achieved immovable status. The new independent was Tom Foxe from Roscommon, representing the local Hospital Action Group there.

Sinn Féin continued to struggle, the party making no forward momentum. The Communist Party ran two candidates who together won less than 400 votes. Three candidates stood in Dublin constituencies on a Gay Rights ticket, winning 1,517 votes.

One of the more interesting groups contesting this election was the Army Wives group. Members of the Defence Forces had not been allowed to form representative groups. In this election the wives of members of the Defence Forces contested three constituencies to air their grievances. The constituencies chosen – Cavan Monaghan, Kildare and Longford Westmeath – all contained large army barracks. The campaign won almost 7,000 votes, the best performance being that of June Kiernan in the Longford Westmeath constituency, who won 3,207 votes.

For reasons best known to himself, William (Abbey of the Holy Cross) Fitzsimon registered himself to contest seven constituencies, five in County Cork and two in Tipperary. For his sins he won 880 votes. He also chose to stand on the same day in Munster for the European Elections, winning 1,789 votes.

Seven political parties were now represented in this Dáil, the most that had ever been represented. This diversity was achieved on a smaller vote. 'Others' won 23 per cent of the vote in 1987, with 17 per cent won in 1989 – both votes being higher than the average vote for 'others' achieved in Dáil elections.

The holding of a general election on the same day as a European Election gave the opportunity of assessing how voter behaviour differed from one to the other. In 1989 it was a significant difference. In the previous European Election (1984), Fianna Fáil and Fine Gael between them won fourteen of the fifteen seats available. In 1989 these parties lost two seats each. The four available seats were spread quite liberally. In the Dublin Euro-constituency, Prionsias De Rossa topped the poll, while Barry Desmond regained a seat for Labour. General Secretary of the Progressive Democrats Pat Cox topped the poll in the Munster Euro-constituency, where T.J. Maher was elected for a third time. In Connacht/Ulster, Neil Blaney succeeded in being elected after his loss in 1984.

Between them, Fianna Fáil and Fine Gael won 53 per cent of the vote in this election. 'Others' won 37 per cent. All the non-traditional parties performed better in the European Election than they had in the general election – some significantly. For the Progressive Democrats, Pat Cox won far more votes in Munster than the party had nationally in the general election. Its national share of the vote was higher than it had achieved in the 1987 general election.

The Workers' Party achieved a 50 per cent bounce over its general election vote. The party, influenced by its media guru Eoghan Harris, ran a striking campaign based on thousands of black and white posters of its leader in a relaxed, jacket-over-the-shoulder pose.

The Green Party had a 150 per cent bounce on its general election performance. This was achieved though running candidates in only two of the four Euro-constituencies. The party's strongest performance was in Dublin where Trevor Sargent came close to winning 40,000 votes, out-polling Mary Harney of the Progressive Democrats (instigator of the Single European Act referendum) while Raymond Crotty also did well there, winning over 25,000 votes. Part of the reason for the spurt of Green Party support was the receiving of party political broadcasts from Britain, where the British Greens ended up winning 15 per cent of the vote.

Sinn Féin did not see much variation between its general election and European Election votes. However, a surrogate candidate in Munster, Fr Paddy Ryan won 30,000 votes. The party seemed more intent in engaging in electoral experimentation, acquiring intelligence for future use. Competing with Paddy Ryan in Munster was the Cork based Meitheal – People First, which won 16,000 votes.

The votes counted from both sets of elections, attention then turned to the business of forming a government. This would prove to be a difficult task. Fianna Fáil was seven seats short of an overall majority. Even when combined, Fine Gael and Labour were thirteen votes short. A multi-party of approach of 1948 would be even more ideologically fluid in 1989. For Fianna Fáil the unthinkable had to be grasped – the prospect of dropping its long-held insistence on governing alone.

Just as a return to 1948 seemed unlikely, the other potential of a grand coalition between the Civil War parties was thought heretical. Fine Gael leader Alan Dukes at least broached the subject, proposing what he knew would be unacceptable to Fianna Fáil – an equal share of cabinet seats, with a rotating office of Taoiseach.

The focus centred on a combination that made mathematical sense – a pairing of Fianna Fáil and the Progressive Democrats. This was mathematically possibly, but there was a huge trust chasm between the two parties. Mary Harney suggested in a radio interview that the PDs could vote for a Fianna Fáil candidate. Other PD TDs continued to voice their opposition to Charles Haughey continuing as Taoiseach. The question also remained whether the PDs remained bound to its pre-election pact with Fine Gael, which its parliamentary party agreed to do. This would mean that the opening day of the new Dáil could not be conclusive on the choosing of a new government.

And so it proved. On 29 June, the Dáil reconvened. Seán Treacy was re-selected as Ceann Comhairle. Nominations for Taoiseach were taken for Haughey, Dukes and Spring. Each was defeated. Opposition leaders insisted on Haughey resigning as Taoiseach, having failed to gain majority support in the Dáil. Haughey demurred but eventually accepted the constitutional position, submitting his resignation to the President. He would continue as caretaker Taoiseach. His preference remained a minority Fianna Fáil government supported from the outside by the Progressive Democrats.

Haughey's assumptions and unwillingness to surrender power was not playing well with the smaller party. Despite this, a meeting was organised between representatives of the two parties to discuss what possibilities existed. For the Progressive Democrat team (represented by Bobby Molloy and Pat Cox) coalition had to be one such possibility. For Fianna Fáil this represented a precondition the party would not accept. Playing hardball, Haughey stated that the only alternative would be another general election that he would 'request' from the President. A short Dáil sitting on 3 July had opposition leaders challenge Haughey on this creative interpretation of the Constitution.

Within Fianna Fáil, while not being publicly admitted, the idea of another general election that might see the party returned in an even more weakened position did not have universal acceptance. Opinion polls indicated that there was more support for a coalition government of some form instead of another general election. A face-to-face meeting between Haughey and O'Malley gave the go ahead for their negotiating teams to meet again, on terms that included talking about the possibility (if not the expectation) of coalition.

The talks, over the course of a week, moved towards a positive outcome. On 12 July, almost a month since the general election had taken place, a Taoiseach was elected and a new government formed. The Progressive Democrats would hold two cabinet positions – Des

O'Malley as Minister for Industry and Commerce and Bobby Molloy as Minister for Energy. Both had previously been Fianna Fáil ministers. O'Malley had not sought nor was he offered the position of Tánaiste. Later, Mary Harney would be appointed a Minister for State at the Department of the Environment.

Attention now moved to the composition of the next Seanad. The only new independent filled a vacancy left by Mary Robinson at Dublin University. Elected in her stead was Carmencita Hederman, who had enjoyed a high profile as Lord Mayor of Dublin during the city's millennium celebrations in 1988. The Taoiseach's nominees contained no Northern Ireland representative and no cultural emissaries. Eight of the nominees came from a Fianna Fáil background, leaving space for three PD Senators. Martin Cullen had been a TD for Waterford. He was joined in the Seanad by Helen Keogh and John Dardis, chosen by their party with an eye to future elections.

The first half of 1990 saw Ireland hold the Presidency of the European Community. It was a perfect stage on which Charles Haughey could strut. He had designated this to be a 'green' presidency, reflective of growing public interest in the environment. The two European Council meetings held in Dublin were held at a time of historic change in the world. The fall of the Berlin Wall in 1989 had brought about the prospect of German reunification. Eastern European countries were beginning to embrace democracy. February saw the release of Nelson Mandela from prison in South Africa after over twenty-seven years of captivity.

A side effect of a Green Presidency was some government attention being given to environmental issues. The Green Party had been campaigning strongly on the issue of air quality in the capital, following the deadly smogs experienced in Dublin in the 1980s. Newly appointed Minister of State for Environmental Protection, Mary Harney, took up the issue within government. She secured agreement that regulations be put in place banning the sale or distribution of bituminous coal in the Dublin area. She later introduced legislation creating an Environmental Protection Agency.

Local elections were due to be held during the summer of 1990, but again they were postponed. Something about impending legislation to bring about local government reform was cited as a reason. There was an election in 1990, however. President Patrick Hillery was approaching the end of his second term in office. It irritated some that no public election had been held in Ireland since 1973 and that in 1990 surely such an election should take place.

Elements within Labour (a party that had never contested a Presidential election) led by Michael D. Higgins talked up the prospect of creating a contest. In the minds of the promoters, Noel Browne would be the ideal candidate. Not so ideal in the mind of the party leader Dick Spring, who had been doing his own thinking on the matter … the conclusion of which thinking being that Mary Robinson would be a better candidate. Neither Browne nor Robinson were members of the Labour Party. Browne had resigned from the party in 1975, Robinson in 1982.

Spring's view prevailed. A technical difficulty existed in that the Labour Party did not have enough Oireachtas members and needed twenty to nominate. Workers' Party TDs and independent Senator Brendan Ryan helped make up the numbers. As a party, the Workers' Party endorsed Robinson's candidacy. The Green Party was also supportive, although the party's only TD, Roger Garland, was not. Her nomination allowed her to be the first in the field.

The Mary Robinson campaign was a Labour Party initiative, largely financed and managed by the Labour Party, for an independent candidate. Early arguments within the campaign were about branding. Labour insisted that its terracotta rose logo be used in all promotional material. Those around Mary Robinson reacted against this, but the Labour hierarchy prevailed. For them the branding of the campaign represented ownership of the campaign.

Fianna Fáil viewed the Presidency with proprietorial interest. Each previous holder of the office, with the exception of Douglas Hyde, had had Fianna Fáil associations. Coming forward on this occasion was the then Tánaiste and Minister for Defence, Brian Lenihan. Within Fianna Fáil he had been challenged by his cabinet colleague, John Wilson, but Lenihan ended up being the preferred candidate. Undoubtedly popular, Lenihan projected a peculiar personality, which combined an obvious intelligence with an ability to say foolish things. He once talked about 'the futility of consistency'. Another of his contentions, made as part of an argument in favour of emigration, was that Ireland was too small an island to be able to offer a living to so many people.

Fine Gael was not very willing to see a Presidential election happen, Now that it was happening there was an obligation on the party to produce a candidate. Party leader Alan Dukes felt the candidate chosen had to be distinct. He chose Dublin West TD (a constituency shared with Brian Lenihan) Austin Currie. Currie had come into politics in the Republic, after a long career in Northern Irish politics (as an SDLP representative), stretching back to the civil rights movement in the 1960s. His candidacy could help define where Northern Ireland stood in the politics of the Republic.

The campaign would be the most vitriolic, most personality-based of any Presidential election that had yet been held. During a radio debate, the Minister for the Environment Pádraig Flynn (and like Mary Robinson from County Mayo), stated that he found it hard to reconcile her 'new found interest in her family' with her previous life. It was seen as a scurrilous attack that engendered a significant amount of sympathy for Mary Robinson, especially among women voters.

Campaigning of this type was helping Mary Robinson be seen as the more likely to challenge Brian Lenihan. Lenihan had already done much to undermine himself. In May he gave an interview to a Masters student, Jim Duffy, who had been working on a thesis on the Presidency of Ireland. In this interview, Lenihan confirmed that in January 1982 he, Charles Haughey and another cabinet colleague, Sylvester Barrett, stating individually and together they had repeatedly phoned Áras an Uachtaráin, seeking to pressurise President Patrick Hillery to refuse a dissolution of the Dáil to allow Fianna Fáil to form a new government without a new election. This was acting unconstitutionally.

Lenihan had denied these charges on television. *The Irish Times* ran a news story saying it was aware of information that contradicted what Lenihan was saying. Fine Gael held a press conference attended by Jim Duffy, where extracts of the interview tape were played. Under pressure, Brian Lenihan appeared on the main television news, where he admitted 'on mature recollection' that he had not been consistent in his accounts of what had happened. He intensified his apologia by looking not at his interviewer, but directly into the television camera.

Fine Gael sought to make further political capital out of this by tabling a motion of no confidence in the government. The Progressive Democrats, which had been neutral in the campaign up to now, stated the party would leave government unless Brian Lenihan resigned from government. Lenihan refused. Haughey initially had been reluctant to act, but eventually insisted that Brian Lenihan was obliged to leave the government. In making this intervention the Progressive Democrats could no longer be seen as being neutral in this campaign. If the party believed Lenihan was unfit to be a member of cabinet, it was hardly suggesting that Irish citizens should select him as their first citizen.

With all of its running on this issue, or maybe because of it, Fine Gael was not gaining any advantage. When the votes were counted Lenihan topped the poll with 44 per cent of the vote. Mary Robinson came in a close second with 39 per cent. Austin Currie was a distant third with 17 per cent. After Currie's transfers, Robinson was successful on a 53 to 47 margin.

The relatively poor performance of Fine Gael in the election saw pressure being brought upon the leadership of Alan Dukes. A motion of no confidence was moved against him. Sensing its likely success, Dukes resigned before the taking of the vote. John Bruton announced his willingness to replace Dukes. One of the younger members of the parliamentary party, Ivan Yates from Wexford, put himself forward. When senior members Michael Noonan and Jim Mitchell announced their intentions not to stand, while indicating their support for John Bruton, Yates stood aside. Without a vote, John Bruton had become leader of Fine Gael.

Parallel with these changes in Irish politics, a significant change was occuring in neighbouring UK. After eleven years in office, hugely impacting on Irish and European relations, Margaret Thatcher was deposed from office. Her attachment to the deeply unpopular community charge (poll tax) policy was making some in her party consider her an electoral liability. Her growing antipathy towards the EU was not shared by most of her cabinet. In the end, her departure still caused surprise; particularly surprising was its brutal nature.

Her successor, John Major, seemed in many ways Thatcher's polar opposite. He would soon realise the scale of the ongoing difficulties in Northern Ireland; while holding a cabinet meeting at his official residence at 10 Downing Street in February, the IRA managed to fire a number of mortar shells in its direction, hitting nearby buildings.

A number of reviewed judgements in British courts were contributing to some sense of hope that different approaches to Northern Ireland might follow. In 1989 the Guildford Four had their convictions quashed. In 1991 the same uncertainty about forensic evidence saw the quashing of sentences of the Maguire Seven and the quashing of the convictions of the Birmingham Six.

These decisions would inform political debate, although local issues would predominate, with the holding of the delayed local elections. Between them, both Fianna Fáil and Fine Gael lost seats, eighty of these by Fianna Fáil. Labour enjoyed a post-Robinson rejuvenation, winning thirty extra councillors.

The Progressive Democrats standing 126 candidiates won thirty-seven council seats in its first set of local elections. This was significantly more than the number who declared for the party after its foundation. There were sixty Green Party candidates, leading to thirteen councillors being elected, the first elected for the party at this level of government. Ten of these councillors were elected within the Dublin area, with others elected in Kildare, Wicklow and Cork..

The Workers' Party added four councillors to its total, now standing at twenty-four, elected from eighty-two candidates. Sinn Féin found itself literally decimated with its ten councillors being reduced to nine, from the sixty-four candidates it put forward. Republican Sinn Féin stood seven candidates and succeeded in electing one councillor. That success was in County Longford, in an area that had elected the party leader Ruairí O'Brádaigh as an abstentionist TD in 1957. The party remained unregistered, committed only to contesting local elections.

A new entry on the Register of Political Parties was the Independent Socialist Party in Sligo Leitrim. That was the political organisation of Declan Bree, who had been a councillor since 1974. Eighty-one independent councillors were elected from the 308 independent candidates who contested. Neil Blaney's Independent Fianna Fáil won five of the six seats the organisation had held on Donegal County Council.

One party that did not contest these elections was the Democratic Socialist Party. This was because the party no longer existed. In 1990 the party had decided at the behest of its leader Jim Kemmy to merge with the Labour Party.

On Dublin Corporation (later Dublin City Council), Labour, Fine Gael, The Green Party, The Workers' Party and independent councillors formed an alliance to support each other's nominees for the position of Lord Mayor of Dublin. Under this arrangement Tómas Mac Giolla of the Workers' Party, John Gormley of the Green Party, and the long-standing independent Seán 'Dublin Bay' Loftus would each become Lord Mayor. The independent councillors would later come to a similar arrangement with Fianna Fáil, which saw the independent Brendan Lynch achieve the office.

The local elections twelve years previously had seen the beginning of the end for Jack Lynch. And so it proved for Charles Haughey. Its impact was not immediate. Much like the Russian monk Rasputin, it was proving almost impossible to politically kill Charles Haughey. The way was open declaration by his Minister for Finance, Albert Reynolds, that as and when the vacancy arose, he would be a candidate for Taoiseach.

The summer recess bought Haughey some time. When parliamentary life resumed, four young Turks within his parliamentary party – Noel Dempsey, Seán Power, M.J. Nolan and Liam Fitzgerald – moved a vote of no confidence against him. Reynolds and his supporters, seen as enabling this putsch, were removed from the cabinet. Minister for Foreign Affairs, Gerry Collins, appeared on television news appealing to Albert Reynolds not 'to burst the party'. Haughey won the subsequent vote of confidence by 55 votes to 22. This fourth challenge to his leadership seems to have been the most comfortable to rebuff.

His replacement Minister for Defence, Jim McDaid, was photographed outside the Four Courts supporting an escaped Maze prisoner who had avoided extradition. Fine Gael complained about the inappropriateness of this. The Progressive Democrats seemed similarly appalled and the party demanded McDaid's resignation. After little more than a day in office, McDaid resigned.

The stakeholder to Haughey's term of office was his once close colleague, Seán Doherty. Having lost his Dáil seat Doherty was elected to the Seanad. He further succeeded in being elected its chief presiding officer, the Cathaoirleach. As with his Dáil counterpart, the Ceann

Comhairle, his was an office that was supposed to be above and beyond politics. But Doherty had a story to tell and he wanted to tell it. His first attempt was made through an interview held on his local radio station, *Shannonside*. The import of what he was saying was not picked up on during that interview. His second attempt was by appearing on the RTE Network Two programme, *Nighthawks*, an irreverent niche programme. On this he told the programme's presenter Shay Healy that the phone tapping of journalists' phones, that he had endorsed as Minister for Justice, was known by many cabinet members, including Haughey. After filming he stressed the importance of what he said when talking to the presenter, telling him he had said something that night he had not said before.

The media began to get the message that Doherty was attempting to impart. As a media storm broke, Doherty laid low for ten days. He reappeared at a press conference where he provided the postscript to his story. Not only were his actions as Minister for Justice approved, he also provided the transcripts of bugged conversations with the head of the cabinet, the Taoiseach Charles Haughey.

For the PDs this was too much. O'Malley confronted Haughey, insisting on his resignation. Haughey stated that it was his intention to resign, only he wanted the space to choose when to announce. On 30 January 1992, he announced he was stepping down as leader of Fianna Fáil. The following ten days were used to select a new Fianna Fáil leader, who would become the next holder of the office of Taoiseach.

Albert Reynolds made himself available immediately. It was expected he would be challenged for the position by Bertie Ahern. Ahern had been identified by Haughey as a possible successor. He had described Ahern as '*the most skilful, the most devious, the most cunning of them all*'. The Reynolds camp had identified a chink in Ahern's armour. Michael Smith, a supporter of Reynolds, made a public aside that the people of Ireland would want to know where their Taoiseach went home to each night. This was meant as an oblique reference to Ahern's marital status. The hint seemed enough to discourage Ahern's candidacy. On 11 February 1992, Haughey resigned as Taoiseach, quoting Shakespeare's Othello that he 'had done the State some service'.

18

The One-Sheet Man

Anyone expecting a smooth transition into office for Albert Reynolds would soon be disabused of that notion. Firstly, Reynolds had unfinished business within Fianna Fáil. In appointing his first cabinet, he announced eight new ministers. Similarly, nine Ministers of State were replaced.

Secondly, the flawed wording of the Pro Life-Anti Abortion ammendent to the Constitution from 1983 had created its first problematic case. The 'X case' established the right of Irish women to an abortion, if a pregnant woman's life was at risk because of pregnancy, including the risk of suicide. The case involved a fourteen-year-old girl, identified as 'X', who had been the victim of a statutory rape, becoming pregnant. Threatening suicide, her family wished that she travel to procure an abortion. The Attorney General Harry Whelehan sought a High Court injunction (which was granted) preventing the journey of the girl. The Supreme Court overturned the High Court judgement on a four-two majority, establishing circumstances in which abortion could take place in Ireland.

The third 'welcoming present' in Albert Reynolds's in-tray was the Beef Tribunal. Presided over by Justice Liam Hamilton, this tribunal had been established in 1991 to examine how an export credit scheme on the export of beef products was being administered.

The State was guaranteeing payments to companies exporting to Iraq (then engaged in a long-running war with Iran). One company (Anglo Irish Beef Producers, owned by Larry Goodman) was the overwhelming beneficiary of this scheme. The then minister responsible for administrating the scheme was Albert Reynolds. The opposition TD who was challenging him on how the scheme was being administered was Des O'Malley. Public hearings were taking place questioning those who had knowledge of the scheme. Reynolds and O'Malley would soon each give testimony.

Relations between the coalition parties were not helped by Reynolds referring to his government being 'a temporary little arrangement'. At the Fianna Fáil Ard Fheis, a newly appointed minister, Brian Cowen, was trying to press the buttons of the party faithful, alluding to the Progressive Democrats by stating: 'If in doubt, leave them out.'

Meanwhile the Workers' Party seemed to be going in an opposite direction. After its best ever election in 1989, debate began on its future philosophical direction. Party leader Proinsias De Rossa wanted the party to have more of an acceptance of free-market economics, combined with a distancing from doctrinaire Marxism. Arguing two different directions were De Rossa and the party's long-time (although now former) general secretary, Seán Garland.

Among the areas of contention were accusations that the Workers' Party, or elements within the party, had been engaged in counterfeiting. Another cause of embarrassment was the regular sharing of fraternal greetings between the Workers' Party and the Workers Party of the People's Republic of North Korea.

In February 1992 a special convention of party members voted on De Rossa's proposals. They were defeated by nine votes. A week later De Rossa and five other TDs left the Workers' Party. Earlier in the year, De Rossa had decided to concentrate on his Dáil seat. He transferred his European Parliament seat to colleague, Des Geraghty, who also decided to leave the Workers' Party, taking with him the European seat. Only long-time former leader, Tomás Mac Giolla, remained as a Workers' Party TD.

The new party went under a working title, New Agenda. It hoped to attract some TDs and others from the left wing of the Labour Party. One who actively engaged with the possibility was Kildare TD Emmet Stagg, who at that time was estranged from the Labour Party having resigned its whip. In the end he chose a Labour future. By the time the party held its founding convention in March 1992, New Agenda had evolved into Democratic Left. The party defined itself as such:

> a democratic socialist party. We believe that the idea of socialism coupled with the practice of democracy provides the basis for the radical transformation of Irish society. We aim to be a feminist party. An environmental party. A party of the unemployed and low-paid. A champion of personal freedom. A friend and ally of the third world. An integral part of the European Left.

Muddying the water in all this was the desire of the government to pass a new European Treaty bringing into being a European Union. Known as the Maastricht Treaty, it was a complex document outlining the anticipated future direction of the European Community. Included in its provisions were means by which a single European currency would be brought about, provisions that seemed light on the type of fiscal co-ordination that would be required.

Opposing the referendum in the Dáil were Democratic Left and the Green Party. Their economic and political arguments were sidelined as the Taoiseach, Albert Reynolds, had but one campaigning tool. He kept repeating that a Yes vote in Ireland would see Ireland being given £6 billion in cohesion funds from Europe. A huge majority voted Yes when the referendum was held on 18 June. Twelve days earlier Denmark had said No. They and not Ireland would be Brussels's problem.

Attention then focused on the Hamilton Tribunal. In giving his testimony, Reynolds referred to the testimony that O'Malley had given as being 'dishonest'. O'Malley and his cabinet colleague Bobby Molloy resigned from cabinet. The Progressive Democrats left government. The temporary little arrangement had proved very temporary indeed – ten short months.

A general election was held on 25 November. The momentum coming up to the election was very much with the Labour Party. Party leader Dick Spring had been spending his time widening as well as deepening his party's appeal. Part of this process was the absorption through mergers of smaller left-wing groupings into the Labour Party. This process had begun in 1990 with the merger with Jim Kemmy's Democratic Socialists. In 1992 Cllr Declan Bree and his Independent Socialist Party (Sligo Leitrim) were also brought into the Labour Party.

To be held simultaneously with the general election was a multi-question referendum that sought to tackle the issues brought about by the X case. Two questions related to reaffirming and reasserting the rights to travel and to receive information. The third question sought to limit the definition of the health of a pregnant woman, to exclude psychological health, in assessing the termination of a pregnancy.

The continual although never definitive preoccupation with the issue of abortion in Irish politics helped develop a new subset of political involvement, that of religious-based political parties. In the 1991 local elections, an unregistered grouping stood fourteen candidates under the banner of the Christian Principles Party. None were elected. In 1992 this organisation formally registered with the Registrar of Political Parties, for the purposes of contesting future elections, taking as its new name the Christian Centrist Party.

The election was a disaster for Fianna Fáil. The party lost nine seats and slipped below 40 per cent of the votes for the first time since 1927. Fine Gael, in its first election under John Bruton, lost a similar level of support as Fianna Fáil, while losing even more seats (ten). The big winner in this election was the Labour Party, which more than doubled its presence in Dáil Éireann, now standing at thirty-three TDs. This would be the party's highest ever representation in any Dáil, although its vote share at 20 per cent did not pass the 22 per cent of the vote it had won in 1922. The scale of the Labour success led commentators to entitle this the 'Spring Tide' election, as the party's leader, Dick Spring, was the focus of so much of the campaign.

The Progressive Democrats could take some satisfaction in its performance. Despite having been in government the party bounced back, going from six seats to ten. There was a slight decrease in the party's vote share, as the party took a more strategic approach in running fewer candidates. Back in the Dáil were Michael Mac Dowell (Dublin South East) and Martin Cullen (Waterford). Former party General Secretary, now MEP, Pat Cox, added TD to his political portfolio, winning the seat that had been held by Pearse Wyse in Cork South Central. New to the parliamentary party was Liz O'Donnell (part of the party's local election cohort in 1991) who was elected in Dublin South. Having served as a Senator, Helen Keogh was elected for the party in Dun Laoghaire.

That PD gain in Dublin South was at the expense of the Green Party. Roger Garland had been targeted since he had been elected. When complaining how an extradition process was being followed on Sinn Féin IRA activist, Dessie Ellis (on which he was legally correct), he left himself open to be charged by Mary Harney of being a 'fellow traveller' of the IRA, a charge that never played well in South Dublin, causing considerable political damage to Garland.

Garland's situation had not been helped either by the independent candidacy in his constituency of Richard Greene. Greene had been a Fianna Fáil activist who annoyed party ministers with a preoccupation with policy on extradition. He was also possessed of a deeply conservative mindset on social issues. He was invited by Garland to contest the local elections on behalf of the Greens. He achieved the distinction of becoming the first Green candidate to be elected to a County Council. His tenure as a Green Councillor was a short and difficult one. He resigned on discovering that most Green party members did not share his perspective on social issues.

It might have happened, at this stage, that the Green Party would have largely disappeared from Irish political life. The party's vote share remained static but was now spread more thinly over more candidates. It was the Labour Party underestimating its likely success that threw an unexpected lifeline to the Greens. In the Dublin North constituency, which had been a three-seater but now had an additional seat, Labour stood the highly popular Seán Ryan, on his own. Without a Labour Party colleague to transfer to, Ryan's surplus helped to elect Trevor Sargent.

This election had come too soon for the Democratic Left. Three of the breakaway Workers' Party TDs failed to be re-elected – Joe Sherlock, Pat McCartan and Eric Byrne. One shaft of light was the election of a new TD Liz McManus in Wicklow, a constituency her husband John had contested a number of times for the Workers' Party.

Together, Democratic Left and the Workers' Party won about 70 per cent of the vote they had achieved in 1989. This impacted worse on the Workers' Party, whose vote share was a quarter that of Democratic Left. The party was defending one seat, that of sixty-nine-year-old Tomás Mac Giolla in Dublin West. He seemed well placed to retain the seat when transfers placed him ahead for the final available seat on the tenth count. There he would stay until the fourteenth and final count, when a transfer from Brian Lenihan to his Fianna Fáil colleague, Liam Lawlor, put Lawlor fifty votes ahead.

Presiding officer for that count was Dublin County Council official George Redmond, who would achieve future renown through his investigation by the Flood Tribunal and ultimate conviction for corruption. This has led retrospectively to the forming of conspiratorial thoughts by some. The Workers' Party had one other strong performance by Martin O'Regan in Waterford, where he polled 3,000 votes. The party now had a significant presence in only these two constituencies. A sideshow at the Dublin West count was the first electoral involvement, under a Militant Labour banner, of Joe Higgins. He won 1,407 votes.

Previous colleagues in Sinn Féin were not performing any better. Running nearly a full slate of candidates, the party saw no major increase in its vote. None of its candidates were coming close to being elected, although in the Cavan Monaghan constituency there were some signs of hope. Six years into its 'armalite and the ballot box' strategy, the party in the Republic was making no perceptible forward movement.

The newly registered Christian Centrist Party ran five candidates in this election, in the constituencies of Cork North Central, Donegal North East, Dublin North West, Dublin South Central and Wicklow. None of its candidates breached four figures in their votes. The national total received by the party was 3,413 votes.

A yet to be registered party, the Natural Law Party, put forward nine candidates. Part of an international movement promoting the practice of transcendental meditation, its message did not seem to resonate. The collective support of its nine candidates was 728 votes.

The number of independents in Dáil Éireann increased to five, with the election of Johnny Fox in Wicklow. A well-known publican, he had decided to run as an independent when he could not secure a nomination from Fianna Fáil. Also standing in the Wicklow constituency was the established Dublin University Senator, Shane Ross, testing the waters unsuccessfully as a Fine Gael candidate.

The strategy regarding the three-question abortion referendum became unstuck. The intention was to encourage voters to vote yes, yes, yes. Many voters felt bemused that they were being asked to reassert basic rights of information and travel. On the substantive questions, voters were unconvinced. The threat of suicide and the psychological well-being of a mother had to be taken into account if a pregnancy was being terminated.

All votes counted, attention turned to how a government could be formed. After some tick-tacking with Democratic Left, which Labour wanted in government, a formal meeting was organised between John Bruton and Dick Spring in the Constitution Room of the Shelbourne Hotel ten days after the election. The final result had just been confirmed and after a series of recounts the final seat had been given to Fianna Fáil's Ben Briscoe over Democratic Left's Eric Byrne by the narrowest of margins.

Bruton was slow to recognise the changed dynamic. These were now two parties of comparable size. Bruton also did not realise how the humiliation Labour felt it had experienced in the previous FG Labour government would make Dick Spring feel even less willing to bend to Fine Gael's whims. Bruton wanted a government that included the PDs, a centre right administration. Labour's preference was to include the Democratic Left – creating a centre left government. Neither Fine Gael nor the PDs were willing to have Democratic Left in government. At a later meeting which included Des O'Malley, Spring repeated not only his insistence that Democratic Left should be involved, but that he should serve two years of a five-year term of government as Taoiseach.

Unofficially a number of senior Labour Party TDs, working through Ruairí Quinn, were having a parallel discussion with Fianna Fáil. These talks indicated that Fianna Fáil was prepared to accede to the vast majority of Labour's demands in order that a government could be formed.

Neither set of talks was completed by the time the Dáil reconvened. On 14 December the House met to elect Seán Treacy to continue in his role as Ceann Comhairle. The nominations for Taoiseach were taken, with Albert Reynolds, John Bruton and Dick Spring offerered for assessment. Reynolds gained the predictable support of Neil Blaney. The Progressive Democrats supported the candidacy of John Bruton. Backing Dick Spring were Democratic Left, Trevor Sargent of the Greens and independent Tony Gregory. With no successful candidate, the Dáil voted itself grace time to allow an opportunity for a Taoiseach and a government to be agreed.

In the meantime, Albert Reynolds felt he had procured an ace that would greatly increase his prospects. After a European Council summit in Edinburgh he returned to Dublin to claim that his boast during the Maastricht referendum that Ireland was due receive £6 billion in European Cohesion Funds was being exceeded and that the country would instead be receiving £8 billion. In this he was being somewhat economical with the truth. More money would, indeed, be made available, but over a longer time period.

Des O'Malley, in a phrase half intended to amuse and half meant to create a fear of the unknown, said likely Labour minister Michael D. Higgins 'would go mad in government'. It did not make Labour TDs more inclined to work with the PDs.

Before a final vote on the selection of a Taoiseach, Albert Reynolds made one final decision. Appointed as Ireland's new European Commissioner was Pádraig Flynn as the Irish representative on the European Commission. After his performance in the Presidential election, that was one appointment with which the Labour Party did not want to be associated.

On 12 January 1993 the Dáil met, six weeks after the general election to take a conclusive vote. Albert Reynolds was elected Taoiseach on a vote of 102 to 60. Fianna Fáil and Labour were joined by Neil Blaney and Tom Foxe. Johnny Fox and Tony Gregory abstained. The cabinet formed included six Labour ministers. New government departments were created to facilitate Labour coming into government – the Department of Equality and Law Reform and the Department of Arts, Culture and the Gaeltacht.

Nobody would have predicted this government, with a beaten Taoiseach subsequently getting the highest vote received for a nominee in a Dáil vote. Labour was experiencing its greatest moment of triumph. This was traditionally the moment that Labour began to turn in on itself.

In February 1993 a new Seanad was elected. For the first time in an age, 'others' were successful in being elected through the vocational panels. John Dardis and Cathy Honan were elected on behalf of the Progressive Democrats. Joe Sherlock was elected for Democratic Left. These candidates were elected because of a voting pact between the Progressive Democrats, Democratic Left and the Green Party – parties with no shared philosophies but with a mathematical capacity to work the system. The author of this book shared in this process, being the Green Party 'guinea pig'. He stood in the Cultural and Educational panel – a good vote but distant from a seat.

In the university constituencies new independents included Joe Lee replacing Brendan Ryan on the National University of Ireland panel. Mary Henry replaced Carmencita Hederman on the Dublin University panel. The Taoiseach appointed only one independent Senator from his eleven appointees. This was Gordon Wilson, whose daughter was killed in the atrocity of the Enniskillen bombing.

An early sign of the new government working well together was the passage of legislation decriminalising homosexuality, acting on the European Court of Human Rights *Norris v Ireland* decision. The bill was piloted through the Oireachtas by the Minister for Justice, Máire Geoghegan Quinn.

A new government settling into place gave Des O'Malley pause on what he should be doing in relation to the party he helped found. He decided that after nearly eight years in charge it was time for someone else to lead the party. He gave approval on his intentions to his original co-conspirator, Mary Harney. A possible challenger for the position, Pat Cox, found himself in Vienna when the announcement was made. This gave Harney an early opportunity with her parliamentary colleagues. When a vote was taken, Harney was a clear winner. Cox became deputy leader of the party. Harney's selection was undoubtedly historic. She would be the first directly elected leader of an Irish political party.

In Northern Ireland, murderous events continued. An IRA bomb on Shankill Road killed ten people. Retaliation followed with the killing of eight people in a pub at Greysteel, County Derry. These acts seemed to strengthen the resolve of the British and Irish Governments to bring forward an effective initiative to end the bloodshed. In December the British Prime Minister John Major, and the Taoiseach, Albert Reynolds, agreed and published *The Downing Street Declaration*, a joint framework on progressing towards peace in the region.

It was an election year in 1994, with elections for town councils and the European Parliament. A number of by-elections (the first in a decade) were also held. The positioning for these elections produced some interesting results within a number of political parties.

As PD leader, Mary Harney was hoping that Pat Cox would become more involved in national politics, allowing Des O'Malley to have his political swan song in the European Parliament. In contesting the general election Cox had told the voters of Cork South Central that in seeking a seat in Dáil Éireann he would not seek re-election to the European Parliament at the subsequent election. Unhappy at how he been treated in relation to the leadership of the PDs, he began to re-think his position. In May he resigned from the Progressive Democrats to announce his attempt to retain a seat in the European Parliament. In doing this he reversed his promise to Cork South Central voters, now saying that if re-elected to the European Parliament he would resign his seat in Dáil Éireann.

The turnout for the European Elections was lower than the previous elections, as the 1989 elections were held at the same time as a general election. A number of seats were won by independents and 'others', following that election. This time around, it was these seats that were re-allocated. Fianna Fáil inched upwards, winning one additional seat. Fine Gael stood still, holding its four seats. Likewise Labour, with its single seat. It was the Green Party that was the story of this election, winning two seats it never held before. One independent was elected and that independent was not T.J. Maher, who had retired at this election. His replacement came from Munster. So the big story from the Munster Euro-constituency was the performance of the first-time Fianna Fáil candidate, Brian Crowley. Son of former Fianna Fáil TD, Flor Crowley, Brian had been appointed to The Seanad by Albert Reynolds in 1993. A wheelchair user, after a series of childhood accidents, he scored over 84,000 votes, 35,000 votes ahead of his nearest competitor.

It was expected that the only other story from Munster would be the contest between Des O'Malley and Pat Cox. That tale did not disappoint. After the first count O'Malley was less than 4,000 votes ahead. He remained ahead until the ninth of the twelve counts, when a transfer from a Catholic values independent candidate, Nora Bennis (who had performed well) put Pat Cox ahead. Cox also did better than O'Malley from the transfers of Labour's Jim Kemmy. This surprised some because Kemmy and O'Malley shared the same Dáil constituency. Cox was also from Limerick. He had taken his first political steps there as an unsuccessful local election candidate for Fianna Fáil. In the end Cox's margin of victory over O'Malley was less than 3,000 votes.

No one had seen the Greens coming. Despite the large votes amassed by Trevor Sargent and Seán English in 1989, there was a feeling among political commentators that these votes were a one-off because of circumstances that only existed then. The party on this occasion contested the four Euro-constituencies, the first time it was seeking a preference from every voter in the country. As a strategy, it seemed to work well. The 1989 totals were added to in the Dublin and Leinster Euro-constituencies, bringing about the election of Patricia McKenna (who topped the poll in Dublin) and Nuala Ahern. The party won over 90,000 votes, 8 per cent of the national poll.

The votes received by Democratic Left, Sinn Féin and the Workers' Party differed little from the votes the parties had received in the general election. The now officially registered Natural Law Party stood a candidate in each of the four Euro-constituencies winning 5,000 votes, 0.4 per cent of the national poll.

The 1994 local elections held on that day involved Urban District Councils and Town Commissions. There were 744 seats contested. The location of these councils was outside of the main metropolitan centres. The demography of these areas was more favourable for some political parties over others. Two-thirds of the vote went to either Fianna Fáil, Fine Gael or Labour. Two-thirds of the remaining vote went to independent candidates, who won 159 seats. The seats won by other parties were as follows Sinn Féin (twenty-four); Progressive Democrats (eighteen); Democratic Left (eleven); Green Party (six); Workers' Party (one) and South Kerry Independent Party (one). The Natural Law Party stood one candidate who won seventeen votes.

Two by-elections were also held on that day. There had been a vacancy in Mayo West for eighteen months, since Pádraig Flynn had been appointed as European Commissioner. The size of the government's majority made it arrogantly indifferent about filling the vacancy. Pádraig Flynn's daughter, Beverley was chosen as his successor. She topped the poll on the first count but was less than 600 votes ahead of Fine Gael's colourful county councillor, Michael Ring. There was a strong performance from an independent candidate, Paddy McGuinness, who won

21 per cent of the vote. It was his transfers that helped give Michael Ring a substantial victory.

The second by-election was in Dublin South Central. Dr John O'Connell had resigned his seat. Having been a Labour TD, an independent TD, the Ceann Comhairle of the Dáil, joining Fianna Fáil losing his Dáil seat, becoming a Fianna Fáil Senator, then ultimately becoming a Fianna Fáil government minister, he may have felt that it was unlikely that he would ever be back at the top table. He was one of the few members of the Oireachtas who was not dependent on a public salary to maintain a living. As the publisher of specialist titles – including *The Irish Medical Times* – his financial future was already assured.

His was a second government seat that was being challenged. The frontrunner for the seat was Eric Byrne of the Democratic Left. Having fallen short at the longest election count at the previous general election, his profile was the strongest of any of the candidates in this by-election. It did not surprise that he topped the poll, far ahead of his nearest challenger. Neither did his ability to attract transfers surprise. This was a by-election where the collective 'others' vote was more than the combined Fianna Fáil-Fine Gael-Labour vote. Eric Byrne's election made mathematically possible Dick Spring's preferred Fine Gael-Labour-Democratic Left government that he looked for in November 1992.

The poor electoral performance of the government parties was being somewhat offset by good news from what increasingly was being referred to as the Peace Process. In August the Provisional IRA announced a cessation of military activity. This was followed in October by a similar statement by the Combined Loyalist Military Command. A tripartite meeting at Government Buildings between Albert Reynolds, John Hume of the SDLP and Sinn Féin's Gerry Adams (whose secret talks could be said to have begun the peace process) marked another important step in seeking peace.

The government could have and probably should have fallen in August, with the publication of the Beef Tribunal (Hamilton) report. Having first received the report as Taoiseach, Albert Reynolds blocked its release until he had prepared a personal defence. The findings supported many of the accusations that had been tabled against Reynolds, including those that had originally been made by Dick Spring. Trust within the government had been significantly undermined.

Whatever electoral and political difficulties were being experienced by the government parties seemed to be paralleled by the Progressive Democrats. When Pat Cox resigned from the PDs, the party leadership panicked, contacting PD TDs who supported Cox for the leadership. TDs like Peadar Clohesey and Martin Cullen were contacted and asked if they were staying with the party. With Martin Cullen, it seemed such fears were well placed. By September, Cullen had left the Progressive Democrats to become a Fianna Fáil TD.

In October the government rolled out a piece of its peace process strategy. A Forum for Peace and Reconcilliation held its first plenary session. Chaired by former independent Dublin University Senator (by now an eminent jurist) Catherine McGuinness, weighted delegations attended from Fianna Fáil, Fine Gael, the SDLP, Labour, Sinn Féin, the Progressive Democrats, the Alliance Party of Northern Ireland, the Democratic Left, the Green Party, Independent TDs, Independent Senators, the Workers' Party, and, in a personal capacity, Senator Gordon Wilson.

Also in October, for the second time (the other being a 1991 ITV *World in Action* programme which asked the questions that brought about the Beef Tribunal) UTV's *Counterpoint* broadcast both sides of the border, highlighted negligence within the Irish State. In this instance it was Church and State collusion centring around the protection of a serial child abuser called Fr Brendan Smyth.

November saw two Cork by-elections being held. If he believed in omens, Albert Reynolds would have been aware that two Cork by-elections speeded the end of the career of Jack Lynch. The Cork North Central by-election was brought about by the early death of the popular Labour TD, Gerry O'Sullivan. His daughter Lisa was chosen to defend the seat. The chief challenger, although not immediately obvious, turned out to be Kathleen Lynch of the Democratic Left. Kathleen, while from the north side of the city, had been elected a councillor and had contested a number of elections for the Workers' Party Democratic Left, south of the river. Her unpretentious style was winning over voters in this by-election. She topped the poll, 300 votes ahead of her Fianna Fáil rival, Billy Kelleher. It was where she needed to be. Transfers were always more likely to help her eventual success.

The by-election in Cork South Central had come about by Pat Cox MEP fulfilling his (secondary) promise to resign his Dáil seat should he be re-elected to the European Parliament. The contest was expected to be a straight fight between two former TDs, John Dennehy of Fianna Fáil and Hugh Coveney of Fine Gael. An opinion poll during the campaign showed that the Green Party candidate Dan Boyle was contesting second place with Fine Gael's Hugh Coveney. Coveney rebuffed Boyle's challenge, but still required Boyle's transfers to claim the seat over Dennehy. Among the other challengers was the once and future independent National University of Ireland Senator Brendan Ryan, seeking to become an independent TD. This by-election also saw the first appearance of the Christian Solidarity Party. The 1,700 votes won by its candidate, Catherine Kelly, were the equivalent of votes won here by the Labour and the PD candidates. The party's name was a redesignation of the Christian Centrist Party that had contested the 1992 general election. The Solidarity title was meant to indicate an affinity with the campaigning group, Family Solidarity, a group linked with anti-abortion and family values causes.

After four by-elections in 1994 the government parties had lost three seats. Labour candidates had performed particularly poorly. Despite these political setbacks, Albert Reynolds, head of a government that had still to deal with the fallout from the Beef Tribunal, or with the State's far from adequate response to the clerical abuse of children, had chosen the day of the counts of the Cork by-elections to have the cabinet (without the presence of any Labour ministers) approve the appointment of the Attorney General, Harry Whelehan (who had dealt with the Brendan Smyth case) to become President of the High Court.

Whelehan was sworn into office on 15 November. Dick Spring and other Labour cabinet members resigned from government the following day. Whelehan resigned his office on 17 November, but the damage had already been done. Albert Reynolds resigned as leader of Fianna Fáil on 19 November, replaced by Bertie Ahern. At first it seemed that a Fianna Fáil–Labour arrangement might be renewed. However, on the cusp of such an agreement Spring and his team decided to throw in their lot with Fine Gael and the Democratic Left. On 15 December John Bruton became Taoiseach, forming a new government without a general election being held. A special Dáil committee sitting in the Dáil chamber under the chairmanship of Fianna Fáil's Dan Wallace drew significant daytime viewership figures when examining these events.

The new government consisted of eight Fine Gael ministers, six Labour ministers and and a single Democratic Left minister (Proinsias De Rossa). The junior ranks were increased to accommodate the demands of the three parties. Fine Gael was allocated nine ministers of State, Labour five and Democratic Left three. One of these, Pat Rabbitte, would be known as a super junior, given the right to attend but not vote at cabinet meetings. Four of the six Democratic Left TDs now held ministerial rank.

Politically 1995 was a pause for breath after the frenetic activity of 1994. There was one by-election held that year. A number of significant political deaths occurred in 1995. Independent TD from Wicklow, Johnny Fox, died. Independent Senator Gordon Wilson passed away. During his brief time in the Seanad, the man who bore no ill-will nor grudge impressed many with his quiet dignity. He was replaced in the Seanad by the well-known Northern Ireland journalist, Sam McAughtry. He sat as an independent Senator, having been recommended for nomination by the Democratic Left. September saw the deaths of Brian Lenihan, former Tánaiste and presidential candidate, and of Neil Blaney, fulcrum of the Independent Fianna Fáil organisation in Donegal.

The Wicklow by-election took place in June. The Fox organisation put forward Johnny's daughter, Mildred, as his successor. She topped the poll on the first count, and was never likely to be caught by her Fianna Fáil challenger, Dick Roche. Another strong independent performance was that of Nicky Kelly. Kelly had been in prison having been convicted for taking part in the robbery of a railway train. He was released on a Presidential pardon, his conviction seen to be a miscarriage of justice. Although standing in this by-election as an independent, he had once been a member of the IRSP.

A further interesting sideline was the candidacy, on behalf of Democratic Left, of John McManus, husband of then TD Liz. His election would have seen a husband and wife elected for the same constituency within the same Dáil. The Fianna Fáil–Fine Gael–Labour poll at this by-election was 47 per cent of the vote, being another sign of changing times.

A new entry appeared on the Register of Political Parties. It was for a new party called Muintir na hÉireann. Built around the profile and the personality of Richard Greene (an independent councillor who had had orginally been elected for the Green Party), its unique selling point was Greene's blend of being anti-abortion and anti-extradition.

The peace process moved fitfully in Northern Ireland. David Trimble became leader of the Ulster Unionist Party, determined to take on Ian Paisley for the leadership of the wider unionist community. A touchstone issue was the right of Orange Order marches to walk along 'Queens' highway. One route from Drumcree to the centre of Portadown town passed a nationalist enclave on Garvaghy Road. Despite being asked to take an alternative route the march went on its 'traditional' route, ending in Portadown, with Paisley and Trimble raising each other's arms in triumph. Later that summer Gerry Adams was telling a rally in Belfast that the IRA 'haven't gone away you know'. So there was still a journey to travel.

In Dublin, the Rainbow government (a not particularly appropriate, but now widely used name for the Bruton administration) agreed to put to the people, once again, a constitutional referendum to remove the legal prohibition on divorce. Nine years earlier the proposition had been comprehensively defeated. This time opinion polls seemed to indicate that another result might be possible.

A fly in the ointment was a court action taken by Green MEP Patricia McKenna challenging the government on using public money to persuade people to take a particular position when considering constitutional referenda. The action was overturned in the Supreme Court on a four-to-one majority. An important democratic principle had been established, a principle that many in Irish politics, then and since, have never really accepted.

One week later the referendum was held. On the following day when the votes were being counted, the result was uncertain until the last constituency had submitted its returns. The referendum was passed by a margin of 9,114 votes, or 0.56 per cent of the poll.

On 9 February 1996 the IRA ceasefire came to a shuddering halt with the bombing of the Canary Wharf financial district in London. One person was killed and forty people injured. Sinn Féin continued to have a presence on the Forum for Peace and Reconciliation. Later in the year a Garda detective called Gerry McCabe was shot dead in the aftermath of an IRA bank robbery in Adare, County Limerick. At this time hope seemed further away than ever.

Outside of IRA violence, confidence in public safety was severely dented when crusading journalist Veronica Guerin was shot dead in her car by a passing motorcyclist. Guerin had been exposing the criminal gangs that were flooding Dublin with hard drugs, creating a multi-million pound criminal business.

An issue that had plagued the Rainbow government since it was formed was how the government, the Department of Health, and most particularly its Minister, Michael Noonan was dealing with how agencies of the State had supplied contaminated blood products which led to serious health issues and the eventual deaths of many victims. Bridget McCole from Donegal was seen as the victim most representative of this crisis. The way in which she was dealt with by official Ireland was seen by many as cold and offhand. By 1995 the government had been forced to establish a Tribunal of Inquiry, which sat for the first time in 1996.

The by-elections on foot of the deaths of Brian Lenihan and Neil Blaney took place in April. In Donegal North East, Fianna Fáil ended Independent Fianna Fáil's continued Dáil presence. Neil Blaney's brother Harry came close to retaining the seat but found himself being beaten by Fianna Fáil's Cecilia Keaveney. The irony of this defeat was that Cecilia's father Paddy had been the victor of an earlier Donegal by-election, on behalf of Independent Fianna Fáil.

In Dublin West an extremely varied field of candidates led to a very split vote. In topping the poll Fianna Fáil's Brian Lenihan Jr had less than half the vote he needed to pass the quota. He was closely chased by Joe Higgins who was standing under a Militant Labour banner. Since his explusion from the Labour Party, Higgins (and those around him), had engaged in street politics, identifying and fomenting issues on which political support would be built upon public discontent. For Joe Higgins in this by-election that issue was water charges.

After the first count Lenihan was ahead of Higgins by 252 votes. The total Fianna Fáil Fine Gael vote was 41.5 per cent of the total vote. Given the narrowness of his first-count lead and the distance that still had to be bridged to reach the quota, Brian Lenihan's win in this by-election was quite remarkable. Tomás Mac Giolla continued to contest here for the Workers' Party, winning another solid (10 per cent) vote, but Higgins's performance meant he had slipped further down the pecking order in relation to the left-wing vote.

In November 1996 a constitutional referendum to allow for a tightening of the bail laws was promoted. The demand for the referendum had been induced to create an impression of a political response. Most voters were indifferent and less than 30 per cent of the electorate took part. Those that did participate approved the measure on a three-to-one margin.

Neither by-election was for a government seat, so the Dáil arithmetic remained unaffected. The next cleavage would occur in the largest party in government, Fine Gael. The Department of Transport, Energy and Communication would not ordinarily be the first choice of investigative journalists looking for evidence of political corruption. The Minister at that department, Michael Lowry, was attracting much attention to himself for how he was going about his duties.

First elected as a TD in 1987, he had established a high reputation as a fundraiser in Tipperary. He had been associated with helping the local GAA organisation pay off money for the development of Semple Stadium in Thurles, within a short time period. The holding of the Féile music festivals was a key part of that strategy. Asked to play a similar role within Fine Gael, Lowry managed to eliminate a £3 million debt held by the party.

It was Lowry's ability to raise funds for personal use that would prove to be his eventual undoing. A key decision to be made by his department was one to grant a second mobile phone licence. The successful bid was to come from an Irish company, ESAT Digiphone, owned by Denis O'Brien. The success of the bid provoked questions about the efficacy of the process. Those questions would be later asked at a different forum.

It was the news that Dunne Stores, through principal shareholder, Ben Dunne, had paid for a £200,000 extension to Lowry's house (built without planning permission), that eventually forced Lowry's resignation as Minister. At a press event announcing his resignation, where both attended, Lowry referred to the Taoiseach, John Bruton, as 'My best friend. My best friend forever'.

In February 1997 another tribunal of inquiry was established. It came to be known as the McCracken Tribunal after its sole member, High Court judge Brian McCraken. The remit of the Tribunal was to investigate payments given to Charles Haughey and Michael Lowry. One of the motivations in establishing the Tribunal was to remove these issues from political debate – debate that was focused on an upcoming general election. The Tribunal began taking evidence in April.

John Bruton called this election for 26 June 1997. Twelve registered political parties contested this election, more than had contested any previous election. Labour was not looking forward to this election with as much enthusiasm as others. The party did not seem to be earning reward for its participation in either government in which it had taken part since 1992. Having won an additional eighteen seats in 1992, its total would be sixteen seats lower. Fianna Fáil won an additional ten seats (although the party still remained below 40 per cent of the national vote). Fine Gael won an extra seven seats, coming out of government in a far more healthy state than either of its former partners.

The other partner, Democratic Left, did not have a particularly happy election. The party lost two seats when their two by-election victors (Eric Byrne and Kathleen Lynch) failed to win through in a general election. There was no upward trajectory in the party's vote.

At least Democratic Left could get some satisfaction from being equal in size to the Progressive Democrats in the Dáil chamber. For the PDs this was an extremely poor election. The party remained static in terms of its vote share, a vote share that had elected ten TDs in 1992 only elected four in 1997. Re-elected were party leader Mary Harney, Des O'Malley (now the only PD TD in Limerick East), Bobby Molloy and Liz O'Donnell in Dublin South. The party had lost two seats through defections in 1994. Seats lost at this general election were those of Michael McDowell (who in his four elections had been elected in, out, in and out); Helen Keogh in Dun Laoghaire (a constituency that had also taken a yes-no approach to the PDs; Mairín Quill in Cork North Central and Peadar Clohessy in Limerick East.

The Green Party doubled its votes (albeit from a low base) and eventually doubled its seats. The long count of the 1997 election involved Michael MacDowell of the Progressive Democrats and John Gormley of the Green Party, in the Dublin South East constituency. Gormley had been twenty-seven votes ahead of MacDowell at the final count, before a series of recounts had every mark on every ballot paper re-examined. This process saw Gormley pulling further away. Eventually MacDowell conceded.

The election saw forward progress for the Greens, although the expectation created by the European elections in 1994 had not been met. The party was especially disappointed that the vote gained in the Cork South Central by-election was not repeated.

Despite the breakdown in the IRA ceasefire, Sinn Féin, eleven years after its 1986 Ard Fheis, had finally made a breakthrough in having a candidate elected to sit in Dáil Éireann. The election of Caoimhghín Ó Caoláin in Cavan Monaghan was as much due to his nursing the constituency than to any upsurge in the Sinn Féin vote, which still remained at a modest level.

An eighth political party was represented after Militant Labour. Fresh from its near success in the Dublin West by-election, Joe Higgins and his associates registered as a political party called the Socialist Party. The party was not related to the party of the same name that existed in the 1970s and 80s. Nor was it linked the Roddy Connolly's communist linked party of the 1920s. Joe Higgins's Socialist Party succeeded where none of those parties had, by having him elected. Four other colleagues also stood but none was elected.

Six independents were elected to the Twenty-eighth Dáil, making this the most diverse Dáil that had ever been elected. Tony Gregory was elected for the fifth successive election. Mildred Fox repeated her by-election success in Wicklow. Harry Blaney did better than his by-election experience, regaining the Dáil seat his brother had held since 1948. Another Donegal independent was Thomas Gildea, elected on foot of a campaign opposing the government's attempts to stop the unlicenced rebeaming of television signals.

Formerc government minister Michael Lowry was re-invented as a poll-topping Tipperary independent. That sixth independent would introduce a pinch of surrealness to the incoming Dáil.

Jackie Healy Rae had, over the course of several general elections, been Fianna Fáil's director of elections for the Kerry South constituency. His local reputation was that he was expert in the art of electioneering. In 1997 he felt it was his turn to be a candidate. When Fianna Fáil's lead candidate John O'Donoghue stymied a nomination, it led Healy Rae to declare and then become elected as an independent. He topped the poll sixteen votes ahead of O'Donoghue. His strong Kerry accent and comb-over hair would become a trademark of the incoming Dáil.

The outgoing Ceann Comhairle Sean Treacy retired at this election. Tom Foxe, the independent who had been elected with the support of the Roscommon Hospital Action Group, failed to retain the seat, his vote diluted in a new constituency, Longford Roscommon.

Others tried but failed to be elected. A new entrant to the field of religious identity politics was the National Party, founded by and formed around Nora Bennis, who had performed strongly in the 1994 European elections. The party stood sixteen candidates, winning 19,000 votes. Nora Bennis, as party leader, stood in the Limerick East constituency, contesting with former leaders of two other political parties (Des O'Malley and Jim Kemmy) and one future leader of another (Michael Noonan). The appearance of the National Party caused concern to the Christian Solidarity Party (CSP), which had changed its name to appeal to Bennis's organisation. CSP led by Gerard Casey ran six candidates winning over 8,000 votes. A third Catholic values-based party, Muintir na hÉireann, did not contest. The party's founder, Richard Greene, had fallen out with the party's officer board, leaving the party to run, unsuccessfully, as an independent in the general election.

It was a terrible election for the Workers' Party, winning less than 8,000 votes. Most of these votes went to the party's Waterford candidate, Martin O'Regan. O'Regan had improved his vote from the 1992 election. He would end up being the fifth-placed candidate for the four available seats in the constituency, without ever really challenging for the seat. Party stalwart Tomás Mac Giolla experienced severe disappointment, losing almost two-thirds of the vote he had won in the 1996 by-election.

A newcomer on the left side of the aisle was the Socialist Workers Party. Older members of this group had operated as a faction in the formers Socialist Labour Party in the early 1980s, having existed since the early 1970s, and subsequent to the SLP's demise, as the Socialist Workers Movement. The decision to become a party was made in 1995, with the formal registration happening before the general election in 1997. Four candidates stood on its behalf, winning around 2,000 votes.

The Natural Law Party ran eleven candidates, winning about 1,500 votes. Advocating a different type of high was the Cannabis Legalisation Party (unregistered). Seeking to draw attention to the issue were two candidates, *Hot Press* journalist Olaf Tyaransen, who stood in Dun Laoghaire, and Tim Murphy standing in Cork South Central. Between them they won 1,000 votes, with Cork seeming to be twice as liberal as Dun Laoghaire.

A quarter of the 1,388 votes won by Cllr Michael Gleeson, standing under his registered party vehicle the South Kerry Independent Alliance, transferred to Jackie Healy Rae, becoming a big factor in his election.

The vacancies created in the Seanad by Senators elected to the Dáil allowed John Bruton to appoint a number of short-term members of the House. Among these was a Democratic Left nominee, Wexford County Councillor Michael Enright. The result of all this diversity was an uncertainty about what kind of government could be formed and who would lead it.

19

The Most Devious, the Most Cunning of Them All

Fianna Fáil had worked the proportional voting system well in its favour. With seventy-seven seats the party was still was six seats shy of a majority in the Dáil. The Progressive Democrats could supply four of those seats. Relationships between the two parties had improved during the two-and-a-half years that they had shared in opposition. Throughout the election campaign both parties stressed that they could work together in government. Labour and Fianna Fáil mutually ruled each other out. Bertie Ahern had said he would not talk with Sinn Féin about in forming a government. Fianna Fáil and the Progressive Democrats seemed to be wishing each other into Leinster House. Negotiations between the parties began on 10 June, successfully completing on 13 June. Then it was a process of convincing a sufficient number of independents, many of whom had come from the Fianna Fáil 'gene pool'.

On 26 June the Dáil met to select a Ceann Comhairle, nominate a Taoiseach and approve a government. Dick Spring nominated his colleague Seamus Pattison, the outgoing deputy Ceann Comhairle, to be accepted for the senior position. The putative Fianna Fáil PD government was happy to see one less opposition vote. Pattison was elected unanimously.

Nominations for the position of Taoiseach were taken for John Bruton and for Bertie Ahern. Bruton received the support of the outgoing Rainbow government plus that of Michael Lowry. The rest of the house divided against him, with the exception of the two Green TDs and the independent TD, Thomas Gildea. In addition to the support of Fianna Fáil and PD TDs were the independents Mildred Fox, Harry Blaney and Jackie Healy Rae. In his (and on behalf of his party) first vote, Caoimhghín Ó Caoláin supported the election of Bertie Ahern as Taoiseach. The rest of the House, with the exception of Thomas Gildea, but including the votes of the Green Party TDs, opposed Ahern's election.

The new Taoiseach got to choose his cabinet. It contained fourteen Fianna Fáil ministers and one Progressive Democrat. The PD minister was Mary Harney, named Minister for Enterprise and Employment. She was also named Tánaiste, the first woman as well as the first Progressive Democrat to hold that office.

Two Ministers of State were also announced, Seamus Brennan as Government Chief Whip and the PD Bobby Molloy as Minister for State at the Department of the Environment. His was a 'super junior' position with the right to attend cabinet but not vote. A number of days later Liz O'Donnell was made a Minister of State at the Department of Foreign Affairs. Three of the four members of the PD parliamentary party now held ministerial office, the exception being the party's founder, Des O'Malley.

Seamus Brennan had been a long-time friend of many of the senior TDs. He had facilitated meetings for them as they considered whether they should form a new party. Brennan chose to stay in Fianna Fáil as a supportive presence in government. Of a similar bent was the newly appointed Minister for Finance, Charlie McCreevy. He would have been looking forward to implementing those PD-influenced sections of the programme for government that sought to reduce the higher rate of income tax, corporation tax and the halving of capital gains tax.

What the PDs would have been less happy about was the appointment to cabinet of the minister for a day, Jim McDaid, whose removal from office the PDs had sought in an earlier administration. The appointment of their former colleague Martin Cullen as a Minister of State cannot have been too comfortable either.

The general election in Ireland had been preceded a month earlier by a significant change in British politics. A New Labour government had been formed under a fresh-faced Prime Minister, Tony Blair, who appointed an enthusiastic Secretary of State for Northern Ireland called Mo Mowlam.

The new mandates of Ahern and Blair seemed to give new impetus to the peace process. In July the IRA announced the renewal of its ceasefire.

Gerry Adams agreed to sign the Mitchell Principles that committed Sinn Féin:

To democratic and exclusively peaceful means of resolving political issues;

To the total disarmament of all paramilitary organisations;

To agree that such disarmament must be verifiable to the satisfaction of an independent commission;

To renounce for themselves, and to oppose any effort by others, to use force, or threaten to use force, to influence the course or the outcome of all-party negotiations;

To agree to abide by the terms of any agreement reached in all-party negotiations and to resort to democratic and exclusively peaceful methods in trying to alter any aspect of that outcome with which they may disagree; and,

To urge that 'punishment' killings and beatings stop and to take effective steps to prevent such actions.

These principles were devised by George Mitchell, who had been since 1995 a Special US Envoy on Northern Ireland, appointed by the US President, Bill Clinton.

The McCracken Report was published in August and it found that Michael Lowry was *knowingly assisted* by Ben Dunne in evading tax. The Tribunal also found that Charles Haughey had deliberately obstructed its work. Criminal proceedings against Haughey would follow these charges, but they were withdrawn on foot of public comments made by the Tánaiste, Mary Harney, which were deemed to have prejudiced any likely prosecution. Other findings would form the basis of a new Tribunal of Enquiry – the Moriarty Tribunal.

Worse was to follow when the Minister for Foreign Affairs, Ray Burke, was publicly accused of accepting bribes to procure favourable planning decisions. He offered a television defence against the accusations, saying he was drawing a line in the sand. That line soon shifted as pressure forced him to resign not only his place in the cabinet, but also his seat in the Dáil. These events would lead to the establishment of yet another Tribunal of Enquiry – the Flood Enquiry.

The elections for the Twenty-second Seanad did not produce any electoral breakthrough for others. In the National University of Ireland Brendan Ryan replaced the retiring Joe Lee. The more surprising news was found among the Taoiseach's eleven nominees. Four of these nominations were for the Progressive Democrats, as many members of the Oireachtas as the party had had elected to the Dáil. Returning as an ever-present representative for the party since 1989 was John Dardis. He was joined by defeated TDs Helen Keogh and Mairín Quill. Also appointed for the party was Jim Gibbons Jr, son of the former Fianna Fáil minister and brother of former PD TD, Martin Gibbons.

The only independent nominated to the Seanad by Bertie Ahern was the Northern Irish equivalent of T.K. Whittaker, Maurice Hayes (former head of the civil service in Northern Ireland). Both had come from County Down.

In the interest of disclosure it should also be said that the author was a candidate in this election. With the purpose of discovering the byzantine procedures of a Seanad election, I sought an 'inner' nomination (an Oireachtas nomination). This required the signatures of members of the Dáil or the Seanad. Those of the two Green TDs were easily obtained and I was grateful that Senators Joe Lee and Mary Henry allowed me to continue the adventure. I came within two votes of winning a seat.

September 1997 saw the sad death of Jim Kemmy at 61 years of age. An independent TD and then the leader of his own political party (the Democratic Socialist Party), he had also been the high-profile chairman of the Labour Party. Thoughout his public life he had impressed many with forthright style, and often brutal honesty, while maintaining a warm and decent persona.

One other election, and two other votes took place in 1997. The President, Mary Robinson, would end her term a number of weeks early. She had been approached to become the United Nations High Commissioner on Human Rights and was prepared to accept the position. During her term, she had undertaken a successful official visit to a number of countries in Africa. She also, through her office, played an important role in the Northern Ireland peace process. Her public handshake with Gerry Adams while on a visit to Belfast helped to open many doors there.

Now there would be a vacancy for the office of President of Ireland. Having elected the first female President, most political parties felt that the Robinson template should be used again. Labour was first to reveal its hand. Once again, the party went outside its membership in choosing the anti-nuclear campaigner, Adi Roche. Her candidacy was jointly announced with the Democratic Left and the Green Party, co-sponsors of the campaign.

Fine Gael chose its well-respected MEP, Mary Banotti, grandniece of Michael Collins and sister of former Minister for Justice Nora Owen, to contest. She had overcome another MEP, Avril Doyle, to win her party's nomination.

Fianna Fáil would have an internal contest to decide its nominee. Albert Reynolds had an expectation that he should be the party's candidate. His expectation was not shared by his successor as party leader, Bertie Ahern. The Taoiseach chose a Northern Ireland-born and Northern Ireland-based law professor, Mary McAleese, to put herself forward for the Fianna Fáil nomination.

There were a number of reasons why Ahern believed Reynolds lacked the qualities to follow Mary Robinson as President. When Taoiseach, there were a number of times when Reynolds seemed out of touch with a changing Ireland. His taunt at Fine Gael's Nora Owen '*That's women for you*', had played very badly among likely women voters. More unfair criticism of his use of the word 'crap' was hugely overblown. Ahern's reasoning may also have been personal, given the whispering campaign that had been conducted against him by Reynolds's supporters when Ahern considered challenging for the leadership in 1992.

At the parliamentary meeting making the choice, Ahern went out of his way to display his vote for Reynolds to Reynolds. Among the Reynolds camp this meant that his campaign was doomed. If Ahern had voted for Reynolds then McAleese would already have secured enough votes.

Three candidates had been selected. Ordinarily that would have been enough. No more than three had contested previous elections. The nomination rules, specified by the constitution, made it difficult for others to come forward – difficult but not impossible. The nomination mechanism of getting four County Councils to ratify a candidate had never before been successfully used. Two prospective candidates would seek nomination through this route.

First into the fray was Rosemary Scallon, better known as Dana, the singer who as a 16-year-old had won the Eurovision Song Contest for Ireland in 1970. She had lived for several years in the United States, where she had been successful with Christian media stations. Against the odds, she succeeded in winning the support of five County Councils.

Following her lead was Derek Nally, who had been the General Secretary of the Association of Garda Sergeants and Inspectors (AGSI), but since that position had helped establish the Victim Support organisation, he secured the support of four County Councils. Now there would be five candidates.

Adi Roche had started the campaign enjoying high ratings. These would soon dwindle as her campaign became beset by allegations against her brother and from other charges by disgruntled employees who had worked for her charity. Her effusive campaigning style was as off-putting to some as it was attractive for others. Mary McAleese was also experiencing negative campaigning. Playing on her Northern Ireland background, hostile commentators were referring to her as a 'tribal republican'.

When the votes were counted, Mary McAleese topped the poll with 45 per cent support. She extended her lead in the second count, winning more votes in transfers than had Fine Gael's Mary Banotti. The surprising vote in this election was that of Rosemary Scallon-Dana who won 15 per cent of the vote. This was more the double the vote won by Adi Roche. The token man in the contest, Derek Nally, won 5 per cent of the vote.

Held on the same day as the Presidential election was a constitutional referendum on the subject of cabinet confidentiality. A Supreme Court decision in 1992, responding to a request from a tribunal of enquiry to be able to access cabinet minutes, ruled that cabinet confidentiality was absolute. Work on loosening this principle was begun within the Rainbow government, later finessed by the incoming Fianna Fáil –PD administration. The involvement of five political parties in this process indicated a large degree of consensus. Within the Progressive Democrats this was less clear cut. Michael MacDowell and Des O'Malley pushed for a No vote, arguing that the loosening did not go far enough. Other parties and prominent individuals made similar arguments. The eventual 52 to 48 margin showed that there may have been a degree of misjudgement in how this amendment was framed.

The remaining political drama of 1997 was the selection of a new leader for the Labour Party. Dick Spring had proffered his resignation after the poor general election had been followed by an even more disappointing Presidential election. In a straight fight between the former Minister for Finance, Ruairí Quinn (four years older than outgoing leader, Dick Spring), and former Minister for the Environment, Brendan Howlin (ten years younger than Ruairí Quinn), the campaign ebbed and flowed. The electorate consisted of the party's national executive as well as its parliamentary party. This entitled sixty-four people to vote. These broke 37-27 in favour of Ruairí Quinn.

One of the final pieces of legislation passed by the Rainbow government had been an Electoral Amendment Act. Among the provisions of this act were new provisions introducing the State funding of political parties. These provisions were frozen, not to apply until 1 January 1998. This was to ensure the issue would not cloud the 1997 general election. The Progressive Democrats had opposed the legislation throughout its progression in the Houses of the Oireachtas. Fianna Fáil had been supportive until the general election. Now in government, their collective reservation subsided. However, the funding that had begun had been covered by legislation. It was the smaller parties who were the bigger beneficiaries of this change.

Irish politics was not falling short of drama. In February 1998, the Flood Tribunal, dealing with abuses in the planning system, began its hearings. There were now a number of overlapping tribunals, examining and attempting to expose the actions of those who were being identified as part of a Golden Circle within Irish society. Growing public disquiet had been created by the revelations brought about by the activities of a 'clandestine bank' – Ansbacher.

When it was revealed that Ben Dunne had given over £1 million in payments to Charles Haughey, the public existence of Ansbacher became known. This bank was run by Des Traynor, who had been a managing director of the Guinness and Mahon bank. For privileged customers Traynor established an offshore subsidiary based in the Cayman Islands. There was a distinguished coterie of clients including politicians, professionals and company directors. The Cement Roadstone company (of which Traynor was Chairman) seemed particularly drawn to the attractions of this scheme. This was unlicenced banking activity in Ireland, designed for the purpose of tax avoidance. The assets (the bank accounts) were registered in the Cayman Islands but the money never left Ireland.

One person named on the Ansbacher list was Fine Gael TD and former minister, Hugh Coveney. He was to die, tragically, after falling while taking a cliffside walk with his dogs near his family home. He had closed his account in 1979 and so would not have the opportunity of explaining its content.

In Limerick East and Dublin North, by-elections were held that had been caused by the death of Jim Kemmy and the resignation of Ray Burke. Labour held the seat in Limerick East. The successful candidate, Jan O'Sullivan, had shared Jim Kemmy's political journey, having been a member and a councillor for the Democratic Socialist Party. There was double joy for Labour when former TD Seán Ryan regained a Dáil seat that had been held by Fianna Fáil, by winning the Dublin North by-election.

Losing a by-election was not good for a minority government. Solace existed for the government, despite this small-scale Labour revival, in that no other opposition parties were performing particularly well. In Dublin North the Green Party polled 1,000 votes in a constituency where there was a sitting, high-profile, Green TD. Democratic Left polled well in Limerick East, winning almost 4,000 votes. In Dublin North, the party's candidate won 225 votes. That was a vote that would lead to much soul-searching for the party.

A partial antidote to the public distaste to the now near daily revelations of corruption was coming from the encouraging news that progress was being achieved with the Northern Ireland peace process. After the resumption of the IRA ceasefire and the signing up of various parties to the Mitchell Principles, the Good Friday Agreement was agreed by all parties (with the exception of the Democratic Unionist Party). The contents of the agreement would be put for approval in a referendum, to be held on the same day, in both parts of the island of Ireland.

This referendum took place in May. In the Republic, the Agreement secured the support of more than 94 per cent of those who voted. In Northern Ireland, there was also considerable support for the measure, being approved on a 71 to 29 margin. In Dublin the government also put the most recent changes in the treaties on the European Union (the Treaty of Amsterdam) for consideration on the day. This was a more competitive referendum but still ended up being approved on a 60 to 40 margin.

The Cork South Central by-election was held in October. Hugh Coveney's 26-year-old son Simon was selected as the Fine Gael candidate. The main threat to his election came from Fianna Fáil's Sinéad Behan. Former Labour TD Toddy O'Sullivan polled well, but did not challenge. The Green Party held its general election vote. Transfers from Labour and the Greens helped elect Simon Coveney.

Absent from the Cork by-election was any candidate from Democratic Left. By this stage, the party had entered into talks with Labour on the possibility of merging the two parties. Proinsias De Rossa had made the original approach to Ruairí Quinn, suggesting that a new entity be formed. Labour negotiators would not move on holding on to the party name. The real difficulties existed at local level. Two Dublin constituencies proved particularly difficult, Dublin North West and Dublin South Central. North West was a constituency shared between Róisín Shortall and Democratic Left leader De Rossa. The constituency was due to become a three-seater, because it was felt that two Labour TDs would not be elected there. The potential conflict was averted by De Rossa agreeing not to stand again, preferring to challenge for a European Parliament seat.

The strongest resistance to a merger came from Dublin South Central, where the local Labour TD, Pat Upton, led the opposition. As the merger talks proceeded, these reservations continued to exist. On 12 December the two parties formally decided to merge. Ruairí Quinn was to continue as Labour Party leader. Proinsias De Rossa was given the newly created position of President of the party. From the Democratic Left perspective, the merger seemed to go ahead seamlessly.

Four councillors (three from Meath County Council and one from Carlow County Council) resigned from Labour, along with a former TD (Brian Fitzgerald in Meath).

During its short, life Democratic Left had experienced government, providing capable individuals for ministerial office. It is difficult to identify any particular policy achievement that could be directly associated with the party. Starting a conversation on a National Anti-Poverty Strategy could be considered as one of the party's strongest achievements. The party suffered, as many smaller parties do, in maintaining and developing their internal organisational structures while in government, finding it a constant act of juggling party and government, seemingly having to look two directions at once. An interview with a Democratic Left activist drew a response that 'party headquarters was effectively denied the human resources needed to engage in party building' as 'most experienced paid party workers were reallocated to the job of defending government policy and servicing the party in government'.

The merger between Labour and Democratic Left was little more than two months in place when one of its strongest opponents, Pat Upton TD, died of a heart attack at 54 years of age. His death brought a by-election for the Dublin South Central constituency.

So 1999 would be a year for voting. Local elections, which had been postponed since 1996 (on the pretext of never achieving reform) were held that year, restoring a link with the holding of simultaneous elections to the European Parliament. As an added treat, voters would also get the opportunity to consider a constitutional amendment to reference local government, for the first time in the Constitution. This would ensure the local elections could no longer be postponed again in the future.

The movement in the local elections leant towards Fianna Fáil and Sinn Féin. Fianna Fáil elected twenty-five extra city/county councillors. There would be fifteen new Sinn Féin city and county councillors. At the lower levels of local government, the party performed even more strongly, electing forty-one members to Borough councils, town councils and town commissioners. This gave the party sixty-two elected local government representatives, being the first evidence of the party gaining from a peace dividend.

Labour saw no dividend from its merger with Democratic Left; in fact the party lost seats from its 1991 total. The Progressive Democrats lost one-third of its city and county councillors. Its total number of councillors now stood at thirty-two. The Green Party had a poor local election, and despite running twenty-three additional candidates, the party's vote stood static. Its total number of city and county councillors fell from thirteen to eight, while its total number of local government representatives fell from nineteen to thirteen. One of the Green Party councillors in 1991 was Richard Greene. He had left the Greens (and probably would have been pushed) within a few months. He founded his own party, Muintir na hÉireann, which he disputed with and left. In this election, he was defending the council seat he had won as an independent, but was unsuccessful.

The Workers' Party, which in 1991 included its (not yet) Democratic Left colleagues, ran only about a quarter of the candidates it had put forward in those elections. The twenty-four councillors it had then were now reduced to three, all of whom were members of Waterford City Council. The party also elected a town commissioner in Tramore, a suburb of Waterford. In one Waterford ward it elected two councillors. This was the ward represented by the party's flag-bearer, Martin O'Regan. Elected with him was his party colleague, John Halligan.

The Socialist Party and the Socialist Workers Party each ran nine candidates in these elections, with different impacts. The Socialist Party TD, Joe Higgins, added the title of councillor to his political portfolio. He was joined on Fingal County Council by his colleague Clare Daly, who was elected in Balbriggan. None of the Socialist Workers Party candidates were able to save their deposits.

The same was true for the Christian Solidarity Party, which stood six candidates, none of whom was elected and all of whom lost their deposits. The National Party did not present candidates for this election. Its last appearance had been at the 1998 Limerick East by-election, where its party leader Nora Bennis won in the region of 500 votes. By the end of 1999 the party's entry in the Register of Political Parties would change to have a new name – The Christian Democrats.

The Natural Law Party stood four candidates, none of whom retained their deposits. Independents won 12 per cent of the vote nationally.

This elected eighty-four city and county councillors. Several of these were independent TDs seeking to protect their base – Michael Lowry in Thurles and Tony Gregory in South Dublin Inner City each polled more than twice the necessary quotas in their electoral areas. Independent Fianna Fáil returned four, down from five, councillors on Donegal County Council. South Kerry Independent Alliance helped Michael Gleeson retain his Kerry County Council seat.

The European Elections, held on the same day, delivered dramatically different results. The Progressive Democrats did not contest the elections. Neither did the Workers' Party. The seat allocation showed Fianna Fáil winning one seat less, with independents winning one seat more. This modest change did not come anywhere close to describing the story of this election. It was another extraordinary election for the Green Party. While not on this occasion contesting the Connacht Ulster constituency, the party still amassed 93,000 votes, which comfortably re-elected Patricia McKenna and Nuala Ahern. Ahern's father, Vincent McDowell, was also elected a councillor that day in Dun Laoghaire. With two elected MEPs, two TDs, and eight city or county councillors, the party had quite an imbalanced feel about it.

Sinn Féin, while not electing any MEPs, saw its vote increase from 33,000 to 88,000 votes. Joe Higgins stood for the Socialist Party in Dublin winning around 11,000 votes, which was more that the combined vote of the four candidates for the Natural Law Party. Labour provided some sideshows. In Dublin Proinsias De Rossa defeated his new party colleague, outgoing MEP Bernie Malone, for the one available Labour seat. In Munster a drama preceded the election. Previously independent Senator Brendan Ryan was encouraged to join Labour to become its European election candidate, but was defeated by Paula Desmond (whose mother Eileen had been an MEP) for the nomination.

The most interesting story of the European elections came from Connacht Ulster. This constituency, which had elected Neil Blaney on several occasions, elected a new independent MEP named Rosemary Scallon, Dana, who had benefited from her foray into the Presidential election. Her success would be the first time a Catholic family-values candidate was elected. But it was not an emphatic election. She was chased all the way by another independent candidate, Marian Harkin from Sligo.

The Dublin South Central by-election, also held on this day, saw the third by-election victory in a row for the Labour Party. Mary Upton, sister of the late Pat Upton, was the successful candidate. Voters in Dublic South Central were given four ballot papers on that day. The fourth was for the constitutional amendment on local government. Nationally, the referendum was passed on nearly a four-to-one margin.

The aftermath of the European elections saw the composition of a new European Commission. The Irish Government proposed its Attorney General, David Byrne, as the country representative. This created a vacancy in the office of Attorney General, so Michael McDowell was proposed and accepted for the position. He was not a member of the Dáil, but he had finally become a member of the cabinet.

As the new century and millennium approached, the government could take satisfaction in how the economic indicators were performing. Employment was reducing. Ireland was becoming a country of net migration and low interest rates were stimulating economic activity that was creating record levels of economic growth. This caused the economy to be referred to as the 'Celtic Tiger'.

Where concern was being created was the impression that parliamentary oversight mattered less than the approval of the 'social partners'. Social partnership had been established in 1987. A round table of government, business and employer groups, trade unions and farming organisations, did prove a useful mechanism in helping deal with the public crisis of the 1980s. At a time of seeming economic prosperity this partnership was in danger of becoming a forum for pleasing everyone.

A community and voluntary pillar had been added to the partnership, which at least gave a better consideration of wider societal issues. The *Programme for Prosperity and Fairness* was the agreed shared policy approach for the years 2000–03. It was looser than its predecessors in the areas of wage restraint and control of public expenditure. This challenged the Progressive Democrats' raison d'etre, but the party seemed more than happy with how the Minister for Finance was delivering on its tax-cutting agenda.

It was the area of political corruption that was causing the government, and particularly Fianna Fáil, some difficulty. Having already lost Ray Burke, others would follow resigning the whip, but not their Dáil seats. First in the queue was Kerry North TD, Denis Foley. He had not disclosed the fact that he held an Ansbacher account, and so the Fianna Fáil whip was removed from him. Following him was Liam Lawlor, who had had several run-ins with the Flood Tribunal, being jailed for contempt on a number of occasions (for a period of six weeks) for failing to supply information. It was for failing to supply information to an internal Fianna Fáil standards committee that led to him losing the party whip.

Beverley Flynn, daughter of Pádraig, lost the whip twice during the term of this government. An RTE television documentary, presented by lead reporters Charlie Bird and George Lee, produced evidence that Flynn, in a previous employment as an investment adviser with National Irish Bank, had sold tax avoidance products.

In the Seanad, the Progressive Democrats were mildly embarrassed to lose one of the Senators who had been appointed by the Taoiseach when Helen Keogh felt her ambitions could be better met by becoming a member of Fine Gael.

The first electoral test of the new millennium was a by-election for the Tipperary South constituency. The Labour Party's Michael Ferris had died of a heart attack while on Oireachtas business abroad. His wife, Ellen was chosen as the Labour Party candidate. The victor was an independent candidate, Seamus Healy. Having set up a Workers and Unemployed Action Group, Healy, working from his Clonmel base, had grown his support to a level that helped him to achieve this victory. Within three months this four-seat constituency would again see its complement reduced, after the death from cancer of Fine Gael deputy Theresa Ahearn.

This would not be the only difficulty Fine Gael would experience. After over a decade in position as party leader, John Bruton found himself under siege. A series of stagnant opinion poll ratings was raising discontent within the party. A motion of no confidence was tabled by Michael Noonan and Jim Mitchell. The parliamentary party of seventy-two members divided thirty-nine votes to thirty-three in favour of the motion. John Bruton resigned and a leadership contest followed.

Noonan and Mitchell declared as candidates, as did Enda Kenny and late in the campaign Bernard Allen from Cork North Central. Allen subsequently was the first to withdraw from the contest, to be followed by Jim Mitchell. The parliamentary party meeting saw a straight contest between Noonan and Kenny. Noonan was victorious on a vote of forty-four to twenty-eight.

The Minister for Finance launched an initiative, Special Savings Investment Account (SSIA), where those who would participate were given £1 by the State for every £4 saved. Savings levels in Ireland were poor. Many welcomed the initiative. Few would turn down the prospect of 'free' money. Some warned that the scheme when finished would lead to a difficult to control consumer spending boom. Those fears would prove themselves later to be true.

An interesting legal judgement would prove helpful to smaller parties and independents in the contesting of future elections. The High Court case 'Redmond versus the Minister for the Environment' had been taken by a Wexford builder, who argued that the requirement to place a financial deposit along with a nomination to seek election was discrimination against those on lower incomes who wished to put themselves forward for election. The action was successful. For future elections independents would require other signatures or the option of making a payment. For candidates of registered political groupings, money deposits would no longer be required. For smaller parties this would be of huge assistance in future elections.

Ireland was quickly approaching a new status within the EU, where the country's GDP level would see it changing from being a recipient nation to a country that would become a net contributor to the EU budget. This was the climate in which a further revision of the EU treaties (The Nice Treaty) had to be brought before an Irish constitutional referendum. The government's strategy was to hold a tripartite referendum. Referenda on formally ending the death sentence and for Ireland to come under the jurisdiction of the International Criminal Court in The Hague were also put to the people. The hope was that holding three referenda together would help increase turnout. The underlying strategy was that voters would be encouraged to vote – yes, yes, yes.

Turnout was 34 per cent and voters voted yes, yes, no. The No vote, to the consternation of the political establishment, was on the Treaty of Nice. It was a fillip for those parties that advocated a No vote – the Green Party, Sinn Féin and the Workers' Party. Shocked at this development, the government established a National Forum on Europe, under the chairmanship of independent Senator, Maurice Hayes. The Forum was made up of all political parties represented in the Oireachtas. Northern Irish political parties, the SDLP and the Alliance Party were given observer status, as were the Workers' Party and the Communist Party of Ireland. Representatives of social partnership organisations were also given observer status. Boycotting the earlier work of the Forum, at the behest of its party leader, Michael Noonan, was Fine Gael.

A second by-election in a year was held in Tipperary South. It was a Fine Gael hold for a Fine Gael vacancy. The successful candidate, Tom Hayes, had come second in the previous year's by-election. The Workers and Unemployed Action Group candidate Phil Prendergast also polled well.

The Green Party decided it should have a single party leader (although it had had a Principal Spokesperson since 1992). There was no stipulation that the leader should be a member of the Houses of the Oireachtas. Three candidates put themselves forward – Trevor Sargent TD, Cllr Paul Gogarty from Dublin and Niall Ó'Brolcháin from Galway. In the first membership-based vote for leader, Trevor Sargent won 80 per cent of the vote available to him. Cllr Mary White from Carlow was selected as Deputy Leader. John Gormley became Party Chairman.

In the wider world, the crashing of two jet airliners into the World Trade Center twin towers on 11 September, killing almost 3,000 people, would change the world geopolitical situation for a generation. Ireland's role was incidental but not without controversy as the Irish Government allowed the use of Irish airports, especially Shannon, for the transit of US troops off to military adventures in Afghanistan and later Iraq.

On 1 January 2002 the Euro stopped being a virtual currency and the Irish pound passed into history. Decisions on money supply and the level of interest rates would then be made by a European Central Bank in Frankfurt, not the Central Bank of Ireland in Dublin.

In the European Parliament, Pat Cox's decision to concentrate his parliamentary activities there saw him elected President of the Parliament, one of the key leadership positions within the European Union. He had reached this position by achieving a high profile within the Parliament by being President of third largest parliamentary grouping, the ELDR (Liberal) group since 1998.

His former colleague, Progressive Democrat stalwart Bobby Molloy, was also ruminating on his future, when events appeared to hasten his departure. He became embroiled in controversy when letters from his constituency office pleaded mitigation for the accused in a rape trial. As a result he resigned his position as Minister for State, indicating that he would not be contesting the next general election.

It could be argued that off-loading such economic control was necessary to allow the Irish political system to concentrate on its real policy obsession – abortion. In 2002 yet another constitutional referendum was held on the subject. That referendum sought to end the use of the threat of suicide as a reason for abortion. The measure was defeated on a 52 to 48 margin.

By now Bertie Ahern had brought a minority government to a full term. May 2002 would see whether he would get his political reward. He came close. The party upped its 1997 performance by four additional seats, just two short of an overall majority. Fine Gael found itself in free-fall after this election, coming back with twenty-two fewer seats. Labour received zero bounce from its merger with Democratic Left, securing one fewer seat than both had won in 1997.

The 'others' had a very good election. The Progressive Democrats vote continued to shrink (this time it stood at 4 per cent) but with that vote the party managed to double its seats, now standing at eight TDs. Six of these TDs were not members of the previous Dáil. Michael McDowell stepped in again. Des O'Malley had retired but two members of his family were members of this Dáil – his daughter Fiona was elected in Dun Laoghaire; his cousin Tim held the seat in Limerick East. Bobby Molloy's retirement may not have been as comfortable, but he helped run a brilliant strategy of three candidates fighting amongst themselves and Noel Grealish was the candidate who won. Before the election the party had achieved a coup in attracting the immediate past president of the Irish Farmers Association, Tom Parlon, whose profile helped him to win a seat in Laois Offaly. The final PD seat also came into new territory. A former independent councillor Mae Sexton became a PD candidate, winning a surprise seat in Longford Westmeath.

Gaining 2,000 votes less, but winning its highest number of votes ever won in a Dáil general election was the Green Party, which saw its Dáil presence increase from two to six seats (including the party's first TD outside of Dublin). Joining Trevor Sargent and John Gormley in the Dáil were Ciarán Cuffe in Dun Laoghaire, Éamon Ryan in Dublin South, Paul Gogarty in Dublin Mid West, and Dan Boyle in Cork South Central.

Outpolling both the PDs and the Greens, although not winning as many seats, was Sinn Féin, whose sole TD was joined by four new colleagues. Joining the pioneering O'Caoláin were Martin Ferris in Kerry North, Arthur Morgan in Louth, Áengus O'Snodaigh in Dublin South Central and Seán Crowe in Dublin South West.

Joe Higgins continued to fly the Socialist flag in Dublin West. His council colleague Clare Daly polled extremely well in Dublin North, winning 5,500 votes. The party's other three candidates averaged about 1,000 votes each, winning a national total of 15,000 votes. The Workers' Party slid further. Running seven candidates, only one breached four figures in a national total of 4,000. Waterford continued to be the party's stronghold, but now in an ever-diminishing way. The earlier death of Martin O'Regan was being felt by the party. His successor and Waterford City Council colleague was John Halligan. The Socialist Workers Party ran seven candidates who averaged fewer than 500 votes each.

The Christian Solidarity Party ran twenty-three candidates. Winning fewer than 5,000 votes nationally, the average vote per candidate was little more than 200 votes. This vote was achieved despite its main rival, the National Party, not offering any candidates for this election. The Natural Law Party also had it absence unfelt. The party's last appearance was the 2000 Tipperary South by-election, where its candidate Raymond McInerney won 97 votes.

An unregistered political group, the Immigration Control Platform, stood two candidates who collectively won 1,400 votes. Its lead candidate, Áine Ní Chonaill, had stood as an independent candidate in the Cork South West constituency where she lived and worked as a teacher. In 1998 she founded The Platform, which remained unregistered as a political party. The Platform argued that it existed to highlight what it believed was the intrinsic danger to Ireland in encouraging net migration. In 2002 she and her colleague Ted Neville announced their intention to contest the election under this label. Neville contested the Cork South Central constituency where he won less than 400 votes. Ní Chonaill chose to contest Dublin South Central, an area of the country with a higher proportion of non-nationals living there. She won a little above 900 votes.

It would be the independents who made the greatest advance in these elections. Thirteen independent TDs were elected. Four of the six independents elected in 1997 were re-elected. Harry Blaney was replaced by his son Niall in Donegal North East. In neighbouring Donegal South West, Thomas Gildea, the television deflector candidate, chose not to stand again. Seamus Healy, who had been elected in a Tipperary South by-election, was elected again to serve a full term.

The seven other independent TDs were quite an eclectic group. Paudge Connolly, a candidate for the Monaghan Hospital Action Group was elected in Cavan Monaghan. Independent James Breen in Clare was a disappointed former Fianna Fáil member. Finian McGrath was elected in Dublin North Central. Nominally a member of the Independent Health Alliance (an unregistered umbrella for eight candidates wanting to promote health issues during the election). McGrath had been an independent member of Dublin City Council since 1999. Paddy McHugh, in Galway East, was another disappointed former Fianna Fáil independent. Dr Jerry Cowley was elected on health and rural development issues in Mayo. Eight years earlier he had stood there in a by-election, winning fewer than 400 votes. Marian Harkin parlayed her good performance in the previous European election to win a Dáil seat in Sligo/Leitrim. Dr Liam Twomey was another medic who benefitted from public concern on health, becoming elected in Wexford.

The European election effect, which worked so well for Marian Harkin, brought about an opposite consequence for her successful opponent in that campaign. Rosemary Scallon/Dana sought election to the Dáil by standing in the Galway West constituency. She finished in twelfth position of the seventeen candidates on the first count, being eliminated after the seventh of fifteen counts.

An independent who almost got elected in this election was Kathy Sinnott in Cork South Central. She had gained a national profile through winning a court case on her son's behalf, finding that the State had not provided sufficient resources to meet the care needs of severely disabled children with autism. Cork South Central was the long count of the 2002 election. After a number of recounts, John Dennehy of Fianna Fáil was declared the victor by a margin of six votes.

No longer being a minority, forming a government was done with little difficulty. The Greens attempted to disrupt proceedings by sitting on the government benches, a protest at not being afforded formal group status (standing orders stipulated that seven members was the minimum number needed.). Eventually, Fianna Fáil's Rory O'Hanlon was elected as Ceann Comhairle. Bertie Ahern was re-elected as Taoiseach winning 93 of the 166 TDs available. Five independent TDs also supported his re-election. The Progressive Democrats, with a greater Dáil strength, now would have a stronger place at the cabinet. Michael McDowell became Minister for Justice and Law Reform. Liz O'Donnell found herself replaced as a Minister of State, despite the party having two positions. These were given to Tom Parlon at the Department of Finance and Tim O'Malley at the Department of Health.

Michael Noonan resigned immediately in the aftermath of what had been a disastrous election for Fine Gael. Four candidates presented themselves to be his successor – Enda Kenny, Richard Bruton, Gay Mitchell and Phil Hogan. The electorate was a much-reduced parliamentary party of forty-nine members. The voting, which took place on 5 June, was by secret ballot, with the results kept secret. Enda Kenny was announced as the new leader, elected, it was said, after the first count. One of the first decisions made by Kenny was to end Fine Gael's boycott of the Forum on Europe.

Immediately in the government's in-tray was the report of the Director of Corporate Enforcement, Paul Appleby, into the workings of Ansbacher Bank. Some 200 people, prominent in Irish society, were named. While over €100 million would be clawed back through taxation and fines, no prosecutions would result.

There were no new independents in the Twenty-second Seanad. The Taoiseach nominated four Progressive Democrats Senators. Among these was the ever-present John Dardis, who was also made Deputy Leader of the Seanad (a new position). The new PD Senators were Tom Morrissey from Dublin, a Fine Gael convert, John Minihan from Cork (he would become Chairman of the party), and Kate Walsh from Kildare.

The government's attention was turned towards a second consideration of the Nice Treaty. An appendix was placed on the Treaty that was meant to address the supposed Irish concern with abortion. The real question was turnout. This increased to 49 per cent, up from 34 per cent in the first referendum, giving the government its desired result – a 62 to 38 yes vote. In absolute terms, more people voted No in the second referendum than had in the first.

The Labour Party, having supported the Nice Treaty on both occasions, then engaged in an open ballot of its members to choose its new party leader. Ruairí Quinn had resigned in the aftermath of an uninspiring election performance. Four TDs put themselves forward for election – Pat Rabbitte, Brendan Howlin, Éamon Gilmore and Róisín Shortall. From this group, Pat Rabbitte emerged successful. A separate election saw Liz McManus being elected as Deputy Leader. Three years after the merger, former Democratic Left TDs held all the leadership positions in the Labour Party.

The political preoccupation in 2003 was global disapproval of the US Bush administration, supported by the Blair administration in Britain, who went ahead with an invasion of Iraq, based on an ill-judged justification. Some 100,000 people marched in Dublin, along with millions of others throughout the world against the lack of sanity in this action.

Between January and June 2004, for the sixth time, Ireland held the Presidency of the Council of the European Union. It was a significant presidency and before its conclusion ten new member countries, (some from the Mediterranean, but most from Eastern Europe) became members of the EU.

In Irish politics, Minister for Health Micheál Martin introduced legislation and regulations prohibiting smoking in any work environment or buildings that had public access, making Ireland one of the first countries in the world to enact such public health legislation.

This was an election year, with the coupling of local and European elections. For Fianna Fáil it was one of the party's worst local election performances. Its national vote decreased by 7 per cent, resulting in the loss of almost 130 seats, eighty at city or county level and forty-nine from various town councils. Fine Gael saw no increase in its vote but the party won an additional sixteen seats in city and county councils, winning a further sixteen seats at town council level. Labour saw a marginal increase in its vote, which delivered an extra eighteen city and county councillors. The party did not increase its number of town councillors. Sinn Féin continued its rise towards respectability, winning 125,000 votes, more than doubling its presence in city and county councils, now standing at fifty-four councillors. The party continued to perform even better at town council level with seventy-one councillors now representing its interests at this level of local government. The Progressive Democrats increased its vote by a percentage point in this election. Despite this, the party now had six fewer city and county councillors. This was partially compensated though the election of thirteen town councillors. The Greens outpolled the PDs, ending up with similar results – eighteen city or county councillors and fourteen town councillors, making it the best local government results the party had achieved to date. The Socialist Party held its vote but had two further councillors elected – Mick Barry on Cork City Council and Mick Murphy on South Dublin County Council, both polltoppers. Independent Fianna Fáil was now reduced to two seats on Donegal County Council. The Workers' Party was also reduced to two seats in its Waterford City Council enclave, although its current standard bearer, John Halligan, did top the poll in his electoral area. In Killarney Cllr Michael Gleeson succeeded in being re-elected with his vehicle, the South Kerry Independent Alliance.

Republican Sinn Féin lost its only seat on Longford County Council. The Socialist Workers' Party slate of candidates won 6,000 votes but no seats. After standing twenty-three candidates in the general election in 2002, the Christian Solidarity Party stood one candidate in these local elections who was not elected. After these elections there were 231 independent councillors at all levels of local government, marginally down from 1999.

The European Elections would be affected by the reduction (from fifteen to thirteen) in Irish seats to the European Parliament, as a result of the accession of ten new member countries bringing about a capping of the overall size of parliaments. The thirteen seats were allocated, with Fine Gael being the most successful party, winning five of the seats; Fianna Fáil winning four; Labour maintaining its one MEP, Proinsias De Rossa; Sinn Féin made a breakthrough winning one seat, with two independents being elected.

Sinn Féin won the third largest amount of votes in these elections, shifting close to 200,000 votes. Its seat was won in the Dublin constituency by Mary Lou McDonald, finishing ahead of Patricia McKenna (seeking a third term for the Greens). After a ten-year tenure, there would a no Irish Green presence in the European Parliament. The reduced number of Irish seats with the smaller number of seats available in most constituencies made it a harder mountain to climb for the party. Also in Dublin, Joe Higgins won 23,000 votes for the Socialist Party.

In Ireland East, the constituency that had largely been Leinster in previous elections, Nuala Ahern retired, perhaps sensing the task had become more difficult. In her stead Mary White was the Green candidate. She won 25,000 votes, but no seat. Six independents stood in the Ireland East constituency. Prominent among them was Justin Barrett, who won 11,000 votes. He had come to prominence as part of the Youth Defence group that had formed as a response to the pro-life/anti-abortion referenda, a kind of Praetorian Guard for that side of the argument. Another independent associated with a focused agenda was Liam Ó Gogáin, who stood on a Fathers Rights platform.

Ireland North West was the constituency that approximated to what had been Connacht Ulster. Here the contest was a repeat of the 1999 election. On this occasion Marian Harkin (since a TD) finished 10,000 votes ahead of outgoing MEP Rosemary Scallon/Dana, winning one of the three available seats.

In Ireland South, in what had been Munster, another new independent came to the fore. Pax Cox had chosen not to stand again. Having achieved the highest position in the parliament, the inducement to return may have seemed less. His replacement could not be more unlike him. Kathy Sinnott, who had come so close to winning a Dáil seat in Cork South Central, had established a network of supporters due to her work disability rights activism. She had expanded her platform to speak to pro-life family-values issues.

On this day was also held a referendum on limiting the criteria for Irish citizenship. This referendum was pushed by Michael McDowell, as Minister of Justice, responding to what he felt was growing public concern on Ireland becoming a country of net migration. It was somewhat an exaggerated fear, given the performance of the Immigration Control Platform in 2002. Nevertheless, the referendum was approved on a four-to-one margin.

Bertie Ahern believed that the votes received by Fianna Fáil could not be seen as only a mid-term kicking. He felt changes had to be made. His first decision was to bring an end to the McCreevy era. Charlie McCreevy was sent to Brussels to become the Irish member of the European Commission. A cabinet reshuffle followed, with Brian Cowen becoming Minister for Finance. Mary Harney asked for and was given the position of Minister for Health.

Bertie declared himself a socialist, by inclination if not by practice. Fr Seán Healy of the Conference of Religious in Ireland (CORI), a frequent critic of government policies that were leading to growing inequality, was invited to speak to the Fianna Fáil parliamentary think-in held in Inchadoney, Co. Cork.

In parallel, the leaders of Fine Gael and Labour, Enda Kenny and Pat Rabbitte, met in Mullingar, County Westmeath, to discuss the possibility of presenting a joint programme for the next general election. Their shared intentions were recorded in a document known as the Mullingar Accord. Also around this time, Fine Gael would receive another fillip when Liam Twomey from Wexford, elected as an independent in 2002, applied to become a member of the party.

President McAleese announced her intention to seek a second term of office. After the local elections, there seemed little enthusiasm to have a contested election, and party coffers would have been depleted from the local and European elections. Fine Gael remained silent on the subject. Within Labour, Michael D. Higgins indicated his willingness to be a candidate, but his party leader Pat Rabbitte decided otherwise.

It seemed that there would no election until a Green Party TD (since 2002) announced he would like to be a candidate.

With six members of the Oireachtas, the Greens were well short of the twenty signatories needed to sign nomination papers. A number of independent TDs, Tony Gregory and Finian McGrath, indicated their willingness. Pat Rabbitte, having stood down Michael D. Higgins's ambitions, said Labour could provide nine of the necessary signatories (he did not want to be seen to have provided more than half the required signatures.) With seventeen of the required signatories, finding another three would have been possible.

Being interviewed on RTE Radio by Marian Finucane, Éamon Ryan answered yes directly to a question as to whether he had ever smoked cannabis. In Ireland, in 2004, this was an issue considered significant. It seemed to take the gloss off a candidacy that had been gathering momentum.

More importantly, the Ryan candidacy had only been floated by himself. The Green Party had yet to formally endorse a candidate. This would happen at a National Council meeting of the party being held in Darrara in West Cork. Some of Ryan's Dáil colleagues, most notably Paul Gogarty, were distinctly cool on the idea. Former MEP Patricia McKenna expressed her unhappiness about the party having a candidate reliant on Labour support. While Ryan would have the support of most of those present, the lack of a united party approach made him decide against putting his name forward. As a result, Mary McAleese was elected for a second term as President of Ireland.

In January 2005 former cabinet minister Ray Burke was jailed for six months, having been convicted on a charge of tax evasion, under legislation he himself had introduced. Events like this, along with the ongoing tribunals of inquiry were keeping the issue of political corruption to the fore.

In March 2005, two by-elections were held on foot of European appointments. One was Charlie McCreevy as a European Commissioner (Kildare North), while the other was John Bruton (Meath) who had been appointed the EU ambassador to the US. The Meath by-election was a safe Fine Gael hold. In Kildare North, the victor was Catherine Murphy, who had become an independent (having been a previous candidate for the Workers' Party / Democratic Left), after falling out with Labour's Emmet Stagg who had decided that there was not enough room for two Labour candidates in Kildare North.

The following year (2005) was the year when the Health Service Executive (HSE) came into being. Constructed under legislation that had been introduced by the then Minister for Health Mícheál Martin, the HSE replaced eleven regionally based health boards. Responsibility for day-to-day management was removed from the Department of Health. The thinking behind the change was primarily to improve efficiency, and the secondary hope was to diffuse health as a political issue.

In 2006, Mary Harney decided that after thirteen years as leader of the Progressive Democrats she needed to step down from the post. There had been a level of encouragement over the previous year for her to take this decision. Michael McDowell, in particular, had been anxious that she made this decision. When it happened, he was the only nominated candidate. He became the new and third leader of the Progressive Democrats, also becoming Tánaiste, while Mary Harney remained a member of the government.

Other political activity in 2006 centred around the fallout emanating from the continuing tribunals. In September the *Irish Times* reported, on the basis of a leak from the Mahon (former Flood) Tribunal, that Bertie Ahern, when Minister for Finance in 1993, had received large sums of money (£50,000) from a millionaire businessman. He had admitted as much in an emotional interview on the main television news. He stated he had broken no laws or regulations in doing so. He further stated that the money had been given as an informal loan, despite no interest being attached or any repayments having been made.

Michael McDowell, now the PD leader, insisted that Ahern should repay these monies with interest. It would the first in a number of 'Duke of York' challenges that McDowell would make in the remaining nine months of the life of this government. McDowell's need to assert himself, combined with Ahern's need to defend himself, was making a return to government unlikely.

There was some good news for Fianna Fáil with the ending of its thirty-six-year-long feud in Donegal. Niall Blaney, son and nephew of Harry Blaney TD and Neil Blaney TD, became a Fianna Fáil TD, winding down the operations of Independent Fianna Fáil. Events conspired to make the Progressive Democrats alter its election plans. Kate Walsh, one of the party's Taoiseach's nominees in the Seanad, passed away. Appointed in her stead, and seen as something of a coup, was anti-child abuse campaigner and founder of the One-in-Four organisation, Colm O'Gorman, who was made a Senator.

The Peace Process in Northern Ireland was moving into a new phase. The parties that had been on the fringes in the Unionist and Nationalist communities, the Democratic Unionist Party and Sinn Féin, rose to become first among equals. Ian Paisley became First Minister with Martin McGuinness becoming the Deputy First Minister. It had not been thought possible, but now it was the reality.

Less of a reality was the reaching of a shadowy agreement between the State, represented by the Department of Education, through its Minister, Michael Woods, and several religious congregations on the compensation of victims of institutional abuse. Through this agreement the State met at least half the cost of any potential compensation to victims. Part of the contribution of the religious congregations was met in kind, by making available land and buildings to the State.

In the Republic, attention was turning to the Green Party as a possible party of government. At the party's convention in early 2007 the mood of delegates was decidedly opposed to Fianna Fáil, a mood especially captured in the speech of the party's chairman John Gormley, which came to be defined as the 'Planet Bertie' speech. In this he excoriated Ahern for his constant shifting of position. The speech also contained the ultimate statement of frustration that can be made by a member outside government when Gormley stated 'I can't stand the thought of another five years in opposition,'.

Nevertheless, the party's official strategy was to speak with every party in a new Dáil about the possibility of putting together a government. Party leader Trevor Sargent gave little doubt where his personal feelings lay when he stated that he would resign as party leader rather than lead the Green Party into a coalition with Fianna Fáil.

20

You're Playing Senior Hurling Now

There was an air of unreality about the 2007 election campaign. The underlying theme seemed that times were good, that the electorate was being persuaded as to which political choice would lead to a better land of milk and honey. The narrative was that the good times would keep rolling, the argument being which political grouping would make them roll faster.

The Fianna Fáil-Progressive Democrat programme predicted that average economic growth of 5 per cent per annum would follow. Fine Gael-Labour based their plan on a 4.5 per cent growth. The Greens went with 4 per cent – the figure the Central Bank had said was most likely. *The Irish Times* judged the Greens' economic proposals to be the most realistic.

In 2002 the Progressive Democrats had placed a lot of store in its postering policy. It believed that its *Left Wing Government. No Thanks.* posters had persuaded enough of middle Ireland then to think positively on its behalf. A similarly themed poster was to be unveiled in 2007 in Michael McDowell's constituency, Dublin South East. That day, near Leinster House, political correspondent with the *Irish Independent*, Fionnán Sheehan met McDowell's rival, John Gormley, jokingly asking him if he was going along. Gormley did decide to go.

Thus began the *Rumble in Ranelagh*. Trading insults in front of large assembled press pack, it came across as a reality TV version of *'Who wants to be in Government'*. McDowell detailed what he thought were the

Green Party's failings, but in doing so seemed only to show the many deficits his own party was experiencing.

The election on 24 May saw most political groupings, with the exception of Fine Gael, being dissatisfied with the results. Enda Kenny had helped his party recoup most of the losses it had sustained in 2002. Fine Gael came back to the Dáil with twenty more TDs. Fianna Fáil returned with four fewer. Its partners in government, the Progressive Democrats, lost three-quarters of its Dáil presence. Labour and The Greens stood still. Sinn Féin lost a seat. Joe Higgins of the Socialist Party was a surprise casuality. Many of the independents elected in 2002 did not return in 2008.

Among the Progressive Democrats only Mary Harney in Dublin Mid West and Noel Grealish in Galway West were returned. In his sixth general election Michael McDowell repeated his win-lose pattern for the third time. On learning of his result in Dublin South East he somewhat petulantly resigned his position as party leader, further announcing his withdrawal from political life. Mary Harney resumed as party leader. Lost to the PDs in the Dáil were Liz O'Donnell (a TD of fifteen years standing); two outgoing Ministers of State, Tim O'Malley and Tom Parlon and two more of the new 2002 intake, Fiona O'Malley in Dun Laoghaire and Mae Sexton in Longford Westmeath.

For the Greens, Dan Boyle failed to be re-elected in Cork South Central (winning seven fewer votes than he had in 2002). The party maintained its parliamentary representation through the election in Carlow Kilkenny of its deputy leader, Mary White. Sinn Féin suffered a setback when Sean Crowe was unsuccessful in Dublin South West.

There was a certain solidity in the independent TDs who survived this election. In his twenty-fifth year as a TD, Tony Gregory was undoubtedly the father of the independents in the Dáil. Elected in 1997, Michael Lowry and Jackie Healy Rae had by now established strong roots in their respective constituencies. Finian McGrath in Dublin North Central was the only independent first elected in 2002 to be re-elected in 2007. The fifth 'independent' was Beverley Flynn in Mayo, who had been denied a Fianna Fáil nomination due to her ongoing legal difficulties.

For two TDs elected as independents in 2002 that subsequently joined political parties – Niall Blaney and Liam Twomey – their fortunes would be mixed. Blaney was elected as a Fianna Fáil TD in Donegal North East. Liam Twomey failed to be elected under Fine Gael colours in Wexford.

The Socialist Workers Party had rebranded itself as the People Before Profit Alliance. With this name almost 10,000 votes, but no seats, were won. There were, however, two strong performances, that of it chief spokesperson, Richard Boyd Barrett, who won over 5,000 votes in Dun Laoghaire and Bríd Smyth, winning over 2,000 votes in Dublin South Central. The new title would be registered after the election. The Socialist Workers Party also remained on the register. For several years, this dual registration was maintained.

The Workers' Party compiled 3,000 votes. More than half of these were won by the party's Waterford candidate, John Halligan. The Christian Solidarity Party won 1,700 votes. Unregistered groups Fathers Rights, Immigration Control and the Irish Socialist Network won 1,350, 1,320 and 500 votes, respectively.

Bertie Ahern would have preferred a return of the Fianna Fáil–PD coalition. This combination now had only seventy-nine seats, five seats short of a working majority. A 1997-2002 option of a minority coalition government also seemed unlikely as there were now only five independents, all of whom would not vote collectively or continuingly with such a government. What Ahern needed was a new coalition partner to supplant or to augment the PDs.

Labour would have been his least preferred option, as that would have meant surrendering too many Fianna Fáil seats at the cabinet. Sinn Féin, during the election campaign had been ruled out of any prospective coalition government by every party, with the exception of the Greens. Fianna Fáil had prepared for the possibility of having to deal with the Greens. Its manifesto incorporated verbatim submissions the party had received from environmental NGOs. In an informal conversation after the 'Planet Bertie' speech, Fianna Fáil's Seamus Brennan told John Gormley 'not to be so quick to rule out Fianna Fáil'.

The shadow dancing took several days. A possibility existed of an anyone but Fianna Fáil coalition. The Fine Gael chairman Phil Hogan informally approached the Greens to approach Sinn Féin on its behalf. The approach was rebuffed. Formal talks between Fianna Fáil and the Greens began ten days after the general election. The Fianna Fáil team of negotiators, Brian Cowen, Noel Dempsey and Seamus Brennan, had had several experiences of such situations. The Green team consisted of John Gormley, party general secretary Dónal Geoghegan, and now former TD, Dan Boyle. This would be their first experience of such negotiations. Brennan welcomed the Greens to the experience, telling them: 'Lads, you're playing senior hurling now.'

Only Fianna Fáil and the Greens were involved in these negotiations. If the PDs were involved their arguments were being made by the Fianna Fáil negotiations team. The Greens preferred not to have any PD involvement in government, believing a working majority existed without them. Neither did the party want Mary Harney to remain in cabinet. Fianna Fáil insisted she remain as Minister: for Fianna Fáil she represented a useful mudguard, particularly in relation to unpopular policies such as the co-location of private hospitals in the grounds of public hospitals.

There were similar Green concerns that special government arrangements should not be entered into with any of the independent TDs, as had been the case during the 1997-2002 government. Fianna Fáil could enter any kind of arrangements it wished, but there would not be agreements with the government. Seamus Brennan, who was Government Chief Whip to that government, explained that his method of working with government supporting independents was not to have formal agreements, but to get a heads-up in announcing already agreed government actions in their constituencies.

After six days of negotiations, it was Green Party involvement in any possible government that was uncertain. The party's negotiators removed themselves from the talks, believing that no progress had been achieved. The door had not been shut, but for many in the Greens there was little belief that the party would be asked back to the table. Over that weekend informal contacts resumed, with Fianna Fáil acceding to several Green demands. Formal negotiations resumed with only three days before the new Dáil would resume. Talks nearly broke down a second time when the party key negotiators Noel Dempsey and Dan Boyle were meeting to agree a final draft.

That crisis averted, the finished document was put to the decision-making mechanisms in each party. With Fianna Fáil, in reality, this was

Bertie Ahern, with it ultimately being rubber stamped by its parliamentary party. With the Green Party, approval was needed firstly from its national council to decide to put the question to a special convention of party members.

The final piece of negotiation was done between Bertie Ahern and Trevor Sargent at Ahern's Drumcondra headquarters, St Jude's. This determined what would be the extent of the Green Party's participation in government – the seats at the cabinet table, in which departments, the number of ministers of State, and the number of Green Party members who would sit in Seanad Éireann.

The Green Party members' convention took place at the Mansion House on the evening of 13 June. The party required two-thirds approval for the proposal to enter government. There was uncertainty as to whether this approval would be forthcoming. Those speaking on motion seemed equally distributed, for and against the motion. Patricia McKenna led those arguing against entering government. It was thought that her position would carry many party members. Ultimately, 84 per cent of Green Party members decided that the party should enter government. Immediately upon learning of that decision, Trevor Sargent spoke to those present, announcing he would be resigning as party leader and not accepting any cabinet position, to honour the personal pledge he had made in advance of the general election.

The following day the Green Party became the ninth political party to participate in government in Ireland. It would be a difficult initiation to what would prove a difficult government. Before the Dáil had sat the outgoing Minister for the Environment, Dick Roche approved a controversial decision in relation to the Hill of Tara, a decision the Greens had felt would be made by the incoming (Green) minister.

John O'Donoghue was selected as Ceann Comhairle. This was astute on Ahern's part. O'Donoghue in the cabinet might have proved a friction point with the Greens. During the previous government O'Donoghue had described the Greens as being 'as useful as a slug on a lettuce'. Ahern's election as Taoiseach was safely achieved. He won the support of four of the five independents, the exception being Tony Gregory who voted against. The election made Ahern the only Taoiseach, other than Éamon de Valera, to be elected for three terms in succession. A cabinet would be formed including Green ministers John Gormley as Minister for the Environment, Heritage and Local Government and Éamon Ryan as Minister for Communications, Energy and Natural Resources.

When the Minister of State positions were announced, the outgoing leader of the Greens, Trevor Sargent, was assigned to the Department of Agriculture and Food. The appointment had been expected, but what had not been expected by the Greens was the Taoiseach's decision to increase the number of ministers of State to twenty, to try and placate the demand among Fianna Fáil TDs for positions.

These were early testings of the Greens' willingness to be and stay in government. More worrying news was beginning to develop. In 2006 a record 90,000 housing units were built in Ireland, as many as were being built in the neighbouring UK. This was creating an over supply in housing that brought about a decrease in housing prices. This would feed into the first lowering of taxation receipts for several years. Some commentators were beginning to speak of the economy in negative terms. This commentary led the Taoiseach, Bertie Ahern, to declare that those unhappy with, and talking down, the economy should commit 'suicide'.

The Green Party needed to select a new leader. Putting themselves forward were John Gormley and Patricia McKenna, representing the now two distinct groupings in the party – those who wanted the party to be in government and those who did not. Gormley emerged victorious on a two-to-one margin.

The new Seanad was to have several new members. On the vocational panels, after an electoral arrangement it had entered into with the Labour Party, Sinn Féin had its first member elected to Seanad Éireann. Pearse Doherty, who had come close to being elected to the Dáil in Donegal North East, would become the party's first Senator. On the National University of Ireland panel there was a surprise when the poll was topped by a newcomer, Ronan Mullen, a former press officer for the Catholic Archbishop of Dublin. He would be associated with the family-values approach to politics.

Among the Taoiseach's nominees were six new Fianna Fáil Senators. Two new Progressive Democrat Senators were appointed, as many Senators as the party had TDs. These were former TD Fiona O'Malley, and County Galway councillor Ciaran Cannon. The Greens submitted two names for appointment, after an internal poll among its elected representatives (local and national). Appointed were former TD, Dan Boyle and Wicklow County Councillor, Deirdre de Burca. In the Dáil the Greens had not sought the position of Tánaiste. In the Seanad, Dan Boyle was appointed to the parallel position of Deputy Leader.

The announcement of the eleventh nominee turned many heads. To sit as an independent Senator would be the political commentator/strategist, Eoghan Harris. Harris had been associated with Proinsias De Rossa's 1989 election to the European Parliament (he was a long-time member of the Workers' Party and its earlier incarnations). He had a large involvement with Mary Robinson's successful Presidential campaign in 1990. He was less successful in his stage directing of a Fine Gael Ard Fheis. In the most recent general election he found himself a panellist on *The Late Late Show*, where he delivered a paean of praise towards Bertie Ahern. This was seen as being significant in persuading some swing voters. His reward was a seat in Seanad Éireann.

With the resignation of Pat Rabbitte as party leader, the Labour Party would have its fourth party leader in a ten-year period. Unlike on the previous two occasions, there would be no contest. The only declared and nominated candidate was Éamon Gilmore. He was the second former Democratic Left Workers' Party TD to become leader of the Labour Party.

The Tribunal of Inquiry Into Certain Planning Matters and Payments, known now as the Mahon Tribunal, had suspended its hearings during the general election. This undoubtedly helped Bertie Ahern. When the Tribunal resumed its hearings, the newly re-elected Taoiseach was its first witness. He responded to how and why he received certain payments, some proven and some unproven. He stated that he had no bank account. He responded that some sums of money were whip-arounds from friends, others being gambling winnings. His testimony stretched his credibility to the limit. This made the Greens uncomfortable, but it did not make the party want to cut and run. A strategy had been decided that the party would not respond to the evidence given at the Tribunal. The reaction would be given to the findings of fact as and when they would be made.

A motion of no confidence tabled that autumn had Ahern and Fianna Fáil wanting to place a counter motion criticising the Mahon Tribunal (a tribunal that had been established by the Oireachtas). As the Minister responsible for moving the counter motion, John Gormley insisted no such reference be included.

As the Tribunal moved into 2008 this position would become harder to hold. The appearance of Ahern's long-time constituency secretary, Gráinne Carruth, would prove to be a game changer. Under difficult questioning, she admitted she had made a number of bank deposits on Ahern's behalf. Ahern's response to his long-term employee shocked many. Progressive Democrat Senator Fiona O'Malley was the first public represenative to call on Ahern to explain these discrepancies. She would receive subsequent support from her party leader, Mary Harney. John Gormley for the Greens came late to the party in also asking for a public explanation.

Ahern's response on 2 April was to announce his resignation as leader of Fianna Fáil. He gave notice of his resignation as Taoiseach to be effective from 6 May. The purpose of this delay was to allow Ahern one last lap of glory, to allow him to play on those areas of policy where he had achieved things, especially in relation to the Northern Irish peace process. His greatest hits tour took him to addresses in Westminster, in Washington, then finally the joint opening of a visitor centre at the River Boyne battle site with the First Minister of Northern Ireland, Ian Paisley.

Throughout this itinerary Ahern had ceased to be leader of Fianna Fáil. His successor, by acclamation, would be the Minister for Finance, Brian Cowen. While waiting for the Dáil to vote upon a new Taoiseach, Cowen embarked on his own 'King of the Midlands' tour. Within the Progressive Democrats, Mary Harney decided to use the opportunity of these competing circuses to announce her second resignation as party leader. Senator Ciaran Cannon became the fourth leader of the Progressive Democrats. He would be the first person to lead any Irish political party from the upper house.

These events were distracting all in Irish political life from the need to have an engaged public debate on the future direction of the EU. These changes were being proposed in a new treaty – The Treaty of

Lisbon. For the Green Party, now in government, this treaty would cause some difficulties. In every Irish European Union referendum since the Single European Act, the Greens had advocated a contrarian position, maintaining that the direction was being taken further and further away from a fully democratic Europe. At this time, some in the Greens felt that the provisions of the Lisbon Treaty would correct many of the mistakes brought about through the Nice Treaty.

The party required a special members' convention to approve its position on the referendum. Like the party's entry into government, a two-thirds majority was required. To the discomfort of the party's leadership the convention was two votes short of meeting that requirement. This meant that the Greens as a party could not campaign formally for the referendum. However, the vote did show where majority support lay in the party. Any member, including government ministers, could participate in the campaign as individuals.

On 13 June 2008, the Irish people voted against the Treaty of Lisbon on a 53 to 47 margin. The Green Party, this time in government, found itself again on the losing side. One of the more negative responses by the government to this defeat was to disband the National Forum of Europe, which had been designed to better inform the public on European Union issues.

From 1 July, a new emissions-based system of motor taxation was introduced. Favouring smaller, less polluting cars, the change had been a central Green measure in the first budget of the Fianna Fáil–Green government. It would be larger economic concerns that would concentrate minds for the rest of 2008. The Irish economy had technically fallen into recession after two quarters of negative economic growth. Unemployment stood at its highest level since 1999. Worrying trends in the global economic climate, and the open nature of the Irish economy, meant that things would get worse, a lot worse.

The collapse of the property bubble in Ireland, allied to international concerns caused by the failure of the large US bank, Lehman Brothers, saw the liquidity of all Irish-based financial institutions become severely compromised. Fears existed that some of these institutions might have been on the brink of insolvency. On the night of 30 September the Irish government decided to extend existing state guarantees to cover all liabilities of six Irish-based financial institutions. This guarantee could have created a potential liability to the State of €400 billion. The Dáil began consideration on the legislation to effect this, *the Credit Institutions (Financial Support) Act 2008*, on the following morning. Later, for the first time in its history, the Seanad moved a piece of legislation after midnight, debating all night, finally passing all stages at 8 o'clock in the morning. Fine Gael and Sinn Féin supported the measure but Labour voted against.

The uncertainty created by events surrounding the bank guarantee made the government bring forward its 2009 budget two months earlier. This would be the first budget introduced by the new Minister for Finance, Brian Lenihan. One provision spooked several government backbenchers. It was proposed to tighten the criteria on the free medical scheme for those over 70 years of age. Its announcement brought large rallies outside the gates of Leinster House, in an impressive sign of 'grey power'. Finian McGrath, an independent TD who had supported the election of Bertie Ahern, stated he would be withdrawing his support for the government. Of greater concern to the government was the resignation from Fianna Fáil of its Wicklow TD, Joe Behan, on this issue.

Meanwhile, the newly elected leader of the Progressive Democrats, Ciaran Cannon, was not sensing much enthusiasm from his party's members to surge into the future. At a special meeting held in November, those attending voted by 201 votes to 161 to dissolve the party.

The PDs had perhaps been the most successful of all the smaller Irish political parties in implementing its policy agenda. This in part had been due the length of time and number of terms served in government (the party had spent more time in government than it had in opposition). Its influence has been as much about altering the philosophical approach of Irish politics as it has been about particular legislative achievements.

The party achieved some significant changes in the area of company law, especially in relation to competition policy, but it was in regard to taxation policy that the party achieved its greatest impact. Styling itself as the low taxation party, the PDs while in government succeeded in the reducing the lower and, more significantly for its supporters, the higher rates of income tax. A similar large decrease in capital gains tax was also introduced at the behest of the party.

What the Progressive Democrats failed to do was to put in place the parallel plank of its economic policy – the control of public expenditure. During its periods in government the party oversaw increases in expenditure far in excess of the rate of inflation or GDP growth, so the tax rate reductions that accompanied this were a large element in the creation of the perfect storm which meant the then government was unable to respond appropriately to the economic crisis that occurred in 2008.

Other achievements were the decisions by Mary Harney, later party leader and then as Minister of State, to establish the Environmental Protection Agency and to create a smoke-free zone in Dublin by banning the sale of bituminous coal. However, as these were issues that had been campaigned for externally by the Green Party, it may be the case for another thesis to decide what has the greater effect – those who sign off on legislative change or those who campaign to bring pressure to bear to bring about such considerations.

There has been only one instance of a minor party in government in Ireland initiating and following through on constitutional change. That was the 2004 Citizenship referendum, limiting the right to Irish citizenship that was proposed by the Progressive Democrat Minister for Justice, Michael McDowell. McDowell is associated with a quotation that probably best exemplifies the difficulty that all minor parties have had in the area of policy attainment. Being in government has diverted the attention of minor parties, by their not being able to pay sufficient attention to maintaining party infrastructure. Policy distinctiveness has also been blunted in a collective failure to achieve an identity separate from the government in which they are participating, or indeed from the senior partner in those governments. This McDowell described as the need for minor parties, the Progressive Democrats in particular, to be radical or redundant.

That redundancy came with the decision of Ciaran Cannon to resign both his leadership and his membership of the PDs, choosing to join Fine Gael in April 2009. Noel Grealish would become the final leader of the party until its formal dissolution in June.

The government introduced a supplementary budget in April 2009. Public finances were not being controlled and were in need of correction. Any measure taken to do so would further foment public discontent. These measures were taken a couple of months ahead of scheduled European, local and two by-elections.

Difficulties were growing for the Green Party in its preparations for these elections. In an almost coordinated action, the only Green Party members on Cork City Council and Dublin City Council resigned from the party, in protest at government policies. In Cork, Chris O'Leary would contest the local election as an independent. In Dublin, Bronwen Maher defected to the Labour Party.

The by-elections would be held in Dublin South and Dublin Central. Seamus Brennan, then suffering with ill health, retired from cabinet, when Brian Cowen replaced Bertie Ahern as Taoiseach. Brennan passed away in July 2008. His death removed a calming presence in government, one that was supportive of the Greens. His skill in maintaining the 1997-2002 minority government was seen to be lacking in the later years of that government.

January 2009 saw the death, again at a relatively young age, of Tony Gregory. Despite his early flirtations with Official Sinn Féin and the IRSP, Gregory could be seen as the quintessential independent in Irish politics. He had achieved his greatest renown very early in his career, yet he showed how an individual public representative could bring about a more direct use of resources for his constituents, when required for the purpose of electing a government. The Gregory Deal was also a more honest attempt to rise above standard Irish political clientelism. It was published. It contained measures meant to apply to areas other than Gregory's own constituency. It sought to change policy. Twenty-five years later Tony Gregory was continuing to be elected on its success. His death removed a powerful voice from the Dáil on issues of poverty and drug abuse.

For the Dublin South by-election, Fine Gael pulled a rabbit out of a hat in persuading George Lee, RTE's economics correspondent (the man who was daily highlighting the government's failings with the economy), to stand on its behalf. It was a runaway victory, with Lee winning 53 per cent of the vote. In Dublin Central Tony Gregory's legacy continued, with the election as a TD of a member of his organisation, Cllr Maureen O'Sullivan.

The by-elections were held to coincide with the already scheduled European and local elections. In the European elections, there was much movement in votes and seats. For a start, there would be one less seat available to contest. After Romania and Bulgaria had become EU members, Ireland's European Parliament delegation would be reduced from thirteen MEPs to twelve. Of these, Fine Gael dropped one seat, as did Fianna Fáil (which fell to a 24 per cent share of the vote). Surprisingly Sinn Féin lost its single seat, despite maintaining its national vote. There would also be one fewer independent MEP.

The big winners were the Labour Party whose numbers changed from one MEP to three. In Ireland South, Alan Kelly (a Senator since 2007) beat outgoing independent TD Kathy Sinnott to the third and final seat. In Ireland East the Labour Party persuaded Nessa Childers (daughter of the late president, Erskine Childers, who had once been a member of the Labour Party) to run. Up to a few weeks before that Childers had been a Green Party councillor in Dublin, a position she had resigned 'to spend more time with her family'.

A more interesting political resurrection was that of Joe Higgins in the Dublin constituency. Having failed to be re-elected to the Dáil, this election was his first opportunity to again enter the political fray. Higgins more than doubled his vote from the previous election, leaving Sinn Féin's outgoing MEP, Mary Lou McDonald trailing in his wake. His election helped resuscitate the Socialist Party.

The Green Party, standing in two of the four constituencies, saw its vote more than halved. Its situation in the Dublin constituency was compromised by the decision of Patricia McKenna to stand as an independent against the party's official candidate, Deirdre De Burca.

A new political party was formed and registered for the purpose of these elections. Named Libertas, its three Irish candidates Caroline Symons in Dublin (active in pro-life organisations), Raymond O'Malley in Ireland East (a former deputy president with the Irish Farmers Association), and party leader Declan Ganley were part of a pan-European platform of candidates. Ganley, an Irish businessman who had spent his early life in the UK, had provided many of his personal resources in the campaign against the Lisbon Treaty. Contesting these elections would be the next step in that process. The party won close to 100,000 votes; most of these (67,638) were won by Ganley himself, standing in the Ireland North West constituency. He was unsuccessful and finished a distant fourth for the three available seats.

The local elections created their own series of surprises. Fine Gael became the largest party, surpassing Fianna Fáil. Labour increased its local government presence by around 50 per cent. Sinn Féin maintained its numbers and its own continuing strong presence. The Socialist Party added two councillors to the party's existing four city councillors. The People Before Profit Alliance (a Socialist Workers Party initiative) had five councillors elected, largely in the Dublin area, in this its first outing. Seamus Healy's Workers and Unemployed Action Group elected two county and five town councillors. The Workers' Party again elected two councillors. It lost one councillor on Waterford City Council when its chief vote-getter, John Halligan, left over a policy dispute. In this election he topped his local electoral area as an independent. On Cork City Council, Ted Tynan regained a seat he had last been elected to in 1979 as a Sinn Féin, the Workers' Party candidate.

The number of Green councillors reduced from over thirty councillors to under twenty. At city and county level this was a disastrous election for the Greens. There were now only three Green councillors at this level of government, where there had been eighteen. Michael Lowry boasted that he had more councillors elected than the Greens. The Green vote itself had held up; where seats were being lost was where the party no longer received transfers to the extent it had. This was the price of being in government. As a result, with the exception of Mary White, none of the members of the Green parliamentary party had any local councillors working with them in their constituencies.

Twenty former Progressive Democrats councillors found themselves elected under new designations, mostly Fine Gael but some Fianna Fáil, and some as independents. Not elected was John Wolfe who had registered a political party for contesting local elections. This party was registered as Seniors Solidarity. The intent was to build upon the latent grey power vote that manifested itself during the budget protest. A condition of membership and for becoming a candidate, was to be over 60 years of age. In the 2009 local elections Wolfe was the party's only candidate. He polled a respectable 1,319 votes.

The Christian Solidarty Party had four of its members contest these elections. One candidate, Colm Callanan, stood in ten electoral areas – one in Dublin City Council, all five in Laois County Council and all four in Offaly County Council. The average vote the party received in the thirteen electoral areas it contested was thirty-six votes, a high of 143 and a low of six.

This was an intense political time. Severe public unhappiness with the political system already existed under the worsening economic conditions. Controversies over ethics were tipping other people over the edge. Media investigations on the use of expenses exposed and brought down the Ceann Comhairle, John O'Donoghue. He was replaced by Seamus Kirk from Louth.

With more than enough on its agenda, the government was also planning towards a second Lisbon Treaty referendum. This entailed the Green Party having another members' convention to discuss what the party's position should be. This time the convention voted 214 for supporting the treaty with 107 voting against, precisely the two-thirds majority that was needed. When the referendum itself took place a similar majority in favour was achieved. Unlike the second Nice referendum, on this occasion a significant changeover of votes occurred. On a slightly larger turnout nearly 500,000 more voted Yes, while almost 300,000 fewer voted No.

As part of its willingness to remain in government, the Green Party demanded a review of the programme for government. These negotiations brought significant changes to the programme for government – more political reform measures, local government reforms, protected expenditure in education, removal of tax avoidance mechanisms, the introduction of green taxation measures and further renewable energy initiatives. It was with this review that an Irish government first committed to applying property taxes and metered water charges.

Relationships between the two government parties, never particularly warm, were exposed in these talks. Fianna Fáil tactics were to put, and keep, the Greens in their box. The Fianna Fáil negotiator charged that the Greens only seemed to be concerned with 'hares, stags and badgers'. 'The Greens,' Mary White countered, 'and all you (Fianna Fáil) are con-. cerned with are builders, bankers and bailouts.'

Against this background the government was also struggling with how to deal with non-performing loans and assets that were prohibiting banks to restore their ability to operate. The National Asset Management

Agency (NAMA) legislation was framed to deal with this problem. The proposals were not popularly received, being seen as throwing more good money after bad.

Green Party members were to be brought together for the fourth time since 2007 to decide on the direction of government policy. The Green Party had shown itself to be the most open and engaging of Irish political parties in how it consulted with its members. For others, there would be a sense of disquiet, that such a relatively small group of people was having such an opportunity to influence public policy.

At this meeting two questions were to be decided, the first on a new programme for government, the second on the proposed NAMA legislation. Both required a two-thirds majority. Defeat of either proposal would have meant the party leaving government. The programme for government motion passed with an 84 per cent majority (the same margin achieved when the party had entered government). The NAMA motion passed with a somewhat less but still sufficient 71 per cent in favour. These were difficult decisions, but the party would receive some partial compensation for the soul searching, through acquiring a new member of the Oireachtas. This was after an agreement to alternate the contesting of Seanad by-elections, when former Mayor of Galway Niall Ó'Brolcháin, became the first Green to be directly elected to the Seanad.

Those majorities might not have been achieved a few weeks later when Brian Lenihan presented the 2010 Budget. Included was the introduction of a carbon tax, a key Green policy but not necessarily a popular one. At the heart of the Budget were cuts to many social welfare payments, with the exception of the old age pension. This was a government that seemed intent to dig itself deeper into the mire.

So 2010 became a year of escape. First to bolt was George Lee, after only eight months as a TD, when he possibly became frustrated with the reality of political life. A number of days later he was followed by Green Senator Deirdre de Burca, whose dissatisfaction was a combination of unhappiness with policies being followed by the government; a lack of support received from her party during the European elections; and upset that there would be no Green presence in the cabinet of newly appointed European Commissioner, Máire Geoghegan Quinn.

Within a week there would be a resignation from the cabinet. Minister for Defence Willie O'Dea had survived a vote of confidence in the Dáil over his behaviour in a slander trial with a political rival. That confidence was not absolute. Green Party chairman Dan Boyle tweeted that that confidence was not shared by him. By the following day O'Dea had resigned. Five days later it was revealed that Green Minister of State Trevor Sargent had made contact with the Gardaí about the progress of an investigation in which a constituent of his had been a victim. Believing the perception to be wrong, on an issue that most others would have challenged or ridden out, Sargent chose to resign his office. It would be another two weeks before the fifth and final of this series of resignations. It was another resignation from the cabinet. Martin Cullen, the Minister for Arts, Sports and Tourism, resigned his cabinet post and his Dáil seat, citing medical advice.

Three of these resignations required a cabinet reshuffle. This would leave the two Green ministers holding the same portfolios. It was at Minister of State level that the Greens were determined to effect change. The number of junior ministers was meant to be reduced from twenty to fifteen. Despite this, Brian Cowen was also expected to appoint two new Green ministers of State. These would be Ciarán Cuffe and Mary White. The vacancy brought about by Deirdre de Burca's resignation from the Seanad was filled by Louth councillor Mark Dearey.

The 2010 Green Party convention was meant to see the party stress what it was achieving in government, while dealing with difficult economic circumstances. The party found itself imprisoned in the Convention Centre in Waterford. Outside, 2,000 protestors were letting the party know what they thought of its policies. Most of these protestors came from a recently formed, yet strongly organised group, known as RISE (Rural Ireland Says Enough). The policies causing such risk to rural Ireland was the Dog Breeding Establishment Bill (a bill drafted by a Fianna Fáil minister, which had preceded the Greens being in government) and a bill to ban stag hunting. The intent of the protests was to show that the Greens were frivolous in their legislative priorities, oblivious to economic priorities. The truth was that Green Party spokespeople were more inclined than their Fianna Fáil counterparts to respond to and seek to explain government policies through the media.

The government had some brief respite when the main opposition party began to turn on itself. Richard Bruton moved a motion of no confidence in his party leader Enda Kenny. Most of the Fine Gael front bench declared against Kenny. He overcame the challenge, although the actual result was not publicly released. It was thought that Kenny survived without having confidence from his TDs, securing a victory with the votes of Fine Gael Senators.

The government managed to pass some significant pieces of legislation – a Planning Act and an historic Civil Partnership Act. Later, in retrospect, John Gormley would state that this would have been the time for the Greens to have left government, at a time that some achievements could be pointed to, with Fine Gael in a state of disarray.

Another party that the Greens gave a helping but unwilling hand to was Sinn Féin. That party had taken a High Court action seeking to force the government to move the writ for the Donegal South West by-election, vacant since the election of Pat 'The Cope' Gallagher to the European Parliament in June 2009. Under the separation of powers, the courts had usually taken a position of not interfering with the affairs of the legislature. However, on this occasion, the High Court accepted the argument that it was the democratic rights of citizens that were being interfered with. Fianna Fáil wanted further delay by referring the decision to the Supreme Court (the Attorney General wanted this as well). The Greens insisted that the by-election had to be held. It succeeded, when held later in the year, in electing Sinn Féin Senator Pearse Doherty. His articulate voice would add greatly to, the what had been up until then a fairly staid Sinn Féin team in the Dáil.

Donegal would have one TD fewer with the resignation from the Dáil of former cabinet member, Jim McDaid. A conveyor belt of TDs seemed to be lining up saying they would not be contesting the upcoming general election – Dermot Ahern, Noel Dempsey, Mary Harney and Bertie Ahern included.

By the time the Dáil had returned from its summer recess all such thinking would prove moot. Rumours and uncorroborated reports were circulating that Ireland would have to avail of an International Monetary Fund (IMF) facility. The G20 group of industrial nations was meeting in Seoul in South Korea. Media were reporting that German EU sources were saying that Ireland would have to avail itself of the IMF. It was the Governor of the Central Bank who had revealed that the IMF were coming to Ireland, something that many public representatives still were to hear. Given the loss of sovereignty the presence of the IMF represented, the Greens announced their intention to leave government, but to do so in a timetabled way so that a budget could be agreed. The party believed that the parameters of a programme had to be agreed, so that any incoming government would be governed by that, and not by any glib, populist promises made during an election campaign.

After that, it all became a bit surreal. Brian Cowen saw off a vote of no confidence laid against his leadership of Fianna Fáil. That victory seemed to embolden him. Either by persuausion or contrivance, a number of Ministers resigned their positions. Cowen wanted to appoint six new members of cabinet to a government that had already agreed to shorten its lifespan. Appointing new ministers would, in effect, be asking the Dáil to approve a new government. The Greens said No, resigning their positions in government. This was followed by Cowen's own resignation as leader of Fianna Fáil. He would be replaced by Mícheál Martin who overcame a challenge from Brian Lenihan.

The stage was now set for the biggest reshuffling of the pack of cards that was Irish politics that had ever occurred in a single election.

21

Labour's Way, Not Frankfurt's Way

The general election to elect members to the Thirty-first Dáil took place on 25 February. The 70 per cent turnout showed an electorate at its most engaged. It would result in gains for all the opposition parties, with catastrophic results for the outgoing parties of government. Fine Gael, for the first time in its history, would become the largest party in the Dáil, making a net gain of twenty-five seats. Labour also achieved its highest standing in Dáil, winning an additional seventeen seats. Sinn Féin, made a significant advance although perhaps not as much as the party was expecting. The party still more than trebled its parliamentary party size, over and above the number that had been elected in 2007. The Socialist Party returned to the Dáil, re-electing not only Joe Higgins, but also having Clare Daly elected in Dublin North. The People Before Profit Alliance made its debut in the Dáil, electing two TDs, Richard Boyd Barrett in Dun Laoghaire and Joan Collins in Dublin South Central. There would be fourteen independent TDs, up from five elected in 2007.

Together these groups made gains of sixty-three seats, gains won from Fianna Fáil and the Green Party. Fianna Fáil suffered its worst ever general election result, losing fifty-seven of the seventy-seven seats the party had won in 2007. In Dublin, Fianna Fáil elected only one TD (Brian Lenihan in Dublin West). At least Fianna Fáil would continue to have a presence in the Thirty-First Dáil. The Greens experienced electoral wipeout, losing all six of its Dáil seats. The party hoped that either Trevor Sargent or Éamon Ryan could be elected, while both polled significantly, neither succeeded. Even worse was the failure of the party to meet 2 per cent of the national vote, the level at which state funding of political parties becomes available. The party missed that target by about 3,500 votes or about eighty additional votes in each constituency.

Sinn Féin's new TDs included a returning Sean Crowe in Dublin South West; Sandra McLennan in Cork East; Jonathan O'Brien in Cork North Central (where he topped the poll); Pádraig MacLochlainn in Donegal North East; Mary Lou McDonald in Dublin Central; Dessie Ellis in Dublin North West; Brian Stanley in Laois Offaly; Peadar Tobín in Meath West; Michael Colreavy in Sligo North Leitrim; and finally, party leader Gerry Adams in Louth (previous TD, Arthur Morgan, stood aside on Adam's behalf). The party now had Dáil representatives in every border constituency.

Among the new independents elected was returnee, Catherine Murphy in Kildare North. Former PD TD, Noel Grealish was elected as independent TD in Galway West. Thomas Pringle was elected in Donegal South West. He had been elected as an independent councillor in 1999, was elected a Sinn Féin councillor in 2004, leaving Sinn Féin in 2007 then retaining his council seat as an independent in 2009. The Kerry South constituency elected two independents for the three available seats. One was Michael Healy Rae, replacing his father Jackie. The second was Tom Fleming, a long-standing Fianna Fáil councillor, who had figured that his best chance of being elected to the Dáil at this time was as an independent. In Roscommon South Leitrim, the colourful Luke 'Ming' Flanagan was elected. A county councillor since 2004, he improved his vote twelvefold over his previous general election performance in 2002. Tipperary South was another three-seat constituency that elected two independents. One was Seamus Healy, winning back the seat he had lost in 1987. The other was Mattie McGrath, who had been elected as a Fianna Fáil TD in 2002, leaving the party over what he saw was a letting down of rural Ireland. In the neighbouring Waterford constituency, John Halligan made his breakthrough, being elected as an independent TD. In the previous general election he had been the Workers' Party flag bearer. In Wexford, having decided to contest only six weeks before the election, was the unconventional builder-developer Mick Wallace, who topped the poll. Also working against the template was the cerebral

Stephen Donnelly, elected as an independent in Wicklow, who prior to his involvement in politics had been a management consultant with McKinsey & Company.

Other established parties that contested but did not get candidates elected were the Workers' Party (winning 3,000 votes) and the Christian Solidarity Party (now led by Richard Greene, who was not a candidate) which won 2,000 votes.

A newly registered party was Fís Nua (New Vision). The party was a protest breakaway from the Green Party. Five candidates stood in four constituencies, two standing in the Wicklow constituency. This was the constituency of the party's only elected public representative, Pat Kavanagh, who had been elected as a Green Party town councillor in 2009. Collectively the party's candidates won less than 1,000 votes. Its Dublin South East candidate, Peadar Ó'Ceallaigh (opposing Green Party leader John Gormley), won 18 votes.

Unregistered groups in this election included New Vision (not to be confused with Fís Nua). This was a loose umbrella of independents brought together by Macdara, a son of the former TD, Neil Blaney. Twenty candidates stood in eighteen constituencies, winning more than 25,000 votes. Its sole success was that of Luke Flanagan in Roscommon South Leitrim. Another group The People's Convention ran a number of candidates in Cork constituencies, polling around 1,500 votes.

An umbrella group of a different sort was the United Left Alliance (ULA) which won cumulatively 59,423 votes and five seats. The ULA comprised the Socialist Party, the People Before Profit Alliance, the Workers and Unemployed Action Group and Sligo North Leitrim independent candidate Declan Bree. These groups campaigned seperately but sought to present a united front. It was the intention to operate that way in the new Dáil.

The government formed was a Fine Gael–Labour coalition. It would the government with the largest majority ever. New Taoiseach Enda Kenny had a ninety-vote majority on being elected. The new government came into office with a great deal of public goodwill. This was added to by visits to Ireland by Queen Elizabeth II and by US President, Barack Obama.

The new government was presented with the final report of the Moriarty (Payments to Politicians) Tribunal. Among its main findings were that Michael Lowry 'secured the winning' of the 1995 mobile licence for the businessman Denis O'Brien; that O'Brien had made two payments to Lowry that totalled IR£500,000, further supporting a loan of IR£420,000 secured by Lowry, a benefit equivalent to a payment; that Lowry imparted substantive information to O'Brien which was 'of significant value and assistance to him in securing the licence'; that Lowry deceived his Cabinet colleagues and thus not only influenced, but delivered a positive decision for Esat Digifone; that a $50,000 donation to Fine Gael was made through Telenor on behalf of Esat Digifone; that Lowry sought to influence a hike in the lease for Telecom Éireann headquarters following a request from Ben Dunne. This was found to be 'profoundly corrupt', with Lowry being criticised for his 'cynical and venal abuse of office' and his refusal to admit the impropriety of his financial arrangements with Denis O'Brien and Ben Dunne. Michael Lowry remained a member of Dáil Éireann.

A radically different Dáil would become mirrored by a radically different Seanad. Fianna Fáil's losses during the 2009 local elections made this inevitable. On the vocational panels Sinn Féin became the beneficiaries of this. Thanks to its own strengthened presence in local government, Sinn Féin elected three Senators – Trevor Ó Clochartaigh from Galway, Kathryn Reilly from Monaghan and David Cullinane from Waterford. On the Dublin University panel, a new independent Senator was elected. He was the Trinity transport economist, Seán Barrett.

The eleven Taoiseach's nominees announced presented several interesting choices. Four of the eleven nominees had direct political affiliations, three Labour Senators and one Fine Gael Senator. Seven of the nominees would sit as independents in the Seanad. These included former World Champion athlete, Éamon Coughlan; the artistic director of the Abbey Theatre, Fiach MacConghail; Martin McAleese (dentist and husband of President Mary McAleese); the founder of Lily O'Brien Chocolates and co-founder of the Jack and Jill Foundation charity, Mary Ann O'Brien; the broadcaster Marie Louise O'Donnell; children's rights advocate, Jillian van Turnhout; and the co-founder of the community education organisation – An Cosán, Katherine Zappone. Most of these members would sit together as a separate independent grouping in the Seanad, largely supporting the government's legislative programme.

After a period of introspection, the Green Party went about choosing a new leader. Three candidates presented themselves for consideration – party activist Phil Kearney, Kilkenny councillor, Malcolm Noonan and the former Minister for Communications, Energy and Natural Resources and one-time TD for Dublin South, Éamon Ryan. It was Ryan who was given the mantle to proceed. Working with him as Deputy leader was Catherine Martin.

The party also got some solace with the election of Steven Agnew to the Northern Ireland Assembly, retaining the North Down seat that had been won by Brian Wilson in 2007. Since 2005 the Green Party had operated as an all-island party, but as autonomous parties in each jurisdiction. Much like in Germany where its Green Party lost its parliamentary representation after German reunification, but did gain representation through its East German affiliate, Bundis 90, Steven Agnew became the Irish Greens' Bundis 90, being the only Green on the island holding a parliamentary seat.

One election the Greens would not be participating in would be the election to replace President Mary McAleese, who was coming to the end of her second term. Unlike the election for that second term, which was uncontested, more enthusiasm existed among most political parties that there should be a public contest to determine who the next President should be – most parties, but not Fianna Fáil. Party leader Micheál Martin had decided Fianna Fáil would not participate, realising that the toxicity of the party brand could lead to another embarrassing defeat. The party did examine the possibility of approaching a high-profile personality. Respected broadcaster Gay Byrne was approached but he decided against.

Fine Gael would conduct an intricate selection procedure to choose its candidate. Some who wanted to be considered were showing an enthusiasm that the party leadership wished to cool. Gay Mitchell, MEP for the Dublin constituency and former TD for Dublin South-Central, expressed the greatest level of enthusiasm. Avril Doyle, former MEP and TD, also announced her candidacy, but she later withdrew from the contest. Two others sought the nomination – Pat Cox, former President of the European Parliament and former Progressive Democrats Independent MEP, and Mairead McGuinness, MEP for the East constituency.

Cox had earlier indicated his willingness to stand as an independent. He applied for and was given Fine Gael membership by the party's national executive, part of a process where he had been encouraged by the party leadership.

A special convention was held on 9 July 2011. Voting was by secret ballot, with an electoral college that consisted of the Fine Gael parliamentary party (TDs, Senators and MEPs) with 70 per cent of the vote, county and city councillors (20 per cent) and members of the party's national executive council (10 per cent). Gay Mitchell was declared the nominee without the results being released.

Labour also had a selection process. Michael D. Higgins, who had been discouraged from standing in 2004, would face challenges from Fergus Finlay (a strategic adviser for former party leader, Dick Spring) and former Senator, Kathleen O'Meara. The electorate were members of the party's national executive, combined with its parliamentary party. Michael D. Higgins achieved a first-count victory to become the party's nominee.

Having talked around the issue for a number of months, Sinn Féin thought it would seize the opportunity and put forward its own Presidential candidate. It chose Martin McGuinness, the Deputy First Minister of Northern Ireland. The party had a slight logistical problem in that with only seventeen Oireachtas members, it was three short of the constitutional requirement to submit a nomination. Further nominators were found in the form of Michael Healy Rae, Tom Fleming, Finian McGrath and Luke Flanagan.

Four candidates would achieve nominations by securing the support of at least four city or county councils. These were Mary Davis, Chief Executive of Special Olympics Ireland; Senator David Norris; former MEP and Presidential candidate Rosemary Scallon/Dana; and entrepreneur and panellist from the Irish version of *Dragons' Den*, Seán Gallagher. Seven candidates would be the largest ever number to contest an Irish presidential election.

Norris had been an early favourite, but two stories put his campaign off course. One suggested that he made an official representation on behalf of a friend and former lover, who was an Israeli citizen. The second was a somewhat esoteric explanation of the practice of man-boy love in ancient Greece. From then the momentum was with Seán

Gallagher, who was seen both as an outsider and a member of Fianna Fáil. A tweet from the Martin McGuinness campaign was read live, not having been verified, by presenter Pat Kenny during a candidates' debate. This asserted that Gallagher had been involved in intimidatory fundraising activity on behalf of Fianna Fáil.

After that, the election was Michael D. Higgins's to lose as he topped the poll. Gallagher was in second place, some 200,000 votes behind. With every subsequent vote he would fall further and further behind. In third position was Martin McGuinness for Sinn Féin, who won the largest number of votes the party had yet won in the Republic. Gay Mitchell won the smallest vote Fine Gael had ever won in any national election (6.4 per cent). He was barely ahead of David Norris in sixth place. The final two candidates, Rosemary Scallon/Dana and Mary Davis won little more than 5 per cent of the vote between them. Michael D. Higgins was then elected as the ninth President of Ireland.

Held on the same day was a by-election in the Dublin West constituency. Brian Lenihan, who had been struggling with pancreatic cancer for the previous two years, died in June 2011. Despite a strong performance by Ruth Coppinger of the Socialist party, the by-election was won by Patrick Nulty of the Labour party.

Despite these victories, it was the Labour Party that was having early jitters in the new government. Willie Penrose resigned his position as Minister of State because of plans to close the army barracks in Mullingar. Tommy Broughan was expelled for having voted against a further two-year extension of the bank guarantee (a measure Labour had originally voted against). Barely six weeks a TD, Patrick Nulty voted against a budget provision, causing his loss of the Labour Party whip. Before the end of 2012 they were followed by Róisín Shortall and Colm Keaveney. Shortall resigned as Minister of State and from the Labour Party due to a dispute as to how the Department of Health was being managed by the Fine Gael Minister, James O'Reilly. Keaveney, who at the time was the chairman of the Labour Party, voted against the Social Welfare Bill, immediately losing the whip. Later, in 2013, Nessa Childers MEP resigned from the party. The daughter of a former President of Ireland and Fianna Fáil minister, an earlier member of the Labour Party, a Green Party councillor, a Labour MEP, would now sit as an independent in the European Parliament.

It was Fine Gael that had suffered the first loss when Denis Naughton voted against the government on a motion to protect services at Roscommon County Hospital. This was an issue that once elected an independent TD from the constituency (Tom Foxe). Naughton might have considered that his political future might need to follow a similar course.

The spotlight remained on Fianna Fáil, however, as the final report of the Mahon Tribunal was published. Bertie Ahern and Pádraig Flynn resigned their membership of Fianna Fáil on foot of the report. It was felt that if they had not they would have been subject to expulsion from the party.

Around this time legislation was passed that made the future composition of the Údarás na Gaeltachta Authority by appointment only. Since 1979 up to seventeen people were elected from various Gaeltacht constituencies. Dominated by Fianna Fáil and to a lesser extent Fine Gael, some independents were elected. It even led to a Gaeltacht-based party cum civil rights group known as Cumhacht – which translates roughly as 'the ability to deliver change'. It was not until 2005 – the last such elections for Údarás – that party affiliations were allowed to appear on the ballot paper. In these elections the Progressive Democrats and Sinn Féin had candidates elected. A Republican Sinn Féin candidate polled well. The Green Party/Comhaontas Glas stood two candidates. Its candidate in the Galway constituency polled moderately well. In the Meath constituency, its candidate polled five votes from the 800 or so votes available, the worst performance of any Green Party candidate in any election.

Back in the Pale the government was being ham-fisted in its introduction of a property tax. Less than half of those expected to register had done so by the deadline date. Thousands protested outside the National Convention Centre, where Fine Gael was holding its Ard Fheis. The news that the party had gained an additional Oireachtas member, through the recruitment in the Seanad of Éamon Coughlan, did little to ease the party's discomfort.

Controversy attached to the opposition when it was revealed that the Wexford independent TD, Mick Wallace, had made a settlement with the Revenue Commissioners, over the non-payment of VAT receipts. Mick Wallace did not resign. The controversy had ramifications for the

Socialist Party, leading Dublin North TD Clare Daly to resign from the party because of the close political relationship she had established with Mick Wallace.

Daly then sat as an independent under the United Left Alliance umbrella. The Socialist Party was also a part of the ULA. Tensions were rising within the alliance. Seamus Healy removed himself, and the association of his Workers and Unemployed Action Group, from the ULA. He cited the failure to criticise Mick Wallace as his reason for leaving. In early 2013, Joe Higgins took his Socialist Party along a similar route. His reason was failure of the alliance to 'collaborate'. What was left of ULA was a triumvirate who typified the new left in Ireland. These three were Richard Boyd Barrett, Joan Collins and Clare Daly. Boyd Barrett and Collins were part of the People Before Profit Alliance. That alliance was an initiative of the Socialist Workers Party (SWP), although Collins was not a member of the SWP. In fact, she had originally been a member of the Socialist Party, from which she resigned. She was elected as an independent member of Dublin City Council in 2004, before setting up a Community and Workers Action Group which she brought into the People Before Profit Alliance. On their behalf she was re-elected as a councillor in 2009 and as a TD in 2011. Clare Daly's involvement with the ULA was the least complex. She had been a long-standing member of the Socialist Party, being elected a councillor and a TD on its behalf. The Socialist Party became part of the ULA platform. Clare Daly resigned from the Socialist Party, but remained with the ULA. The Socialist Party was subsequently to leave the ULA.

Two constitutional referenda were held in 2012. The first was on the European Fiscal Compact, which strengthened the criteria on banks' reserves and the intervention role of the European Central Bank (ECB) in the event of another financial crisis. There was growing concern in Ireland about how the ECB had been dealing with the Irish crisis in particular, but the referendum passed with a healthy majority. The second referendum was a Childrens' Rights referendum designed to insert specified rights for children into the Constitution. Only one-third of the electorate turned out to vote, and while a 58 per cent majority was achieved, the efficacy of the campaign was thrown into doubt by a Supreme Court finding that the Minister for Children had breached the McKenna judgement by actively advocating a certain position on the referendum.

The prospect of another referendum on abortion remained on the table. In 2010 the case *A, B and C v Ireland*, was heard in the European Court of Human Rights (ECHR) which ruled that Ireland had infringed a complainant's rights in not providing clear information on whether she was entitled to an abortion. The Irish Government had a year to present an official response. The new coalition government decided in December 2011 to establish an expert group to examine the impact of the ECHR judgment. On 12 November *The Irish Times* reported the death of Savita Halappanavar in Galway of maternal septicaemia after a miscarriage that had occurred a number of weeks earlier. The story of her death and her husband's emotional response, re-ignited the debate on abortion.

The Government decided legislation had to be enacted. It further decided that before legislation would be drafted, public hearings of the Oireachtas Joint Committee on Health and Children should take place to help inform the contents of a bill that would be produced. The bill, the *Protection of Life During Pregnancy Bill* was produced in April 2013. Fianna Fáil allowed a free vote on the bill. Only five other Fianna Fáil TDs supported the position of party leader Mícheál Martin that the bill be supported. All other parties applied whips. Sinn Féin suspended its TD Peadar Tobin for opposing the bill. Fine Gael shipped the greatest damage when four of its TDs vote against the second-stage reading of the bill. These TDs – Terence Flanagan, Peter Mathews, Billy Timmins, and Brian Walsh – were expelled from the Fine Gael parliamentary party. At the report stage they would be joined by a rising star in the party, Lucinda Creighton, who was obliged to also resign as Minister for State for European Affairs.

Towards the end of 2012 the news was revealed of the death of Minister of State Shane McEntee. He had taken his own life. His death necessitated a by-election in the Meath East constituency. Fine Gael chose his daughter Helen to be its candidate. She was elected without any great difficulty. The story of this by-election was found lower down on the first-count results. Labour had been relegated to fifth place in this by-election. Ahead of its candidate was a candidate for a newly registered party, Direct Democracy Ireland.

The party had three principal aims – to allow citizens to petition for a referendum on any issue through the collection of a certain number of signatures; to allow for the recall of non-performing politicians and to create realistic economic policies based on public debate. Unregistered for the 2011 general election, three of its candidates accumulated 570 votes. The party was one of the few to oppose the Childrens' Rights referendum in 2012. What and who the party represented was somewhat cloaked. In the middle of the Meath East by-election, the Christian Solidarity Party took out a newspaper advertisement stating that the DDI candidate, Ben Gilroy, was 'sound' on the abortion issue.

The Government established a constitutional covention to examine areas where the Constitution could be modernised. It consisted of 100 members: a chairman; twenty-nine members of the Oireachtas (parliament); four representatives of Northern Ireland political parties; and six-ty six randomly selected citizens of Ireland. The inaugural meeting was held on 1 December 2012 at Dublin Castle, with working sessions beginning in late January 2013. The agenda of the convention would be:

- Reducing the presidential term of office to five years and aligning it with local and European elections;
- Reducing the voting age to 17;
- Reviewing the Dáil electoral system;
- Giving citizens resident outside the State the right to vote in presidential elections at Irish embassies, or otherwise;
- Provision for same-sex marriage;
- Amending the clause on the role of women in the home and encouraging greater participation of women in public life;
- Increasing the participation of women in politics;
- Removal of the offence of blasphemy from the Constitution;
- Following completion of the above reports, such other relevant constitutional amendments that may be recommended by it.

Independents from the Dáil and the Seanad were represented by Catherine Murphy and Maureen O'Sullivan and by Jillian van Turnhout. Sinn Féin was represented by Gerry Adams, Mary Lou McDonald and Martin McGuinness. The Greens had a presence through its Northern Ireland Assembly member, Steven Agnew.

Those Fine Gael TDs and Senators who had been expelled from the party over the Protection of Life during Pregnancy Act, (TDs Lucinda

Creighton, Terence Flanagan, Peter Mathews, Denis Naughten and Billy Timmins and two Senators, Paul Bradford and Fidelma Healy Eames organised themselves into an Oireachtas grouping, named the Reform Alliance. Another TD, Brian Walsh from Galway West, chose not to participate.

One government position this new group chose to oppose was the constitutional referendum asking that the Seanad be abolished. This was an issue that the constitutional convention was not allowed to discuss. In opposition, Enda Kenny had floated the idea of abolition of the Seanad, on a whim. It had become, for him, a political priority. Sinn Féin also supported the government's position. Opposed were Fianna Fáil, the Green Party, the Reform Alliance and the Workers' Party. Others, like Michael McDowell, took a high-profile role in opposing the referendum. Opinion polls throughout the campaign showed a big Yes lead, but also a large number of undecided voters. The No victory, on a 52 to 48 result, came as a surprise to many and an embarrassment to Enda Kenny.

A second, less contentionious, referendum was held simultaneously. The proposal to establish an intermediate Court of Appeal to operate between the High Court and the Supreme Court was overwhelmingly endorsed.

The Green Party was experiencing further setbacks in its efforts to achieve a political recovery. Its Clare County councillor Brian Meaney decided to join Fianna Fáil. He was followed by the chairwoman of New Ross Town Council, Niamh FitzGibbon, who threw in her lot with Fine Gael. Defectors from the Greens had now joined Fianna Fáil, Fine Gael, Labour, Sinn Féin and Fís Nua. This left the party with only two county councillors in the whole country.

Towards the end of 2013 it was announced that Colm Keaveney, who had been chairman of the Labour Party before losing its whip, then sitting as an independent TD, had chosen to become a member of Fianna Fáil.

Early in 2014, a long-running campaign in the Dáil, undertaken by Mick Wallace and Clare Daly on what they believed was malpractice within the Garda Síochána, was beginning to bear fruit. It was reported that the Garda Síochána Ombudsman Commission offices were being bugged. This led to the resignation of the Garda Commissioner, Martin Callinan, who had been visited by the Secretary General of the

Department of Justice (sent there by the Taoiseach, Enda Kenny). This led to accusations that the Commissioner had been constructively dismissed, which had been done unconstitutionally without a cabinet decision.

Meanwhile the Minister for Justice, Alan Shatter, had appointed someone who had given him political donations as the Garda Confidential Recipient (a conduit for whistleblowers in the Gardaí to work through). A transcript of a meeting between the recipient (Oliver Connolly) and key whistleblower Sgt Maurice McCabe, was read into the Dáil record by Mick Wallace. The transcript gave the impression that McCabe was being threatened. As a result, Shatter fired Connolly, but not before he had appeared on television with Mick Wallace, revealing that he had information of Wallace's own interactions with the Gardaí. This created an impression that, as Minister, Shatter may have had intelligence gained from Garda sources on opponents that he might be prepared to use for political advantage. The government appointed a State Counsel to review these events. His report (the Guerin Report – later challenged by Shatter) led to the resignation of the Minister for Justice and Defence.

This was the mood music that accompanied the next scheduled round of elections for the European Parliament and for local councils being held throughout the country. Mid-term elections traditionally are difficult for any government in office, as these would prove. The Irish contingent in the European Parliament was being reduced from twelve to eleven, after the accession to membership of Croatia. In the local elections, there would be fewer seats to contest, after legislation that had abolished town councils.

The European elections were now organised in three constituencies – a three-seat Dublin constituency, and two four-seat constituencies Ireland South and Ireland Midlands North West. Fine Gael held its four seats. Sinn Féin had an excellent election, electing three MEPs. Three independent MEPs were elected. Fianna Fáil only succeeded in having one MEP elected. This was despite winning the largest number of votes (outpolling Fine Gael by 425 votes, with Sinn Féin a further 27,000 votes behind). At 22 per cent of the poll this offered little solace. On the other hand the Sinn Féin performance, at close to 20 per cent of the poll, was a record for the party in any election in the Republic. Labour lost all three seats it held. None of those who had seats in 2009 was available to the party in 2014. Proinsias De Rossa retired, Alan Kelly was now a Minister of State, while Nessa Childers had left the party. The Green Party at 5 per cent of the national poll had its best election (in terms of votes) for ten years, close to the number of votes won by the Labour Party. The Socialist Party lost the Dublin seat it had won in 2009 (won then by Joe Higgins, who after his election back to the Dáil in 2009 had been replaced by Paul Murphy). Direct Democracy Ireland ran four candidates (two in Dublin) winning 25,000 votes, without any of its candidates threatening. People Before Profit stood Bríd Smith in the Dublin constituency, the first time the party had contested these elections. She won 24,000 votes, being cited by the Socialist Party as the reason why the party did not hold the seat it was defending. The Catholic Democrats (previously the Christian Democrats, and once the National Party) stood one candidate in the Ireland South constituency who won about 14,000 votes. Fís Nua stood in all three constituencies, and its candidates won on average 1,500 votes each. The Workers' Party did not contest these elections.

Some interesting stories came from each of the constituencies. In Dublin, the Sinn Féin candidate Lynn Boylan, raced to the first seat. It seemed that Brian Hayes of Fine Gael and Éamon Ryan of the Green Party (who had polled quite strongly) would win the remaining two seats. Independent MEP Nessa Childers had been 10,000 votes behind Éamon Ryan after the first count. After a series of eliminations, Childers went marginally ahead of Ryan. Surprisingly, she did better from the transfers of the Fianna Fáil candidate, Mary Fitzpatrick, meaning she would win the second seat with Hayes winning the final seat. The gap between Childers in second and Ryan in fourth was one-third of one per cent of the available votes.

In Ireland South Brian Crowley produced his usual poll-topping performance. He was followed by the Sinn Féin candidate, Liadh Ní Riada, daughter of the late composer Seán O'Riada. There were strong performances from the independent Diarmuid O'Flynn (associated with the Ballyhea Says No protest group, which had organised weekly protests against austerity) and the Green Party's Grace O'Sullivan (a former crew member of the Greenpeace ship the *Rainbow Warrior* bombed by the French secret service in the South Pacific).

In Ireland Midlands North West two of the four seats were won by independents. Matt Carty made it three seats out of three for Sinn

Féin. Marian Harkin held her independent seat. Poll topper was Luke Flanagan TD who had assembled a coalition of voters through his anti-austerity policies, rural decline and the contested rights of turf cutters. Many of these supporters would not have identified with Flanagan's original political positions which centred around a long-running campaign seeking the legalisation of cannabis.

In the local elections, the parties of government lost approximately 200 seats between them. Fianna Fáil became the largest party of government on 25 per cent of the vote. Sinn Féin made a huge advance, winning over 100 seats, now having three times the presence of Labour in local government. People Before Profit won fourteen seats, the same number of their colleagues/opponents in the Socialist Party which decided before these elections to assume a dual existence. The official name of the party became the Stop the Water Tax Socialist Party, while simultaneously registering under the title the Anti Austerity Alliance. The ownership of the water charges issue was central to the progress of the new left. The Green Party made a respectable showing, electing twelve councillors, eight in the Dublin area, three within The Pale (two in Louth, one in Wicklow) with one outlier in Kilkenny. The Workers' Party lost its Waterford bastion, electing only one councillor onto Cork City Council. Later an independent councillor elected to Dublin City Council, Éilis Ryan (daughter of former Senator, Brendan Ryan), joined the party. With the disintegration of the United Left Alliance, two TDs – Clare Daly and Joan Collins – (who had left the People Before Profit) registered United Left as a new party.

Seamus Healy's Working and Unemployed Group elected one person to the newly unified Tipperary County Council, one less than the organisation had elected to the South Tipperary Riding council. Michael Gleeson was again elected to Kerry County Council with the help of his Kerry Independent Alliance. On the same council, the Healy Rae organisation elected two councillors, Danny Healy Rae and Johnny Healy Rae. The People's Convention group in Cork had candidates elected to Cork County Council (Claire Cullinane in Cobh) and Cork City Council (Paudie Dineen, who promptly disassociated himself from the group once he had been elected).

A registered group known as Independents for Equality Movement, a vehicle for Mick Wallace TD, stood four candidates for Wexford County Council, none of whom was elected.

Among those who stood but did not get candidates elected were Direct Democracy Ireland whose nineteen candidates average about 200 votes each. Fís Nua ran six candidates who averaged about 150 votes each. The Communist Party of Ireland ran two candidates, in the first election it had contested in several years, one in Dublin and one in Cork. Together they won little more than 200 votes.

A relatively recently registered party Éirigí stood four candidates. The party, a breakaway from Sinn Féin, was registered to contest local elections, taking a core republican position of not recognising a 'partitionist' parliament. Going into the election the party had two elected representatives, Louise Minihan on Dublin City Council and John Dwyer on New Ross Town Council. Minihan had achieved a degree of infamy by throwing red paint at Mary Harney at a public event some years earlier. Éirigí had none of its four candidates elected.

Two by-elections were held on the same day of these elections. The Longford Westmeath by-election came about through the death of Fine Gael TD, Nicky McFadden. Her sister Gabrielle was elected in her stead. Her strongest opponent was Aengus O'Rourke, son of former Fianna Fáil minister, Mary O'Rourke. Not that far behind was the Sinn Féin candidate, Paul Hogan. Best performing of the five independent candidates was Kevin 'Boxer' Moran, although James Morgan secured more first-preference votes. The official Labour Party candidate finished in seventh place on the first count.

The Dublin West by-election was caused by the resignation of the independent and one-time Labour TD, Patrick Nulty. He had resigned due to reportage of inappropiate internet contact made by him with a constituent. The beneficiary of his action was Ruth Coppinger, who had finished runner up to him in a previous by-election. On this occasion she would be elected. The Socialist Party would now have two members in the Dáil, both representing the same constituency.

The first effect of these sets of elections was to to bring about the resignation of Éamon Gilmore as leader of the Labour Party. It would become effective upon the choosing of a new leader, on which he would also resign as Tánaiste and as a member of the cabinet. Two candidates made themselves available for the first one-member one-vote election held by the Labour Party. These were the Minister for Social Protection, Joan Burton and Minister for State at the Department of Health, Alex White. Burton secured the leadership on a four-to-one margin. Her deputy leader was Alan Kelly, the Tipperary North TD.

In Brussels Fianna Fáil was engaged in another act of repositioning. Party leader Mícheál Martin wanted Fianna Fáil to become part of the Liberal grouping with the European Parliament. This would have necessitated Brian Crowley, the party's sole MEP, surrendering his role as president of the existing group Fianna Fáil had been a part of. Crowley chose to remain where he was. For this defiance he had the Fianna Fáil whip removed. For the first time since 1973, there would be no official Fianna Fáil representative in the European Parliament.

A new European Parliament meant a new European Commission. The government put forward its Minister for the Environment, Phil Hogan, for consideration. In Ireland, Hogan had presided over the implementation of the most unpopular policies of the government – property taxes and water charges. The issue of metering and paying directly for water became the last straw on the camel's back for many people in Ireland. This resistance was strengthened by a somewhat shambolic creation of a new company, Irish Water, which became a repository for much public discontent.

Two Dáil vacancies were created by the election to the European Parliament of Brian Hayes and Luke Flanagan, resulting in by-elections in Dublin South West and Roscommon South Leitrim. Water charges would be the issue in Dublin South West. Sinn Féin had been expected to easily win this by-election, based on votes the party had received in the earlier local elections. The legislation on water charges had been passed and Sinn Féin leaders stated they would comply with the law and pay these charges. Anti Austerity Alliance (Socialist Party) candidate Paul Murphy argued for total defiance of the legislation and continued non-payment. His campaign strategy was the more successful. In Roscommon South Leitrim, Luke Flanagan's chosen successor, Michael Fitzmaurice was successful. Fitzmaurice's main campaign theme was advocating for turf cutters to continue to cut turf on land listed for conservation.

A vacancy in the Seanad arose when Deirdre Clune was elected to the European Parliament. Gerard Craughwell, a former president of the Teachers Union of Ireland, put himself forward as an independent candidate. His initial intention was to contest a symbolic gesture, protesting against the usual practice of the government using its parliamentary majority to secure the election of its chosen candidate. Craughwell gained sufficient signatures for his nomination from members of the 'technical group' and from Fianna Fáil. He unexpectedly won the election after the Fine Gael candidate John McNulty withdrew from the race because of a controversy over the propriety of his appointment to the board of the Irish Museum of Modern Art (IMMA). Both were contesting the Cultural and Educational panel and McNulty requested his appointment to better his cultural resumé.

Within the Dáil the Reform Alliance ceased to exist. At a press conference, behind a banner stating, 'Reboot Ireland', Lucinda Creighton announced her intention to form a new political party. Sitting with her at that press conference was the financial consultant Eddie Hobbs and an Offaly County Councillor, John Leahy. A number of weeks later, she announced the name of the party to be Renua Ireland, Renua being a made up word that did not exist in Irish or in English. From the Reform Alliance, Denis Naughton and Peter Mathews would not be part of the new party, nor would Fidelma Healy Eames in the Seanad. All would continue to sit as independents. The Taoiseach's nominee in the Seanad, Mary Ann O'Brien, indicated her willingness to join the party, but only at the end of her term as a Senator. About half a dozen local authority councillors came to join the party.

Shane Ross along with Michael Fitzmaurice proposed to establish an Independent Alliance, not a political party (and it would not be registered as such either). It comprised the following TD: Shane Ross, Michael Fitzmaurice, Finian McGrath, John Halligan and Tom Fleming; and the Senators Feargal Quinn (who was about to retire) and Gerard Craughwell. Its focus was to offer voters a coordinated approach in selecting independent members of the Oireachtas, and to offer in the event of a hung parliament a vehicle through which independents might participate in government.

Irish politics in early 2015 was devoted to the holding of two constitutional referenda, the most attention being given to the Same Sex Marriage Referendum. All the political parties represented in the Oireachtas supported the proposal, as did the Green Party and the Workers' Party. In the Dáil the sole dissenting voice was that of independent TD, Mattie McGrath. Senator Ronan Mullen led the charge against the referendum in the Seanad. The proposal was approved on a 62 to 38 majority. Its approval was seen a significant milestone in the development of a new Ireland.

The second referendum, one of several proposals made through the Constitutional Convention, was an attempt to reduce the age restriction on becoming a presidential candidate, from 35 years of age to the age of 21 years. By an almost three-to-one margin the proposal was not accepted.

Also held on this day was a by-election to fill vacancy that existed on Phil Hogan being made a European Commissioner. With its first by-election success since 1996, the seat was won by Bobby Aylward, brother of former TD and MEP, Liam. 45 per cent of the vote in this by-election was won by candidates other than those from Fianna Fáil, Fine Gael or Labour (whose candidate finished fifth). Best performing of the others was Kathleen Funchion of Sinn Féin winning close on 11,000 votes. Renua Ireland could be happy with its first electoral outing. Its candidate Patrick McKee, who had been elected as a Fianna Fáil councillor, won 10 per cent of the vote. The Greens won over 5 per cent. People Before Profit and the Anti Austerity Alliance each ran candidates and together they won 7 per cent of the vote. Winning short of 1,000 votes was Peter O'Loughlin, standing on behalf of an as yet unregistered party, Idenity Ireland. The party was far right in nature, linked to a network of anti-Islamic groups in Europe. At the bottom of the poll with slightly above 200 votes was a candidate for the National Citizens Movement. This party was also unregistered, although eventually it would become a part of Direct Democracy Ireland.

In the aftermath of the Same Sex Marriage Referendum, a new party would emerge from within Dáil Éireann. Three independent

TDs, Catherine Murphy, Róisín Shortall and Stephen Donnelly came together to announce the establishment of the Social Democrats. They were seeking a place in the political marketplace between Sinn Féin and Labour, while promoting a nordic model of social democracy. The three TDs adopted a joint leadership approach, stating that the question of a single leader would be examined in the future. Four councillors signed up with the new party.

The new left coalesced but did not merge with each other, with one eye on future speaking rights and another on safe funding gained when a party passes the 2 per cent threshold of votes, so the Anti Austerity Alliance and the People Before Profit Alliance registered as a single political party, although each would keep their own separate structures. The Socialist Party remained on the Register of Political Parties.

Enda Kenny had succeeded in bringing his government to a full five-year term. He would have had strong expectations of returning as Taoiseach (a first for a Fine Gael leader), even if with a reduced majority. He might have expected that he could already factor such losses into his calculations. During the course of government Fine Gael had lost six TDs, Labour had lost four and Willie Penrose had returned to the parliamentary party. A significant Fianna Fáil recovery seemed unlikely. A narrative which pitched Sinn Féin as Fine Gael's most likely competitor would play strongly with Fine Gael's core voters. There was another factor that the outgoing government would have seen as helping its return – the membership of the Dáil was to be reduced by eight members. This reduced the number of constituencies to forty. This necessitated an increase in the number of three-seat constituencies. Taken together these measures would, in theory, have made it more difficult for independents or candidates from smaller parties to be elected.

The results of the general election held on 26 February 2016 surprised most people. Fine Gael lost twenty-six seats, more than it won in 2011, but Enda would still have more TDs than he inherited when he first became Fine Gael leader. Fianna Fáil won an additional twenty-four seats. This was less than half the seats the party had lost in 2011, but it still represented a significant advance. Fine Gael remained ahead of Fianna Fáil if only just, six seats and 1.2 per cent of the national vote. These were now parties of equivalent size.

Moving into third place in Irish politics significantly was Sinn Féin. The party won an additional nine seats. Yet despite this the party had reason to be disappointed. At 14 per cent the party was performing at under the vote achieved by Martin McGuinness in the Presidential election, or the 20 per cent support the party had won during the European Election. The new Sinn Féin TDs included Kathleen Funchion in Carlow Kilkenny; Pat Buckley in Cork East, while previous TD Sandra McLennen, stood down, unhappy at the party's policy of pooling wages and expecting their elected representatives to live on the average industrial wage; Donnchadh Ó Laoghaire in Cork South Central; Denise Mitchell in Dublin Bay North; Louise O'Reilly in Dublin Fingal; Eoin Ó'Broin in Dublin Mid West; Maurice Quinlivan in Limerick City; Imelda Munster in Louth (a second seat for the party there); Carol Nolan in Offaly; Martin Kenny in Sligo Leitrim (replacing Michael Colreavy) and David Cullinane in Waterford (married to Kathleen Funchion). One significant failure was outgoing TD Pádraig MacLochlainn, unable to win a second seat for the party in the new five-seat Donegal constituency.

Labour fell to new electoral depths. In electing seven TDs its parliamentary party was at its smallest size since 1932. Its 6.6 per cent share, the lowest it had received since 1987. The bigger difficulty for the party was that while it had been reduced to fourth position before, the gap between it and Sinn Féin would be, if possible, difficult to close at the next election. Labour was now in danger of never securing third position again.

With this election the combined vote of Fine Gael and Fianna Fáil was, for the first time ever, under 50 per cent of the vote. Taking into account the Labour vote, the 'others' vote in this election was close to 44 per cent, the highest it had been in any general election.

Six TDs were elected under the AAA-PBP banner. Joe Higgins stepped aside at this election. Of those elected in by-elections, Ruth Coppinger and Paul Murphy were returned to serve a full Dáil term. They would be joined by their AAA/Socialist Party colleague, Mick Barry, elected in Cork North Central. On the other side of the fence, Richard Boyd Barrett would be joined by People Before Profit colleagues Bríd Smith in Dublin South Central and Gino Kenny in Dublin Mid West.

The three principals behind the Social Democrats each topped the poll in their respective constituencies, all being elected on the first count.

The party came close to a fourth seat in the Dublin Central constituency, where Dublin City councillor Garry Gannon challenged for the final seat.

The Greens came back, with party leader Éamon Ryan being elected for the Dublin Bay South constituency. Even more impressive was the performance of Catherine Martin, being elected in the three-seater Dublin Rathdown constituency, defeating the former Minister for Justice, Alan Shatter, in the process.

Twenty-three independent TDs were elected, the same number as Sinn Féin. These independents would become categorized into a number of groupings. Independents 4 Change (which had been the Independents for Equality Movement) would be the new home for Mick Wallace, Clare Daly, Joan Collins and Tommy Broughan. The Independent Alliance, unregistered as a political party, endorsed twenty-one candidates. Among them was former Green Party TD, Paul Gogarty, who was unsuccessful. Those who were successful included four of the five outgoing TDs who had formed the Alliance (Tom Fleming had not stood again in Kerry). Joining these would be Seán Canny who topped the poll in Galway East and Kevin 'Boxer' Moran in Longford Westmeath.

Among the independents not in a formalised grouping were the new TDs that included Michael Harty in Clare; Michael Collins in Cork South West; Katherine Zappone in Dublin South West and Catherine Connolly in Galway West. In the new five-seat Kerry constituency, the first two seats were won by the two Healy Rae brothers, Michael and Danny. In Tipperary, three of the five available seats were won by independents.

For Renua Ireland, the dream came to a shuddering end. None of the party's outgoing members of the Oireachtas secured election. A distinct, but none too popular election manifesto seemed to seal the party's fate. The manifesto included a proposal for a flat personal tax rate of 23%. Also included was a three-strikes law which would bring mandatory life sentences into being for those convicted a third time for a serious crime. The only shaft of light for the party was the realisation that it qualified for State funding, after having passed the 2 per cent of the national vote threshold. Within a number of months Lucinda Creighton would announce her withdrawal from political life. The task of breathing future relevance into Renua Ireland would rest with John Leahy, the party's Offaly County Councillor.

Direct Democracy Ireland ran nineteen candidates who averaged about 350 votes each. The Workers' Party put forward five candidates who between them won 3,000 votes. The Catholic Democrats stood three candidates winning 2,000 votes. Fís Nua marginally increased its vote while running three fewer candidates. Its total, however, was 1,124 votes. The unregistered Peoples Convention group won 1,400 votes, standing in two Cork constituencies. Three parties stood a single candidate each. The strongest performing of these was Ken Smollen of the Irish Democratic Party (registered after a breakaway from Direct Democracy Ireland) who won under 1,000 votes in the Offaly constituency. After an absence from a number of elections the Communist Party of Ireland stood a candidate who won under 200 votes. The Communists might reflect that they did outpoll by two votes (in national terms) the representative of the far right, Peter O'Loughlin of Identity Ireland, who won 183 votes in the Cork North Central constituency. A party had registered in September 2015 but did not contest this election. The party, United People, was another breakaway from Direct Democracy Ireland.

The Dáil reconvened on 10 March. At that session a new Ceann Comhairle was selected, Seán Ó'Fearghail, a Fianna Fáil TD from Kildare South. There were another eleven sessions of the Dáil before a Taoiseach and a cabinet was selected. Much of that time was spent avoiding the obvious – that a grand coalition should be formed by the two civil war parties. Neither was willing. The country celebrated and acknowledged the 100th anniversary of the Easter Rising without a government. Somehow that seemed apt.

Fine Gael, as the slighly larger party, was forced into a situation of trying to form a government. It organised a series of round table meetings with interested independents and with the Green Party. This identified those independents who would work with and support a Fine Gael-led minority government. Fianna Fáil indicated it would be prepared to enter into a 'confidence and supply arrangement' with Fine Gael, if Fine Gael could illustate it held the support of the majority of the rest of the House (fifty-eight TDs). On 2 May, Fine Gael and Fianna Fáil reached agreement on a confidence and supply arrangement. Being a relatively short document it is reproduced here in full (Appendix 1).

On 6 May, Enda Kenny was elected Taoiseach under circumstances that he, nor anyone else, would have imagined. He secured fifty-nine votes for his nomination to forty-nine votes against. Nine independents supported Kenny's election – Seán Canney, John Halligan, Michael Harty, Michael Lowry, Finian McGrath, Kevin 'Boxer' Moran, Denis Naughton, Shane Ross and Katherine Zappone. The opposition, less Fianna Fáil and the Green Party, arranged against him.

The cabinet then announced contained three independent ministers – Katherine Zappone, the first independent who had agreed to support the new government was made Minister for Children and Youth Affairs; Denis Naughton, who had been for many years a Fine Gael TD, in this cabinet he would be thought to represent the interests of a sub-set of rural TDs. He would become the Minister for Communications, Climate Change and Natural Resources; and Shane Ross, also once a Fine Gael candidate then subsequently the driver behind the Independent Alliance was appointed Minister for Transport, Tourism and Sport.

Three independent TDs would later be appointed to Minister of State positions. Finian McGrath would be given responsibility for disability issues, arching over three different government departments. He would also be given the right to attend cabinet meetings. John Halligan was appointed Minister of State for Training and Skills. Seán Canney was given responsibility for the Office of Public Works. Eighteen Ministers of State were appointed. This would result in twenty-seven of the fifty members of Fine Gael's parliamentary party holding positions of ministerial rank.

The Independent Alliance had suffered its first casualty, Michael Fitzmaurice, when the Programme for Partnership agreement on forming a government was not to his liking. He abstained on the vote for Taoiseach. The new government listed its key priorities as:

- agreement with the Oireachtas on a reformed budget process, including the publication of a Spring Statement and a new National Economic Dialogue;
- preparation and publication of an Action Plan for Housing;
- establishment of a mobile coverage and broadband task force for rural areas;

- reactivation of the National Treasury Purchase Fund to reduce waiting lists, and the preparation of a new winter A&E plan;
- engagement between government and education partners on new after-school care arrangements.

While partial progress would be achieved, in varying degrees, in each of these areas, the 100 days timetable would be met for none of them.

Kicking for touch and delay would become a sub theme of this new government. It led to a new description, that of a 'new politics'. Changes were made to Dáil procedures. It became easier to establish technical groups for speaking rights. More opposition time was provided to allow for debate of private members' bills. Several of these bills passed initial stages; the amount that eventually pass all stages in both houses will help judge the success of new politics.

The first session of the Twenty-fifth Seanad was delayed because of the inability of the Dáil to select a Taoiseach. The Seanad elections saw Sinn Féin win seven seats on the five vocational panels, its strongest ever Seanad representation. Its new Senators, joining outgoing Senator Trevor Ó Clochartaigh, were Rose Conway-Walsh (group leader), Pádraig Mac Lochlainn (former TD), Niall Ó Donnghaile (former Lord Mayor of Belfast), Fintan Warfield (former Mayor of South Dublin), Máire Devine and Paul Gavan.

Four independents and a Green Party Senator were elected through the vocational panels. Gerard Craughwell elected in a 2014 by-election, was elected to serve a full Seanad term. Victor Boyhan, a former Progressive Democrats councillor was elected, as was disability rights campaigner, John Dolan. Well-known performer, Frances Black surprised many by being elected. Grace O'Sullivan became the first member of her party to be directly elected at a Seanad general election.

Three new independents were elected through the university panels. Some were less new than others. Michael McDowell resumed his political career, even though he had said he had put it behind him. He was elected on the National University of Ireland panel. Joining him was Alice Mary Higgins, who had been Campaigns Officer with the National Women's Council of Ireland. She also was the daughter of President Michael D. Higgins, himself a former Senator. On the Dublin University panel, the newcomer was a recent President of Trinity College Students' Union, Lynn Ruane.

Five independents were nominated among the Taoiseach's nominees. These were Mary Louise O'Donnell who was re-appointed for a further term; Pádraig Ó Céidigh, founder of Aer Arran and recent National University panel candidate; Joan Freeman, founder of Pieta House suicide charity; Colette Kelleher, chief executive of Alzheimers Ireland and Billy Lawless a Galway born, Chicago-based businessman, chosen to be a representative of the diaspora. Micheál Martin made some of these suggestions on the Taoiseach's behalf, in an early example of new politics.

There were no formal relations between independent Senators and independent TDs. Fine Gael, with less than one-third of the membership of the Seanad, would need to box clever to get its legislative programme through.

For Labour a new party leader had to be found. While any contest would involve a ballot of party members, to become nominated required the ability to be nominated within the parliamentary party. Colleagues were willing to nominate Brendan Howlin, but less willing to support their enthusiastic Deputy Leader, Alan Kelly. His combative style as Minister for the Environment between 2014 and 2016 was seen by many in Labour as contributing to the party's loss of support. With the rest of the parliamentary party holding these reservations, Brendan Howlin became the next leader of the Labour Party without a contest.

In Northern Ireland 2016 was also an election year for members of its new Assembly. The Green Party increased presence in the Assembly with Clare Bailey joining Steven Agnew in Stormont. Also making a breakthrough was People Before Profit with Gerry Carroll topping the poll in the Sinn Féin stronghold of West Belfast. With legendary socialist Éamonn McCann being elected in Foyle, it was an extremely satisfying election for the party. Along with Sinn Féin, the Greens, People Before Profit, the Socialist Party and the Workers' Party were the only political parties operating throughout the island, seeking votes in both jurisdictions.

The 2016 general election in the Republic was the first to be conducted under gender quota rules. These obliged political parties to present their national panels of candidates ensuring that at least 30 per cent of their candidates were of female or male gender. It helped bring the percentage of women in the Thirty-second Dáil up to 22 per cent of the membership, up from 15 per cent in 2011. The percentage of women in the Seanad was 30 per cent.

In a similar vein, the new government hoped the appointment of Noirín O'Sullivan as Garda Commissioner (she had been operating in an acting capacity), would help draw a line under the continuing litany of bad news that had been coming from the force. Her appointment meant that the offices of Chief Justice, Minister for Justice, Attorney General the Director of Public Prosecutions and the Garda Commissioner were now all held by women.

A government that had taken so long to come together moved slowly, continuing on its steep learning curve. Those newest to government, many of the independent members, found it difficult to abandon instinctive ways to oppose proposals that might be publicly thought unpopular. The need for independent ministers to curb this instinct, combined with the frequent obstacles of office, would be a defining question for this government. As Minister for Transport, Shane Ross found himself having to deal with transport strikes within Dublin's tram system (Luas), the capital's bus services (Dublin Bus) and then regional bus services throughout the country (Bus Éireann).

This was all happening in an increasingly uncertain world. The UK Brexit referendum created a possibility that the sales of goods and services to and from one of the country's larger trading partners, would need to be re-thought. The election of Donald J. Trump as President of the United States, another of Ireland's major trading nations, meant that practically everything needed to be recast.

Attempting to fit in with the Trump *zeitgeist* was Justin Barrett, former alumni of Youth Defence and European election candidate. Justin Barrett (closely associated with European neo-Nazi groups), announced his attention to establish a new political party, the National Party, (not to be confused with the Nora Bennis vehicle of the same name, now known as the Catholic Democrats).

The ability of the Social Democrats in Ireland to develop in this environment suffered a significant blow when one of its triad of leaders, Stephen Donnelly, resigned from the party, to sit initially as an independent.

In December 2016 a group of activists engaged with the issues of homelessness took over a vacant office building in Dublin, turning it into a temporary shelter for the homeless. The *Home Sweet Home* group had identified Apollo House, believing it to be in NAMA ownership. Celebrity visits, combined with considerable media coverage, brought heightened attention to the issue. The Minister for Housing Simon Coveney had requested his ministerial portfolio in Kennedy-esque terms (not because it was easy, but because it was hard). Housing agencies, in particular the voluntary bodies, were grateful for the enhanced publicity, yet frustrated that campaigners seemed unaware of the work these groups were doing on the ground. After a month, and on foot of a court order, the occupation of the building ended. The campaign had been successful in highlighting the pre-eminent issue in the country of the time.

In March 2017, the AAA/PBP re-registered as a political party. The Socialist Party component of the group ditched its AAA alter ego and replaced it with a new title – Solidarity. A separate entry for the Socialist Party continued to remain on the Register of Political Parties.

Government hopes that the official appointment of Noirín O'Sullivan as Garda Commissioner would bring an end to a scandal-strewn period in the history of the force were proving unfounded. In February 2017, reported in the *Irish Examiner* newspaper and through an RTE *Prime Time* television broadcast, revelations were made as to how key whistleblower Maurice McCabe was treated in the aftermath of the scandal. This included being reported (wrongly) to Tusla, the Child and Family Agency, for child sexual abuse. Undeniably angry at learning about these allegations, McCabe threatened to sue the State. The government promised another commission of investigation into these allegations. This would be chaired by Peter Charleton, a Supreme Court judge. McCabe demanded an open and public Tribunal of Inquiry. The government reluctantly agreed to this. The Disclosures Tribunal opened at the end of the month.

This on it own would make life difficult for Noirín O'Sullivan. Ensuing stories about the robustness of Garda statistics when it was learned that hundreds of thousands of phantom breathalyser tests were registered and allegations of financial impropriety at the Garda Training

Centre in Templemore, County Tipperary, would take political and public confidence to new depths.

There would be political ramifications. The 'who said what to whom, and what was known by whom' circus, was soon to have Taoiseach Enda Kenny brought into the ring. He was found to have been economical in his accounts of what he knew and what he told others and when. This miscommunication persuaded some in the Fine Gael parliamentary party that the Taoiseach should provide a schedule to his already announced willingness to step aside. Citing a workload that included a Washington visit to the new US President, helping to develop an EU response to Brexit, and dealing with the consequences of the collapse of the Northern Ireland Assembly, he was unable to accede to such requests immediately.

The Northern Ireland Assembly had collapsed because of a scandal concerning the structuring of a renewable energy scheme that had been administered at the time by First Minister, Arlene Foster. The resulting election was to elect a smaller assembly of ninety members reduced from 110. Sinn Féin leader and Deputy First Minister Martin McGuinness did not contest that election due to illness (he died on 21 March 2017). Michelle O'Neill was appointed in his place.

In the election, Sinn Féin came within one seat of the Democratic Unionist Party in becoming the largest party in the new Assembly. The Greens held on to their two seats. Gerry Carroll came through West Belfast again for People Before Profit, but Éamonn McCann's tenure in elective politics would prove to be short lived.

In Dublin, the water charges issue was dripping to a conclusion that brought the whole situation back to where it had started. The Expert Commission, sought by Fianna Fáil under the confidence and supply agreement, had reported. The specially convened Oireachtas committee examining the report would pit Fine Gael (and to a lesser extent the Green Party) against the rest.

This was the stage when Enda chose to make his exit. On 18 May he announced his resignation as leader of Fine Gael, putting in place the procedures needed to select a successor. That was the first Fine Gael leadership contest where the parliamentary party ceded part of its decision-making to local authority representatives, and to general members of the party. The weightings were 65 per cent for the parliamentary party, 10 per cent for local authority representatives, with 25 per cent of the vote being given to general party members.

Two candidates, expected to contest, revealed their interest. Both represented a generational change, not only in Fine Gael, but also in Irish politics. Simon Coveney (44) and Leo Varadkar (38 and son of an Indian immigrant) faced each other with the prospect of becoming the fourteenth head of government in Irish political history. While not much distinguished the two candidates in policy terms, each took a different philosophical approach. Coveney sought to bring the party back to its (never implemented) *Just Society* policy document. Varadkar wanted to represent 'those who got up early in the morning'. Early declarations by most of the parliamentary party seemed to almost hand the election to Varadkar. Nevertheless, Coveney won almost two-thirds support from the members of the party, significant but not enough to turn over Varadkar's already significant lead. On 2 June Leo Varadkar was declared the eleventh leader of Fine Gael.

He would lead a party that remained a major party, in a political system at its most diverse – a system subject to huge volatility. Fine Gael's previous general election results had been a loss of twenty-six seats, a gain of twenty-five seats, a gain of twenty seats, and a loss of twenty-two seats. Its main opponent is a political party with which it has few policy differences and with whom seeking common political cause will studiously be avoided, as the sum will always be less than its parts.

Fianna Fáil has achieved levels of support that no other Irish political party has had, or is ever likely to have. It has also experienced the steepest fall in support of any Irish political party, in a single election. Its recovery since 2011 speaks to an organisational institutional memory that should help the party maintain itself into the future. In 2026 the party will reach the milestone of being the first, and only, Irish political party to have achieved one hundred years of continuous existence through its elected public representatives. It is extremely unlikely, however, that it (or any other Irish political party) will ever be a 40 per cent plus party.

Sinn Féin 'Mark VI' (each earlier version being a different and distinct party) should be happy with the progress it has achieved since its political birth in the early 1980s. If the party finishes ahead of Labour at the next general election it will have broken the template that has existed since the foundation of the State. The party still needs to cross several political rubicons to maximise its potential. While the party has been becoming more transfer-friendly, a significant portion of the electorate is immune to voting for it all. It may take a change of leadership to unlock that potential. The ultimate test for the party will be when, and if, it participates in government in Dublin. Such an experience would test the party's new-found support.

Labour has recovered from impossible situations before. The party's current plight sees it further behind than it has been before. The political landscape is littered with alternatives for the voters to flit between, alternatives that would not have existed at previous times of crisis for the party. The tendency of the left to be self-critical and go to war with itself has not helped. Nor has a global political environment, where social democracy is suffering in many countries, been of assistance.

The new left also has decisions to make about where it sees its future. A registered party that exists as two parties, a group that sits in the Dáil as a single party, which outside the chamber campaigns as two separate parties, a floating organisation with joint sponsors (the Socialist Party and the Socialist Workers Party) having their own separate and distinct existence. The politics of 'No' has served the nebulous politics of the new left well. However, the overriding question for Solidarity People Before Profit is how long can the politics of 'No' be used sustainably. The secondary question the new left needs to respond to is what are the circumstances, if any, in which they would be willing to participate in government, in order to advance their political priorities?

The Green Party has regained a foothold in Dáil Éireann. That in itself is an achievement. The first smaller party to have been in government, to have lost and then regained its representation in the history of the Dáil. The party has always traded on a niche image. It has struggled against stereotypes, yet is dependent on those in the electorate with a higher standard of living, and who have had access to further education. Geographically, a concentration of support in South Dublin has created something of a political ghetto for the Greens. The pendulum effect of the party performing better during better economic times needs to be addressed. The solace the party has received in the past from being part of an international movement is lessening. Internationally, a new generation is re-addressing what Green politics is. One indicator of where and how the party may find itself has been the decision by US President Donald Trump to remove the US from the Paris Agreement on Climate Change. Having a nemesis is helpful for any political movement.

The defection of Stephen Donnelly from the Social Democrats eventually to Fianna Fáil (in February 2017) has stymied the party's progress. Donnelly, while never seeming the best fit as a social democrat, did provide a level of intellectual gravitas, which, while not lacking in other Soc. Dem. TDs, Catherine Murphy or Róisín Shortall, their skills in direct campaigning were not shared by Donnelly. At least the Social Democrats triad of Donnelly, Murphy, and Shortall gained mandates from the electorate. The difficulty for the party is that it has yet to have an elected local authority base. Now with a half a dozen councillors (none of whom have been elected under a Social Democrats banner), becoming and remaining relevant until the 2019 local elections is a singular challenge for the Social Democrats.

Renua Ireland is a political party that has two elected representatives, both county councillors, neither of whom were elected as Renua representatives. Born out of an Oireachtas rebellion in Fine Gael against the Protection of Life During Pregnancy Act in the 2016 general election, the party pushed on individual conscience in relation to abortion. Since then it has been emphatically anti-abortion. The party seems to think that this represents the potential for political growth despite twenty-five years of failure of religious-based parties. Where an opportunity does lie is in the distinct low tax, low public expenditure grounds discarded by the Progressive Democrats, but maybe Leo Varadkar has now closed those doors?

The Workers' Party had a poor general election in 2016, one of series of poor elections that party has had since it lost Dáil representation. Despite that, the party was beginning to gain something of a higher profile through involvement in campaigns on public housing. Other registered political parties – Direct Democracy Ireland, the Irish Democratic Party, the Communist Party of Ireland and United People do not seem to be gaining any public or social media attention.

One comforting aspect of the Irish political system has been the failure of the far right, through the politics of race, to make an impact.

Populism in Ireland has been channelled through groups which have claimed a left-wing inclination. The performance of groups like the Immigration Control Platform and Identity Ireland have been derisory. Others like the National Party (Justin Barrett) have talked about but have chosen not to enter the electoral field.

The Irish voting system – Single Transferable Vote Proportional Representation (STVPR) – allows for the election of a greater number of independent candidates than most democratic countries in the world. However, the only directly comparable system is Malta, which uses the same electoral system but does not elect the same proportion of independents. Therefore, in Ireland there must be cultural factors that account for the prevalence of elected independents. Independents in Ireland have created the impression of being both a local chieftain and the local *file* (poet), feared by chieftains as well as challenging their role. Independents have played these dual roles well, that of being king of the castle and the voice of the people. Because of these conflicting roles, independents were associated not with challenging but with intensifying the many failings of the Irish political system – those of clientelism, parochialism, nepotism and patronage.

Twenty-first-century Irish independents are more complex. They look for the support of others in proto-party structures. To belong, but to be independent. To make decisions, while being able to oppose. The next chapters will be more than interesting.

Appendix 1

A Confidence and Supply Arrangement for a Fine Gael-Led Government

This document outlines the 'Confidence and Supply' arrangement between Fine Gael and Fianna Fáil to facilitate a Fine Gael-led minority Government and the agreed policy principles that underpin that arrangement. Fine Gael will seek to agree separate policy commitments in a broader range of areas with other Oireachtas members as a basis for a comprehensive Programme for Government.

Core Principles for the Confidence and Supply Arrangement for a Fine Gael Led Government

This is a document that outlines the confidence and supply arrangement to facilitate a Fine Gael-led minority Government.

Subject to the ongoing implementation of the attached policy principles:

Fianna Fáil agrees to:

– abstain in the election of Taoiseach, nomination of Ministers and also the reshuffling of Ministers;
– facilitate Budgets consistent with the agreed policy principles attached to this document;

– vote against or abstain on any motions of no confidence in the Government, Ministers and financial measures (eg money bills) recognised as confidence measures; and

– pairing arrangements for EU Council meetings, North South meetings and other Government business as agreed.

The Fine Gael–Led Minority Government agrees to:

– accept that Fianna Fáil is an independent party in opposition and is not a party to the Programme for Government;

– recognise Fianna Fáil's right to bring forward policy proposals and bills to implement commitments in its own manifesto;

– publish all agreements with Independent Deputies and other political parties in full.

– allow any opposition Bills (that are not money bills) that pass 2nd stage, proceed to Committee stage within 10 working weeks;

– implement the agreed policy principles attached to this document over a full term of Government;

– have an open approach to avoiding policy surprises; and

– introduce a reformed budgetary process in accordance with the OECD review of the Oireachtas along with the agreed Dáil reform process.

Should an event arise that has potential to undermine this agreement efforts will be made to have it resolved by the two Party Leaders.

It is agreed that both parties to this agreement will review this Framework Agreement at the end of 2018.

It is agreed that the final arrangements will be a written agreement signed by the respective Party Leaders.

This is a political agreement and is not justiciable.

Policy Framework for a Confidence and Supply Agreement to Facilitate a Fine Gael-Led Minority Government

Ireland's Economy

- Maintain our commitment to meeting in full the domestic and EU Fiscal rules as enshrined in law.
- Facilitate the passage of budgets presented by the Government within these rules and which are consistent with the policy principles contained in this document.
- To address unmet needs introduce budgets that will involve at least a 2:1 split between investment in public spending and tax reductions.
- Base health expenditure on multi-year budgeting supported by a 5 year HSE Service Plan based on realistic, verifiable projections.
- Introduce reductions in the Universal Social Charge (USC) on a fair basis with an emphasis on low and middle income earners.
- Establish a 'Rainy Day' Fund.
- Maintain Ireland's 12.5% corporation tax, and engage constructively with any measures to work towards international tax reform while critically analysing proposals that may not be in Ireland's long term interests.

Industrial Relations and Public Sector Pay
— Recognise full implementation of the Lansdowne Road Agreement in accordance with the timelines agreed and recognise that the recruitment issues in the public service must be addressed as part of this Agreement.
— Establish a Public Service Pay Commission to examine pay levels across the public service, including entry levels of pay.
— Support the gradual, negotiated repeal the Financial Emergency Measures in the Public Interest Acts having due regard to the priority to improve public services and in recognition of the essential role played by public servants.
— Tackle the problems caused by the increased casualisation of work that prevents workers from being able to save or have any job security.
— Respect the Workplace Relations Commission and the Labour Court as the proper forum for state intervention in industrial relation disputes and ensure that both bodies are supported and adequately resources to fulfil their roles.

Securing Affordable Homes and Tackling Homelessness
— Significantly increase and expedite the delivery of social housing units, remove barriers to private housing supply and initiate an affordable housing scheme.
— Retain mortgage interest relief beyond the current end date of December 2017 on a tapered basis.
— Increase rent supplement and Housing Assistance payment (HAP) limits by up to 15% taking account of geographic variations in market rents, and extend the roll out by local authorities of the HAP, including the capacity to make discretionary enhanced payments.
— Protect the family home and introduce additional long term solutions for mortgage arrears cases.
— Improve supports and services for older people to live independently in their own home, including a provision for pension increases.
— Provide greater protection for mortgage holders, tenants and SMEs whose loans have been transferred to non-regulated entities ('vulture funds').

Creating Decent jobs and Supporting Enterprise

– Prioritise regional development across all policy areas.
– Fully implement Food Harvest 2020 and Food Wise 2025.
– Secure the future of family farms and support our fishing industry.
– Seek to introduce a PRSI scheme for the self-employed and provide a supportive tax regime for entrepreneurs and the self-employed.
– Increase capital investment in transport, broadband, education, health and flood defences following the mid-term review of the Capital Plan which is expected mid-2017.
– Examine all options for increased credit availability, competition and quality of service in the banking sector through the development of new and existing platforms.
– Develop a strategy for growth and development for the credit union sector.

Cutting Costs for Families and Improving Public Services

– Reform the public sector to ensure more accessible public services.
– Maintain a humane approach for discretionary medical card provision.
– Develop targeted supports to reduce childcare costs, broaden parental choice and increase supports for stay at home parents.
– Tackle child poverty by increasing community based early intervention programmes.
– Increase and ring-fence €15m in 2017 in funding for a National Treatment Purchase Fund to urgently address waiting lists for those waiting longest.
– Reduce primary school class sizes; reintroduce guidance counselling to secondary schools and increase financial supports for post graduate students with a particular focus on those from low income households.
– Take all necessary action to tackle high variable interest rates.
– Seek to alleviate pressures affecting household budgets across energy, childcare, medical and insurance costs.

Tackling Crime and Developing Community Services

– Increase Garda numbers to 15000, invest in CCTV and mandate the Policing Authority to oversee a review of the boundaries of Garda districts and the dispersement of Garda stations.

– Increase funding to LEADER.
– Strengthen the Social Inclusion and Community Activation Programme (SICAP) and develop new Community Development Schemes for rural areas and reactivate and increase funding to RAPID areas through the Local Authorities.
– Improve services and increase supports for people with disabilities: particularly for early assessment and intervention for children with special needs and provision of adult day services.
– Fully implement 'Vision for Change' in the area of mental health.
– Strengthen and develop cross border bodies and services in Northern Ireland and implement the 'Fresh Start' agreement.
– Establish a Judicial Appointments Commission to identify the most suitable candidates for judicial office.
– Ensure that local Government funding, structure and responsibilities strengthen local democracy.
– Increase investment in the Irish language.

Bibliography

Bell, J. Bowyer, The Secret Army: A History of the IRA, 1916–1970. Not Avail, 1970.

Benoit, Kenneth, and Michael Laver, 'Estimating Irish party policy positions using computer wordscoring: The 2002 election – a research note,' Irish Political Studies 18.1 (2003): pp. 97–107.

Blondel, Jean, 'Party systems and patterns of government in Western democracies.' Canadian Journal of Political Science 1.02 (1968): pp. 180–203.

Bolleyer, Nicole, 'The Irish Green Party: from protest to mainstream party?.' Irish Political Studies 25.4 (2010): pp. 603–623.

Bolleyer, Nicole, and Diana Panke, 'The Irish Green Party and Europe: An Unhappy Marriage?,' Irish Political Studies 24.4 (2009): pp. 543–557.

Boyle, Dan, A Journey to Change: 25 Years of the Green Party in Irish Politics, Dublin: Nonsuch Press, 2006.

Boyle, Dan, Without Power or Glory: The Greens in Government, Dublin: New Island, 2012.

Brennan, Séamus, and Eric Murphy, Brennan's Key to Local Authorities, Dublin: Landscape Press, 1986.

Browne, Noël C, Against the Tide, Dublin: Gill and Macmillan, 1986.

Carty, R. Kenneth, Party and Parish Pump: Electoral Politics in Ireland, Waterloo, Ontario: Wilfrid Laurier University Press, 1981.

Chubb, Basil, The Government and Politics of Ireland. Vol 2, Stanford, California: Stanford University Press, 1970.

Clark, Alistair, 'Breaking the mould or fiddling at the edges? Ireland's minor parties in comparative and systemic perspective.' Irish Political Studies 25.4 (2010): pp. 661–680.

Coakley, John, 'Minor parties in Irish political life, 1922–1989.' Economic and Social Review 21.3 (1990): pp. 269–97.

Coakley, John, 'The rise and fall of minor parties in Ireland.' Irish Political Studies 25.4 (2010): pp. 503–538.

Coakley, John, and Michael Gallagher, Politics in the Republic of Ireland, Dublin: Routledge, 1999.

Collins, Stephen, Breaking the Mould: How the PDs changed Irish Politics, Dublin: Gill & Macmillan, 2005.

Coogan, Tim Pat 'The I.R.A.' Dublin: HarperCollins (2000).

Copus, Colin, et al. 'Minor party and independent politics beyond the mainstream: fluctuating fortunes but a permanent presence.' Parliamentary Affairs 62.1 (2009): pp. 4–18.

Costello, Rory, and Robert Thomson. 'Election pledges and their enactment in coalition governments: A comparative analysis of Ireland.' Journal of Elections, Public Opinion and Parties 18.3 (2008): pp. 239–256.

Desmond, Barry. No Workers' Republic! Reflections on Labour & Ireland, 1913–1967, Dublin: Watchword 2009.

Donnelly, Seán, Elections' 99: All Kinds of Everything. Dublin: Sean Donnelly, 1999.

Donnelly, Seán, Elections 2002. Sean Donnelly, 2002.

Dunphy, Richard, and Tim Bale. 'The radical left in coalition government: Towards a comparative measurement of success and failure.' Party Politics 17.4 (2011): pp. 488–504.

Evans, Bryce. Seán Lemass: Democratic Dictator, Dublin: Collins, 2011.

Farrell, Brian. 'Labour and Irish Political Party System – A suggested approach to analysis.' (1970).

Farrell, David M. 'Ireland: Centralization, Professionalization and Competitive.' How Parties Organize: Change and Adaptation in Party Organizations in Western Democracies (1994): p. 216.

Farrell, David M. 'Ireland: a party system transformed?.' Changing party systems in Western Europe. London: A&C Black (1999): pp.30–47.

Feeny Brian, 'Sinn Féin: A Hundred Turbulent Years' Dublin: O'Brien Press, 2002.

Ferriter, Diarmaid. Ambiguous Republic: Ireland in the 1970s, Dublin: Profile Books, 2012.

Finlay, Fergus, Snakes and Ladders. Dublin: New Island Books, 1998.

Gallagher, Michael, 'Party solidarity, exclusivity and inter-party relationships in Ireland, 1922–1977 – evidence of transfers.' (1978).

Gallagher, Michael, Political parties in the Republic of Ireland. Manchester: Manchester University Press, 1985.

Gallagher, Michael, 'Proportionality, disproportionality and electoral systems.' Electoral studies 10.1 (1991): pp. 33–51.

Gallagher, Michael, (ed.), How Ireland voted 2007: The Full Story of Ireland's General Election. Dublin: Palgrave Macmillan, 2008.

Gallagher, Michael, and Michael Laver (eds), How Ireland Voted in 1992. Dublin: Folens Publishing, 1993.

Gallagher, Michael, and Michael Marsh (eds) How Ireland Voted 2011: The Full Story of Ireland's Earthquake Election, Dublin: Palgrave Macmillan, 2011.

Gallagher, Michael, and Paul Mitchell (eds.), How Ireland Voted 2002 Dublin: Palgrave Macmillan, 2003.

Gallagher, Michael, Richard Sinnott (ed.) How Ireland Voted 1989, Galway: Study of Irish Elections University College Galway, 1989.

Garvin, Tom. 'Political Cleavages, Party Politics and Urbanisation in Ireland: The Case of Periphery-dominated Centre', European Journal of Political Research 2.4 (1974): pp.307–327.

Goodwillie, John (Aug/Sept 1983). 'Glossary of the Left in Ireland'. Gralton: an Irish Socialist Review 9: pp. 17–20.

Hanley, Brian, and Scott Millar, The Lost Revolution: The Story of the Official IRA and the Workers' Party, London: Penguin UK, 2010.

Hansen, Martin Ejnar, 'The parliamentary behaviour of minor parties and independents in Dáil Éireann.' Irish Political Studies 25.4 (2010): pp. 643–660.

Horgan, John, Noël Browne: Passionate Outsider, Dublin: Gill & Macmillan, 2000.

Irish Opinion Poll Archive – Web Archive – Trinity College Dublin.

Joyce, Joe, and Peter Murtagh, The Boss: Charles J. Haughey in Government, Dublin: Poolbeg Press Ltd, 1983.

Ray Kavanagh. 'Spring, Summer and Fall: the Rise and Fall of the Labour Party, 1986–99.' Blackwater Press, 2003: pp. 119–120.

Kenny, Shane, and Fergal Keane, Irish Politics Now:' This Week' Guide to the 25th Dáil. Dublin: Brandon Books, 1987.

Laver, Michael, How Ireland voted: the Irish general election, 1987. Dufour Editions, US: 1987.

Laver, Michael, 'Party policy in Ireland 1997 results from an expert survey.' Irish political studies 13.1 (1998): pp. 159–171.

Lee, Joseph. Ireland, 1912–1985: politics and society. Cambridge: Cambridge University Press, 1989.

Little, Conor, Politics on the margins of government: A comparative study of Green parties in governing coalitions. Doctoral Thesis for the European University Institute. 2014.

Lowery, David, et al, 'Policy agendas and births and deaths of political parties.' Party Politics 19.3 (2013): pp. 381–407.

McCullagh, David. A makeshift majority: The first inter-party government, 1948–51. Dublin: Institute of Public Administration, 1998.

McCullagh, David, 'The Reluctant Taoiseach: A Biography of John A. Costello'. Dublin: Gill Macmillan, 2010.

McDaid, Shaun, and Kacper Rekawek, 'From mainstream to minor and back: the Irish Labour Party, 1987–1992.' Irish Political Studies 25.4 (2010): pp. 625–642.

MacDermott, Eithne, Clann na Poblachta. Cork: Stylus Publishing, LLC., 1998.

Mair, Peter, 'The autonomy of the political: the development of the Irish party system,' Comparative Politics (1979): pp. 445–465.

Manning, Maurice, Irish Political Parties: An Introduction, Irish Book Centre, Wexford, 1972.

Manning, Maurice, James Dillon A Biography, Dublin: Wolfhound Press, 1999

Marsh, Michael and Paul Mitchell, How Ireland Voted 1997, Colorado: Westview Press, 1999.

Marsh, Michael, et al, The Irish voter: The nature of electoral competition in the Republic of Ireland. Manchester: Manchester University Press, 2008.

Minihan, Mary. A deal with the devil: the Green Party in government, Maverick House, 2011

Moran, John (1972). 'Local Elections in Cork City (1929–1967)'. Journal of the Cork Historical and Archaeological Society: pp. 124–133

Moss, Warner, Political parties in the Irish Free State. New York: Columbia University Press, 1933.

Murphy, Ronan J., and David M. Farrell, 'Party politics in Ireland: regularizing a volatile system.' Political Parties in Advanced Industrial Democracies Publisher, Oxford University Press (2002): pp. 217–247.

Ní Lochlainn, Aoife, 'Ailtirí na hAiséirghe: A Movement of its Time', in D. Keogh and M O'Driscoll (eds), Ireland in World War Two: Diplomacy and Survival, Cork: Mercier Press 2004.

O'Byrnes, Stephen, Hiding behind a Face: Fine Gael under FitzGerald, Dublin: Gill & Macmillan, 1986.

O'Malley, Eoin, 'Punch bags for heavyweights? Minor parties in Irish government.' Irish Political Studies 25.4 (2010): pp. 539–561.

Potter, Matthew, 'The government and the people of Limerick: the history of Limerick Corporation,' City Council 1197–2006 (2006).

Puirséil, Niamh. The Irish Labour Party, 1922–73, Dublin: University College Dublin Press, 2007.

Sherwin, Frank, Independent and Unrepentant, Newbridge: Irish Academic Press, 2007.

Rafter, Kevin, The Clann: The story of Clann na Poblachta, Dublin: Mercier Press, 1996.

Rafter, Kevin, Democratic Left: The Life and Death of an Irish Political Party, Newbridge: Irish Academic Press, 2011.

Sinnott, Richard, 'Interpretations of the Irish Party System'. European Journal of Political Research 12.3 (1984): pp. 289–307.

Sinnott, Richard, Irish voters decide: Voting behaviour in elections and referendums since 1918, Manchester: Manchester University Press, 1995.

Taylor, Peter, Behind the Mask: The IRA and Sinn Fein, Dublin: TV Books Incorporated, 1999.

Varley, Tony, 'On the road to extinction: agrarian parties in twentieth-century Ireland.' Irish Political Studies 25.4 (2010): pp. 581–601.

Varley, Tony, and Peter Moser, 'Clann na Talmhan Ireland's Last Farmers' Party.' History Ireland (1995): pp. 39–43.

Walker, Brian Mercer, 'Parliamentary election results in Ireland, 1801–1922.' Dublin: Royal Irish Academy, 1978.

Weeks, Liam, 'Minor parties: a schema for analysis.' Irish Political Studies 25.4 (2010): pp. 481–501.

Weeks, Liam, Radical or Redundant: Minor Parties in Irish Politics, Dublin: The History Press, 2011.